An Immigrant Nation Seeks Cohesion

ANTHEM STUDIES IN AUSTRALIAN POLITICS, ECONOMICS AND SOCIETY

This series showcases the most significant contributions to scholarship on a wide range of social science issues, dealing with the changing politics, economics and society of Australia, while not losing sight of the interplay of other regional and global forces and their influence and impact on this region. **Anthem Studies in Australian Politics, Economics and Society** is intended as an interdisciplinary series, at the interface of politics, law, sociology, media, policy, political economy, economics, business, criminology and anthropology. It is seeking to publish high quality research which considers issues of power, justice and democracy and provides a critical contribution to knowledge about Australian politics, economics and society. The series especially welcomes books from emerging scholars which contribute new perspectives on social science.

An Immigrant Nation Seeks Cohesion

Australia from 1788

James Jupp

ANTHEM PRESS

Anthem Press
An imprint of Wimbledon Publishing Company
www.anthempress.com

This edition first published in UK and USA 2018
by ANTHEM PRESS
75–76 Blackfriars Road, London SE1 8HA, UK
or PO Box 9779, London SW19 7ZG, UK
and
244 Madison Ave #116, New York, NY 10016, USA

British Library Cataloguing-in-Publication Data
A catalogue record for this book is available from the British Library.

ISBN-13: 978-1-78308-766-2 (Hbk)
ISBN-10: 1-78308-766-8 (Hbk)

This title is also available as an e-book.

CONTENTS

PREFACE

My personal experience of politics began as a boy in South London, heavily bombarded by Hitler's Luftwaffe and rockets. I came to Australia in 1956 as a newly qualified master in sociology from the London School of Economics. My first host was the Salvation Army in Fremantle as I had no money and was alone. I am grateful to them. Australia was wide open to British migrants then. It was also notably more affluent than post-war England. However, it was rather old-fashioned and conservative and very white. It was protected from others by immigration policies preferring the British and excluding non-Europeans; it was protected from new ideas and controversies by a censorship system based on the Vatican Index of prohibited items administered at the landing place by customs officers; its Sundays were devoted to closing down innocent pleasures such as newspapers, cinemas and above all the consumption of alcohol; it banned birth control and abortion, kept women in a secondary role and made divorce as hard as possible. On the international scale it was protected from potential enemies by the alliance between Britain and the United States, left over from the Japanese defeat. This 'saved' Australia from a tiny band of communists, which got steadily smaller and has now vanished. Potential enemies never attacked.

Melbourne University reflected much of this safeguarded provincialism. Although renowned, it was inbred, with most academics born and raised locally. My later teaching posts have included Canada, Yorkshire and Canberra, with research sessions in Sri Lanka and Vanuatu. But Melbourne started me off as an academic, teaching compulsory Australian Politics One as the equivalent of a base-grade tutor.

My impressions of the world since then have largely come from international travel, which I recommend to scholars who need to get out of their studies for a look at reality. This includes regular returns to London to see the changes in my home town, which is now far more multicultural than anything in Australia; two years teaching in Canada, which showed me that a bilingual, multicultural society can be more intelligent than the officially created Australian model; years of studying and publishing on Sri Lanka, a tragedy which arose from being unable to accept ethnic variety; a field study on bicultural politics in Vanuatu as it came to independence; voyages by bus, car and train through a very wide variety of nations in Europe, Asia, the Americas and the Pacific. To understand the world, you need to go there. Many Australian academics, journalists and politicians should be better informed. It is hard for them to get away as often as they would like. Truly the 'tyranny of distance' has always been a problem. The core perspective in this study is international rather than local. An international perspective was more difficult for scholars until ships were replaced by planes in the 1960s and then by the Internet. This was not their fault.

This is not a 'black armband' history, to use a phrase popularized during the 1980s, except where reference is made to obvious failings, such as White Australia, refugees, racism, Aborigines, the convict system and suspicion of the outside world. Rather it is a historically based discussion of the unique experience of creating a viable modern society from a sparsely populated country by the hard work and serious planning of human beings over 230 years. It is not a 'history book' in the usual sense, but uses historic instances to illuminate issues often spread over many years or even centuries. In the course of two centuries many wrongs were committed, many projects launched and many lives changed. Overlooking much of this could create a false report about building a unique nation at the end of the world. The alternative to black armband has too often been flag-waving. However, Australian academic history is very professional and forms the basis for my own references and studies. These I owe to my colleagues in political science and historical studies in Australia and elsewhere over a period of many years.

Among those who have helped and encouraged me in this effort have been my colleagues in the Australian National University School of Demography and especially Peter McDonald, who invited me to join them. They left me to get on with whatever I was doing, which is a priceless gift in modern academia; earlier colleagues at the University of York, especially David Coates, now in the United States; Ian Hume, now in Wales and bilingual in Chinese and Welsh; Phil Cerny, moving between York and New Jersey; founders of multiculturalism such as Peter Shergold and Sev Ozdowski; Sri Lankan friends like Vinod Moonesinghe and Don S. Abeygunawardena; Olavi Koivukangas; Nonja Peters; Barry York; Eric Richards; Hanifa Dean; Andrew Jakubowicz; and many others, including the contributors to my three encyclopedias of 1988, 2001 and 2009; the late Andrea McRobbie, who ran the office, before moving to the United States; and Liz Wayman (now in Los Angeles), who created the amazing illustrations for each of them. Their work has been maintained by Gillian Evans into the present, for which I am very grateful. I should also like to thank the Anthem Press copyeditor for all their very careful work.

With the passage of time, many whom I knew are no longer with us. A special note should be made of Jerzy Zubrzycki, Charles Price and Oliver McDonagh, who were a continuing influence on my early work on immigration, as were many others. Many friends and allies of multiculturalism had to put up with undue criticisms and misunderstandings from those who always wanted things to stay as they once were. As Prime Minister Malcolm Fraser put it: 'Life was not meant to be easy'.

My final thanks for everything must always go to my dear wife, Marian Sawer, without whose continuing support I would have given up years ago.

ABBREVIATIONS

AHRC	Australian Human Rights Commission
ALP	Australian Labor Party
ASIO	Australian Security Intelligence Organisation
ASIS	Australian Secret Intelligence Service
AWU	Australian Workers Union
CIA	Central Intelligence Agency (USA)
DPs	displaced persons (1940s)
FECCA	Federation of Ethnic Communities' Councils of Australia
FBI	Federal Bureau of Investigation (USA)
GRU	Soviet military intelligence organisation
HREOC	Human Rights and Equal Opportunity Commission
IOM	International Organization for Migration
ICAC	Independent Commission Against Corruption (NSW)
ISIL	Islamic State of Iraq and the Levant (Daesh)
IWW	Industrial Workers of the World
KGB	Soviet intelligence organisation
MVD/NKVD	Soviet domestic security committee
MI5/MI6	British intelligence services
NSW	New South Wales
PNG	Papua New Guinea
RSL	Returned Services League
SIEV	Suspected Illegal Entry Vehicle
UKIP	United Kingdom Independence Party
UN	United Nations
UNHCR	United Nations High Commissioner for Refugees
WA	Western Australia

INTRODUCTION

Australia is a nation of 25 million people, living in relative affluence in a mainly 'European' society, thousands of miles from Europe. Its area is the same as the continental United States. Hardly anyone lives in most of Australia because of desert conditions. Only a minority can trace their own local origins as far back as two hundred years. Its allegiance is nominally to Queen Elizabeth (the Queen of the United Kingdom and the Queen of Australia). Its political system is a federation with parliamentary democracy. At least a million Australians enjoy dual citizenship from somewhere else. Its closest neighbours are New Zealand, Indonesia, Papua New Guinea, Malaysia, Singapore and Timor, to which few Australians travel more than once or twice. Its favourite overseas holiday resort is Bali. Long-distance friends are often in London or Los Angeles. All of this makes Australia distinctive.

Australia has a wide range of interesting writing about itself. Some of this repeats old stories from the past, like the Gallipoli landing, Ned Kelly and Captain Cook raising the British flag. Unlike other countries its history contains no local set battles, no military invasions, no great inventions, very few great leaders, no dictators, no revolutions and not much out of the ordinary except its unique flora and fauna. As the Chinese allegedly say, 'Happy is the country with no heroes'. Struggles against distance and climate mark the early days, but science and technology are conquering much of this. The economy is classified as fourteenth in the world. Its population is spread over an area as large as the continental United States, but mainly located in a dozen cities.

The world is changing fast in Australia's neighbourhood. In this book I have tried to examine problems in sustaining a comfortable, stable democracy by using often rigorous means, retaining the friendship of its neighbours while often misunderstanding their peoples, leaders, beliefs and religions. These problems go back to the British imperial inheritance, relationships with the Indigenous peoples and with the neighbouring Asians, insensitivity about immigration and refugee policies, White Australia and beyond, reliance on Britain or the United States, and fear of Islam and China. Some of these issues go as far back as Cook's mission from Georgian England and right up to current instability and worrying changes in the United States and Asia. The recent testing of intercontinental missiles by North Korea adds to justified anxieties.

This study concentrates on the continued social engineering of the origins, size and character of the Australian population and the responses forced upon governments by changing external circumstances. The successful creation of a stable, planned and prosperous society over the past two centuries has involved control of important social elements, from the Indigenous population to social critics and political deviants. While immigration and nation-building have been presented as rationally planned, they cannot remain insulated from domestic and foreign influences and crises. As in other 'settler societies' there was brutality and insensitivity, especially in convict policy and in the treatment of Aborigines. This has been apparent with the refugee detention policy of recent years and was inherent in the occupation of land for the benefit of British settlers and later immigrants, regardless of prior inhabitants or use.

There are few other societies whose rulers have so consistently determined the character of their populations over such a long period, certainly not the United States or even Canada. This has included reliance on convict labour for 65 years, the preferred choice of free settlers from the United Kingdom for over a century; the threat to control during the gold rushes of the 1850s; the popular pressure for democratic institutions and trade unions for 80 years; the White Australia policy for 70 years; the continuing dilemma of Aboriginal integration (to the present); and the impact of multicultural migration and asylum since 1945. Few developing societies are so closely located near heavily populated and less-developed neighbours, requiring sensitive international relations and diplomacy.

The present approach is loosely that of 'social history'. The book generally proceeds in chronological order from the initial convict colony of New South Wales through a series of chapters dealing with policy and events rather than with individuals. The emphasis is on the official search for a 'cohesive' society and the events that bring this aim into question or adhere to a different objective. These include organizations and influences that have often appeared as serious critics of current policies and controversial alternatives (such as White Australia, socialism, multiculturalism, refugee policy and Aborigines).

The text is divided into two parts: Part I examines changes in culture and society from the convict period to the recent past. It analyses British influence and the role of government, the impact on the Indigenous people, the deliberate planning of the White Australia policy and the post–World War II intake of refugees. Part II takes up post-1945 developments, the effect of ending White Australia and the preference for British immigrants, and the spread of problems in the Asia–Pacific region following the dissolution of empires after 1945. It criticizes the shift of Australia's immigration policy towards mandatory detention for controlling refugee intake. It concludes with a discussion of the impact of Islam on Australia, and the growth of security laws and practices within a democratic system.

Part I

Chapter 1

PRISONS IN THE PACIFIC, 1788–1850

Modern Australia was founded in 1788 as a prison in the Pacific, far enough away from Britain for its inmates to be unable to escape (although a few did). Its long-term planners in London had rejected previous disastrous sites in Africa but were anxious to secure Britain's existing interests against the French in the Indian Ocean and the South Pacific (Christopher 2010; Atkinson 1997). This required a reserve of British settlers and defenders and a well-developed military base. The first-generation convicts were not normally locked away, as there were no custom-built prisons for them. Massive constructions such as Fremantle Gaol or Port Arthur came later. Prison stations outside Sydney, such as Port Macquarie, Moreton Bay, Macquarie Harbour, Norfolk Island and the Newcastle coalmines, were more stringent and feared than the relatively liberal arrangements in Cumberland County defended by historian John Hirst in *Convict Society and Its Enemies* (Hirst 1983, 1988). A much longer and quite different account of the system is that of Robert Hughes in *The Fatal Shore* (Hughes 1987). A statistical analysis by Stephen Nicholas and Peter Shergold (Nicholas 1988) argues that convicts to New South Wales were relatively skilled and literate and were a useful workforce. Van Diemen's Land (later Tasmania) was more rigorous than New South Wales and continued its convict system longer. Convicts were normally put to constructive work relevant to building a permanent society as part of the expanding British Empire. This followed a tradition of convict and indentured labour in other British colonies, but it did not use slavery as in the Caribbean or North America. Convicts and Aborigines were nominally British subjects, governed by British law. Australian origins lay in coercion but not formal conquest.

When necessary, convict discipline was maintained by floggings, transfer to stricter locations or chain gangs working on the roads and public works. Guarding and policing were often provided by other convicts. The British military saw their role as defence and preventing rebellion and (for its officers) making money. Convict numbers reached a peak of 27,831 in New South Wales in 1836, and 46.4 per cent of the recorded population in 1828. In Van Diemen's Land numbers peaked at 28,459 in 1848 and 47.1 per cent in 1819.

Convicts transported to Australia between 1788 and 1868 totalled 160,000 (Robson 1965). Convicts were a major part of the white recorded population and were overwhelmingly male (Robinson 1985, 1993; Daniels 1998). Convicts sent to Western Australia between 1850 and 1868 numbered 9,600, were exclusively male and included many drawn from the industrial areas of Lancashire, Yorkshire and the Midlands. A request that no Irish should be sent was ignored.

As in all repressive systems, some controllers could be more vicious than others. Patrick Logan of Moreton Bay (Brisbane) has gone down in song and story as particularly brutal and was eventually killed by Aborigines in 1830. At the other extreme was Alexander Maconochie, superintendent of Norfolk Island from 1840 to 1844. His radical reforms were well in advance of contemporary thinking. The degree of repression often depended on the colonial governors sent out for limited periods by the government in London. Convict life under Lachlan Macquarie was more liberal than under Ralph Darling (1825–1831), for example. However, this liberalism was criticized by the Thomas Bigge commission of enquiry, published in England in 1822 and 1823. This led to a series of administrative reforms, including further assignment of convicts to farmers and landowners (Hirst 1983).

In theory convicts enjoyed the same common law rights as enjoyed in England and Wales. But these were not very liberal in practice. By the 1830s *transportation*, as shipment of convicts to Australia was termed, was being attacked as 'slavery' both in England and New South Wales. Convicts could not be bought and sold, unlike the slaves in the US system until the civil war of the 1860s. Australia never had slavery, but it had many similar practices into modern times. What it also had was repression of the indigenous population as rigorously as in the United States, but without the use of overwhelming military force. The rapid decline in Aboriginal numbers was largely due to infectious diseases (Campbell 2002). Many were hunted down and shot, especially in Queensland, which did not become a distinct colony until 1859. The British government and humanitarians in England deplored this oppression, but had limited influence on settler society, which was at a distance of several months' sailing.

Many convicts were on a seven-year term, which could be reduced for good behaviour. It could be modified by the grant of tickets of leave, which allowed participation in the labour market and greater mobility. Many were forbidden to return to Britain but could build a new life in the colonies of New South Wales and Van Diemen's Land, often starting as labourers assigned to farmers (Alexander 2010). Murderers were normally hanged in Britain, so they did not arrive. Radicals such as Irish nationalists were sometimes treated lightly when they were of middle-class origin like Smith O'Brien and Joseph Holt.

After massive protests in Britain, six farm labourers from Tolpuddle (Dorset), transported in 1834 for forming a union, were returned to England three years later (Marlow 1971). Unions had been freed from the restrictive *Combination Acts* in 1824. It was no longer illegal to form one, but being charged with taking an illegal oath made transportation questionable.

Eventually, time-expired convicts moved into Victoria and South Australia, in neither of which were they welcomed, instead scorned as 'Van Diemonians'. Both these colonies had laws by the 1850s to prevent migration from Tasmania. Convicts, former convicts and their children comprised the majority of white Australians until the 1830s, when they began to be replaced by immigrants assisted with public funds from the sale of lands. Immigrants were encouraged to bring families and contributed to reducing the heavy male imbalance caused by the convict system (Oxley 1996; Robinson 1993). Many convicts had also formed families, started farming and commerce, and they were admitted rather reluctantly to the classes 'born free', meaning never a convict. Polite society, centred around the Government Houses of Sydney and Hobart, was usually closed to former convicts. The *South Australian Act of 1834* specifically banned the entrance of convicts into the new colony, with limited effect (Pike 1967). Wealth mattered more than origins, in contrast to Britain, where the two were closely interrelated. As long as the convict system lasted, Australia could not be described as a 'cohesive' society. Convicts and their families could always be identified by their ship of arrival. They were predominantly male labourers, with some middle-class forgers or embezzlers.

Misbehaving convicts could be locked into chain gangs, which mainly laboured on roads and public works. A few were imprisoned on small islands in Sydney Harbour, such as Garden Island. Others were sent to isolated prisons on Norfolk Island or at Port Arthur and Macquarie Island (Tasmania). Escape from these was almost impossible. Isolated penal stations at Newcastle, Port Macquarie and Moreton Bay were all more rigorous than the major centres at or near Sydney. Tasmania (Van Diemen's Land) was regarded as especially repressive, with an isolated island in Macquarie Harbour on the remote west coast (Reynolds 2012). In very serious cases, recalcitrants were hanged. More common was flogging, not prohibited for females until 1817, and used on boys as well as adults. Although transportation ended in 1840 in New South Wales and in 1853 in Tasmania (VDL), it was continued in Western Australia until 1868 (for male convicts only).

Prisons in the Pacific were central to the first 60 years of British settlement. (Shaw 1977; Robson 1965). The discovery of gold in the 1850s created several decades of free and uncontrolled immigration, with some ineffective restrictions on the Chinese by governments or employers (Victoria 1855). This came to an end throughout the united country with the *Immigration*

Restriction Act in 1901, the first major law of the Commonwealth (Simms 2001; London 1970; Tavan 2005). Without saying so, this created the White Australia system of excluding all immigrants not of European origin. About half the free settlers from the British Isles were assisted with the passage money; these settlers were selected in Britain or Ireland and paid for by funds raised from land sales in the Australian colonies (Charlotte Erickson 1994). Many were also given support for removal expenses by the English Poor Law system, reformed in 1834 around the new workhouses. Australian employers were critical of those chosen, as they had been of the convict labourers. Skilled workers in mining and the construction trades were not eligible for assistance, but were often paid passages by employers or trade unions.

While many former convicts created respectable and constructive lives, others were recruited into outlaw gangs of 'bushrangers', who flourished between the 1820s and 1880s (White 1975). Ned Kelly, like many other criminals, was the son of a convict, and his family was in regular conflict with the police (Macfarlane 2012). Assisted immigrants, however, normally established stable families and were selected with that in mind. Preference was given to agricultural workers for a century. Recruitment during the first Australian century was designed by colonial governments to ensure a predominantly British and Irish population of mainly working-class people, drawn from convicts, assisted immigrants and gold-rush arrivals. Traditional views of Australia were developed within that context and still influence many popular stereotypes. This produced a planned society, although not one without continuing problems.

Chapter 2

THE BRITISH INHERITANCE

The complex but controlled society of today, created after World War II, followed in a historic tradition of bureaucratic nation-building (S. Macintyre 2015). This began with the convict settlement of New South Wales from 1788 to the 1840s and then built on a system of state-assisted British and Irish immigration, which lasted from the 1830s until the 1970s. Other Europeans were not excluded before 1901, but were not encouraged, except for Protestant northern Europeans from Germany and Scandinavia (Koivukangas and Westin 1999; Tampke and Doxford 1990). From 1901 until the early 1970s no one was allowed to settle permanently who was not of white European origin, with some very limited exceptions, including some already there (Tavan 2005). Although other states around the Pacific had similar or related policies, none pursued them as rigorously as the new colonies of Australia (Lake and Reynolds 2008).

Such imported labour as had been, or continued to be, introduced included Muslim camel drivers from the north-west of the British Indian empire (the 'Afghans') (Bouma 1994; Cigler 1986). Pacific Islanders were recruited for the sugar cane plantations of Queensland and northern New South Wales, but were returned to their islands in 1906 (Corris 1973; Wawn 1893). By 1945 only 1 per cent of the population were not of white, European origin, together with less than 2 per cent from the Indigenous Aboriginal people who had lived in Australia for countless thousands of years. Both of these populations were declining in numbers by federation in 1901. Public policy was designed to maintain this decline (Markus 1979; Palfreeman 1967; Price 1974).

There is a contrast between Australia's early development of parliamentary democracy (Hirst 1988), its later ratifying of international conventions protecting human rights and the right to seek asylum, and its reluctance to extend such rights to minorities – ranging from the early convicts to the current asylum seekers. Unlike similar democracies, Australia does not have a bill of rights, either in its constitution or its legislation. In current debates and public analyses Australian culture is often credited with a basis in British liberal tradition and common law and/or the Judeo-Christian ethic and eighteenth-century Enlightenment (Gascoigne 2002; Broadie 2003; Herman 2003). These analyses are essentially social myths that treat the development of the past 250 years in favourable and even flattering terms. They are seldom analysed in detail and often serve the purpose of obscuring other less attractive inheritances, such as the denial of equality to unpopular minorities or individuals. Most elected politicians were anxious to sustain and expand the control of their parliaments and to mobilize the majority population, if necessary, against minority groups and opinions. Australia and Britain were not liberal democracies in the sixty founding years of the colonies, but neither were they autocracies. They were less directly influenced by the Enlightenment than many European societies or the United States. However most of their governors believed in rational planning, if not in formal democracy. For most of the convict period 'democracy' was officially rejected by governors as the bloodstained and unstable system imposed on France by the revolutionaries in 1795.

The so-called Judeo-Christian inheritance is a recent artefact coming from the United States. Previous Australian generations probably learned more about Greek and Roman cultures, as in Britain. This alleged inheritance is designed to distinguish majority ideals and practices from those of other 'alien' minorities and especially Muslims. Both the Jewish and Christian religions have important bases in the same Old Testament texts as Islam, a fact that is usually ignored or unknown. Most of the popular generalizations about Australia assume a much greater degree of uniformity than can be detected on closer inspection (Bouchard 2008; Hartz 1964). For two centuries two alternative Christian systems competed for public support, agreeing on many moral issues, but disagreeing on church discipline, private morality, educational systems and limitations on personal behaviour (Breward 2001). These Protestant and Catholic systems derived their clientele from Britain and Ireland, respectively. State control of immigration developed rapidly, only frustrated during the gold rushes by huge increases in population and private wealth. State selection was made more important by the need to sustain a cohesive society, while recruiting a labour force from overseas – one that would be useful, obedient and British.

The British inheritance is well documented (Bridge and Fedorowich 2003). But it is also less obvious and uncontested than it was as recently as the government of Sir Robert Menzies. Its lasting benefit is the English language and all those works of literature, knowledge and ideas that most Australians see as sustaining their way of life. Yet changes in ethnicity caused by mass immigration have reduced the British element in the population from over 95 per cent in the 1940s to less than 70 per cent by 2000. British subjects, apart from New Zealanders, ceased to have privileged immigration status in 1978.

A varied population of just over one million British-born remains, the largest number in such a diaspora outside the United Kingdom (Jupp 2004). The great majority of these have the vote, including an elderly residue who are not Australian citizens, but arrived while British subjects and Australian citizens had equal rights and privileges. The British diaspora is remarkably assimilated but still retains some old loyalties (Hammerton and Thomson 2005).

Prior to 1949 British subjects were treated as equally Australian unless they were 'Aboriginal natives of Asia, Africa or the Pacific'. Since then Australian citizenship has become increasingly obligatory for the franchise, passports and visa-free admission. Temporary residents, whether students, workers or visitors, may change their status entirely at the discretion of the Australian government. Citizens have no inalienable right to a passport. This remains the property of the Australian government and may, in rare but increasing cases be denied to them. By 2015 politicians were talking of removing passports from citizens thought to be active in support of Islamic extremism and having dual citizenship. Inhibiting this was the realization that dual citizens may number several millions, the largest group being from the United Kingdom. However, a growing number were stopped at the airports from travelling to the Middle East and a few of these had their passports cancelled. The threat of losing citizenship altogether now hangs over anyone believed to be involved in terrorism overseas. As proposed, this will be subject to a ministerial rather than a judicial decision.

It is still worth asking which traditional values influenced modern Australia in its formative century between 1788 and the 1880s. Many believe these laid the foundations for current beliefs and practices. To start with, the Judeo-Christian ethic was neither uniform nor uncontested over those years. Jewish influence was small and often denied by the great majority (Getzler 1970; Medding 1968). Christianity was seriously divided between Catholics, Anglicans, Presbyterians and Methodists, all of them competing for support and disagreeing on basic issues (Breward 2001; Hogan 1987). In contrast to the English inheritance, no denomination was officially established over any other (Border 1962). Anglicanism remained the numerical majority for 150 years (Frame 2007). But it lost any monopoly status by the 1830s, any constitutional role, except through the monarchy, by 1901, and its numerical domination by the 1950s. It is now outnumbered by Catholicism and challenged by Nonconformist and Pentecostal beliefs. The religious inheritance was fragmented from the early nineteenth century. Just as recent ecumenical cooperation brought the major denominations together, they were challenged by evangelical and fundamentalist beliefs (mainly from the United States), versions of Orthodoxy from the Balkans and Middle East and a variety of non-Christian beliefs and reforming secularism (Carey 1996; Mol 1971).

The early social, political and cultural inheritance from Britain is hard to recognize as having much connection with modern Australia (Davies 2000). In 1788 the United Kingdom was another world. Ireland had its own parliament until 1801 and policies imposed by its Protestant rulers were designed to drive the Catholic majority from their religion and Irish-speaking homelands. Scotland was recovering from its last rising, only 43 years before. Its failure destroyed any hopes of replacing a Protestant German monarch with a Scottish Catholic one. Many rural English were illiterate, while Celtic majorities in Ireland, Wales and western Scotland did not speak English. In rural societies there were hierarchical systems dominated by landowners with political and social power. Thousands of the rural poor were expelled from their homes in Ireland and Scotland, to be placed on ships to Canada or Australia (Richards 1985). Until the 1850s many coming to Australia were convicted felons. Ireland and the Highlands of Scotland both suffered from famines in the early nineteenth century, destructive of whole societies in western Ireland, where about one million starved to death in the 1840s (Keneally 1998). There was a regular stream to North America and a smaller one to Australasia (Erickson 1994; Richards 2008; Haines 1997: Harper 2003; Richards 2004). Most were economic, rather than persecuted, refugees.

There is not much from these societies that can still be directly traced in modern Australia. The English–British inheritance was planted in Botany Bay by military and civilian officials. It spread from there to cover the whole continent by the 1850s, however thinly. It drew on British practices and attitudes that are unrecognizable today in modern Australia. Some linger on only in televised and in sanitized visions of Old England. Hierarchy was central to this vision. Members of the British Parliament were elected by small minorities of male property owners. The hereditary House of Lords provided most of the cabinet ministers and prime ministers until late in the nineteenth century. Thirty dukes owned the majority of landed property, including huge estates in Scotland and Ireland. Until 1872 voting was open, which gave the agents of the aristocratic candidates a good opportunity to discipline their tenant farmers. Agricultural labourers did not have the vote until the 1880s, and women only enjoyed the full franchise by the late 1920s. The Australian colonies were well ahead of the United Kingdom in all of this. Reforming ideas came from Britain, but reforming reality was shaped in Australia, often by British immigrants.

The challenge to conservative institutions came with the influx of gold seekers to Victoria in the 1850s (Serle 1980). Unlike the planned intakes of convicts and assisted immigrants, bureaucratic controls broke down in the face of massive population increases drawn from throughout the world. The focal point for radical change was on the gold fields around Ballarat (Bate 1979;

Blainey 1969). The formulation of political objectives through the Ballarat Reform League drew not only on the British Chartists, but also on French, Irish and American radicalism. Conflicts between gold diggers and authority over compulsory mining permits escalated into the armed attack on the miner's stockade at Eureka in 1854 by forces drawn from the police and the British Army (Molony 1984; FitzSimons 2012). The swearing of allegiance to the Southern Cross flag was taken by authority as a direct repudiation of the British Empire and its queen, which had not been the intention of the miners' leaders (FitzSimons 2012). Authority was particularly fearful of the several hundreds of Americans, heavily armed and radically republican, who had come over from the California gold fields. As with radical movements in Britain, officials put the blame for disorder on foreigners.

Following the military attack on the Eureka stockade in December 1854 and the consequent deaths, injuries and captures, the colonial authorities put on trial such leaders as they could identify and created an official enquiry into the problems that had been revealed. The result was not what had been intended. Trials by jury led to all the accused being found not guilty of treasonous attack on the imperial system (Molony 1984). Rather than condemnation or execution, the eventual result was to consolidate a series of political reforms, extending the franchise to miners and laying the foundations of an elective democracy well in advance of the British model (Hirst 1988). The programme of the Ballarat radicals shaped many of the changes in the later years of the 'golden age' (Blainey 2008; Hill 2010) and were shared by other liberals.

Conservative British political and social traditions survived in Australia after the first hundred years partly as formal decoration or modified copies. Australian parliaments were elected by limited manhood suffrage from the late 1850s, except in Tasmania and Western Australia. The secret ballot developed at the same time and became known as the 'Australian ballot' in the United States and Britain. Women were enfranchised without the violent struggle that marred British politics right up to 1914 and did not fully succeed until 1928. The rule of law or parliamentary government are often quoted as derived from England. However, they were advanced more quickly in Australia by local initiatives. They were not obstructed by the British aristocratic system. Some relics remained well into the twentieth century, including nomination or property franchises for the upper houses of state parliaments. These have all gone, and the Queensland upper house was abolished altogether in 1922.

By many standards Australia rejected and moved ahead of the British inheritance. By the end of the nineteenth century it could present itself as a paradise of democracy and social equality. Yet the British model was not unimportant. What, if anything, did Australia inherit of British traditions of hierarchy and inequality? One obvious inheritance until the 1850s was the existence of transported convict labour, which Britain had been using in its colonies since the seventeenth century. Convicts were British subjects and could not be legally bought and sold. Britain illegalized slavery in the United Kingdom from 1807 and finally abolished slavery throughout the empire in 1833. But convict transportation continued in Australia and peaked in numbers after the British abolition of slavery. Politicians were divided over slavery, although less violently than in the United States. Transportation did not finally end until 1868 in Western Australia. Even so, many convicts were still under life sentences, while others had worked their ticket of leave. Some became quite prosperous. Most did not. Australia was never an equal society, but it had an egalitarian ethos largely derived from the humble origins of transported convicts and assisted immigrants, the majority of the first generation of settlers. At the same time, it was developing an upper class based largely on land ownership, as in the United Kingdom, if more modestly, and on professional immigrants from Britain. These tended to define Australia in terms of loyalty to the British Empire, but not necessarily to British Conservatism. The term 'Conservative' was not used by Australian political parties, 'Liberal' being preferred as in Britain until the end of Queen Victoria's reign in 1901.

As convict labour declined it was replaced for many by indentured labour, which bound workers to their employer. They were also bound by Master and Servant Acts based on the British model, but adopted by local parliaments. These were ended in Australia after political agitation (Saunders 1982). Indentured labour, which had been adopted for imported Pacific Island labourers, was specifically forbidden in the *1901 Immigration Restriction Act* of the new Commonwealth. By then Australia had a strong trade union movement, based on British models, but with more influence because of continuing labour shortages in some regions and industries. Trade unions were well represented in parliaments from 1891, which was not the case in Britain until 1906.

Prejudice remained against convicts and their descendants as did hostility against governors who encouraged them. Australia could not be a cohesive society until the convicts had faded from memory. It was one of the contradictions of this new society that it was founded in coercion and punishment, while many of its leaders believed sincerely in freedom and liberty. It was also founded in an ambivalent attitude towards the Aboriginal inhabitants. Dispossession was common in Britain, from the forced emigration of Scottish and Irish peasants to the private enclosure of common lands. These policies were protected by law and were at their height in Britain during the founding years of Australia.

Aboriginal dispossession was extensive and disruptive. It had the full support of elected politicians as well as settlers. Australian land was vested in the Crown and all uncultivated land was described as 'waste lands' for distribution to potential farmers and British landowners. Having no visible political or legal systems or borders, Aborigines had no effective rights over land they regarded as theirs. One British tradition was that only land that had felt the plough could be owned by someone. This remained the case for land not already alienated, whether in northern or western deserts or the Torres Strait Islands. By the 1990s, vast areas of uncultivated ground were eventually acknowledged to be Aboriginal land, including major parts of the Northern Territory, Queensland and Western Australia. Generations of Aborigines had been unable to benefit from this major change, which was gained by political campaigns and legal decisions. Most alienated land never returned to Aboriginal claimants.

One feature of British society that had an indirect influence on Australia was the Poor Law system (Griffin 2014; Rose 1971). Instituted by Queen Elizabeth I in 1601, this provided for each of the hundreds of English and Welsh parishes to sustain their poor and elderly at a very modest level. It was drastically amended in 1834, largely due to the costs of supporting an increasing population from parish rates. Entitlement was replaced by coercion. Poverty was punished under the new union workhouse system, where it had been subsidized under the previous parish system. Newly built workhouses practiced 'punishing the poor' by incarcerating those unable to support themselves in large, sex-segregated buildings, where conditions were planned to be worse than remaining outside. This never became universal, and was strongly opposed in industrial areas, where several workhouses were burned down, and outdoor relief favoured. Until the English system was finally ended in 1929 and the workhouses closed in 1948, the local basis of poor relief and the ultimate threat of the workhouse disciplined the elderly and the unemployed. This system was resented even more strongly in Ireland than in England and was abolished in the Irish Free State in 1923 (Gray 2009). Scotland had a distinct system of outdoor parish relief. Australian reaction against such systems prompted the very early institution of basic welfare provisions in Australia, even before Britain (S. Macintyre 1985). However, the development of compulsory Aboriginal locations from the 1890s kept the workhouse principles of mandatory residence, behaviour restrictions, control of the workforce and its remuneration and strict discipline.

The principle of punishing people, by making their situation worse than it might otherwise have been, was revived in dealing with unvisaed asylum seekers on the basis of 'no advantage', in the twenty-first century. Australian welfare in general owes much to the British model. But there was never a complete workhouse system, and British immigrants would have objected to one. The principle of 'punishing the poor' was, however, well understood and implemented during economic depressions. Mandatory road works were used in depressions in exchange for basic payments. Roads that had once been built by convict chain gangs were extended and improved by the unemployed in the 1930s. Punishing the poor was revived for immigrants in the 1940s with inadequate housing and services for displaced persons and British-assisted migrants. They were officially urged to be grateful for what they were receiving, which was often disused army huts (Sluga 1988).

British influence was, and remained, contradictory. Many were indifferent to the fate of convicts, immigrants and Aborigines, while others such as Caroline Chisholm and St. Mary McKillop, both Catholics, saw them as deserving subjects of Victorian Christian charity. Imported diseases, imprisonment and armed repression reduced the Aboriginal population to less than 100,000 by 1900. British governors held prestigious if limited power. British-born politicians were common until the 1920s, and appointments from Britain continued to be made for academics, lawyers, clergy, businessmen and public servants. A large proportion from these classes were also of English and Scottish Protestant origin. Australia remains a monarchy with the approval of a majority of Australians. These decorative reminders of British privileges were only gradually eroded. A few remain, centred around the monarchy, parliament, the law and some universities. Protestant prime ministers such as Bruce, Menzies and Howard were Anglophiles. The seven Catholic prime ministers were not to the same degree, if at all.

Chapter 3

WHITE AUSTRALIA AND THE GOLDEN AGE

The second half of the nineteenth century corresponds with the most expansive period of the British Empire under Queen Victoria. Its successes in Australia lay largely with the new colony of Victoria. This relied neither on convicts nor on assisted immigrants for most of this period, being peopled by many thousands seeking gold from 1851 (Hill 2010). The Victorian population increased sevenfold between 1851 and 1860. (Blainey 1969, 2008). Over half-a-million made it the largest of all the Australian colonies by 1860, a position it retained until 1895. Thousands were living in tents in the early years, but Melbourne, Geelong, Ballarat, Bendigo and many other towns were well built and even impressive cities by the time the depression of the 1890s struck (Serle 1963; Bate 1979). Goldfields around central Victoria provided much of the wealth and were worked mainly by recent immigrants, not all of them British.

The 'golden age' began inauspiciously, with the 1854 rebellion at the Eureka stockade in Ballarat. (FitzSimons 2012; Molony 1984). Although it was put down by the military, as it would have been in England, its long-term effect was the extension of the franchise to males and the election of miners' leaders to the Victorian parliament. Eureka underlined how fragile was social cohesion in a society that was rapidly growing and mobile. Wisely, the colonial administration saw that creating a popular parliament and broadening the distribution of land was likely to absorb social resentments. Rather than repression, the New South Wales government implemented changes already planned before the uprising, as did the new colony of Victoria.

The nineteenth century was characterized by much excitement about increased population. London prided itself on being the largest city in the world, at the head of the largest empire in world history. New South Wales drew ahead of Tasmania quite rapidly, was passed by Victoria between 1854 and 1895, with Queensland and South Australia catching up fast from 1870 and West Australia lagging well behind until 1900. By then New South Wales and Sydney had regained the prime position from which they started and that they have never again lost. In the four fastest-moving colonies the motive force was gold, while South Australia and Tasmania had population surges from mining baser metals. Sheep and wheat remained the staple products of agriculture. The majority of Australians lived in rural societies until 1900, but never again (Blainey 2003).

If Australia was consciously colonized to keep it white and British, it was also developed by practical, hard-working men and women, chosen not for their education or origins, but for their ability to conquer physical hardship, vast distances and an uncertain climate. The emphasis was consistently on male roles, but also on modifying the male gender balance of nine to one in the convict days. By the 1830s it was accepted that such a predominantly male society was unhealthy and possibly dangerous. It could only expand steadily by reproduction, even if immigration was consistently pursued. Although there were early intakes of Indian and Chinese labour and later of Pacific Islanders in the sugar cane fields, these were not seen as the appropriate bases for the desired society. The Indigenous population was used for agricultural labour, but lacked the assumed docility of Indians and was declining from imported diseases. Most lived outside a monetary economy and very few were literate or spoke English.

An official priority was to bring out young, complete, families as well as sufficient women to correct the unnatural gender balance. As Edward Gibbon Wakefield, the influential theorist of immigration, wrote in 1849, 'an equal emigration of the sexes is one essential condition of the best emigration' (*A View of the Art of Colonization*). After a controversial intake of several thousand Irish workhouse girls, and doubts about morality on the long sea voyage, policy settled down to bringing out young families. Very young children, who tended to die en route and to be a burden by preventing employment if they lived, were not accepted. Shipboard morality was preserved by rigidly divided accommodation and supervision by a female matron. Despite these precautions, women were arriving in Sydney without funds or protection, inspiring Caroline Chisholm to accommodate them and send them off to bush employers. Women were sought after as domestic servants and were often married within a few months of arrival. In contrast to Britain and Europe, women did not normally work in the fields alongside the men, but took many manual roles on family farms. The itinerant shearing workforce was exclusively male.

Male immigrants were chosen for their skills, especially in farm work, or their strength and health. No sick or disabled immigrants were allowed, a prohibition that still holds today. Skilled workers, such as miners or building craftsmen, were often recruited from Britain by employers. Professionals and white-collar immigrants were not eligible for assistance but could often raise the fare themselves. There was some prejudice against such 'unproductive' people, although lawyers did well, perhaps because of lack of competition. There were very few graduates in Australia and only four small universities (Sydney, Melbourne, Adelaide and Tasmania) by 1901. The 1891 Victorian census reveals that there were less than a thousand graduates in the colony in a population of over a million. Yet with these modest numbers Melbourne sustained an active intellectual life.

This 40-year period (1850–1891) also saw the increasing wealth and power of the British Empire under Queen Victoria, of which the six Australian colonies remained loyal members. Massive immigration continued from the British Isles, often assisted with funds from the colonies and support from London through the Colonial Land and Emigration Commission (Serle 1980). By 1891 the population had passed three million, or almost seven times the number in 1850. Of these, 460,000 were born in England, 228,000 in Ireland and 124,000 in Scotland or, at 812,000, a third of the total population. It was a British society but not just an English one, with 45,000 born in Germany and, more controversially, 37,000 classified as Chinese and 10,000 Pacific Islanders. It was these two peoples who were to provide the fuel for ending the free admission of immigrants to the 'land of gold'.

During this golden age the major cities of South Eastern Australia were transformed. (Serle 1980). Churches were built, banks opened, streets of working-class cottages put up and shopping districts begun in suburbs as well as town centres. Large mansions on the lines of English stately homes were built, especially in Victoria. Wool and gold exports were the basis for an expanding economy. Manufacturing was also expanding in Victoria in competition with British imports. New South Wales followed Britain over free trade, while Victoria, more controversially, favoured protection.

Railway systems were expanded, although they used different gauges in each colony.

Melbourne became the largest city, until the economic crash of 1891 led to its population decline below the level of Sydney. The intellectual life of Melbourne and Sydney had a focus in their respective universities, founded in the 1850s. These were followed by Adelaide in 1874 and Tasmania in 1889. Parliamentary politics also flourished, although corruption was a factor to be deplored by the newspapers. Protestant influence in Melbourne led to legislative prohibitions directed towards alcohol, indecent behaviour, gambling, Sabbath observance and sex (Bongiorno 2012). Education was secularized, with the withdrawal of the subsidies to religious schools, which had been initiated in the 1830s. For the next century the comparative poverty of the Catholic education systems remained as a dividing issue in what claimed to be a cohesive and white British society (O'Farrell 1977). The universities of

Sydney and Melbourne were secular institutions. But their residential colleges were linked to the Protestant churches and private schools. While some smaller cities such as Ballarat, Bendigo and Bathurst survived and prospered, many mining towns simply disappeared or left a few relics to be turned into tourist attractions in later years. Neither the urban nor the rural populations were fully stabilized, but moved around in the search for employment. This led to considerable differences in laws, punishments, education, enfranchisement and entitlements between colonies. There was over a decade between the early granting of the franchise to women in South Australia and its late arrival in Victoria.

Towards the 1880s the two major colonies, New South Wales and Victoria, and to some extent South Australia and Tasmania, had created a class system based on agricultural wealth and commercial profit, in the absence of a long-standing hereditary aristocracy. At the other end of society there were slum conditions in the inner cities and absolute destitution in those Aboriginal societies in direct contact with urban society. Bushranging did not end until the defeat of Ned Kelly at Glenrowan and his execution in 1880 (Macfarlane 2012). Crime within the two metropolitan cities was largely based on slums, as it had been in London in the convict days. Official surveys taken in Sydney in the 1870s also suggested that Irish immigrants were more likely to be involved in crimes of violence. By the end of the 'golden age' many Australians enjoyed a comfortable suburban life. Many others were becoming unionized and able to protect themselves. But there was still a 'submerged tenth' in the cities, as in Britain. From the 1870s this was the target for Christian missionaries in the Salvation Army and other charitable movements with origins in the British slums.

There was still a male preponderance, heavy drinking and occasional violence and rioting. These were directed against Chinese miners at Lambing Flat (NSW) in 1860 and Buckland River (Victoria) in 1857, against early communists in Brisbane in 1918, and spasmodically against Catholics. There was forcible relocation of Aborigines and, in Queensland, an armed force, the Native Police, which were notorious for their attacks on Aboriginal groups, regardless of their behaviour and the nominal law. In Queensland and Western Australia laws were being passed by the 1890s to force Aborigines into the 'protection' of controlled settlements. Aborigines were forbidden entry to Perth until the 1940s. State laws tried to categorize Aborigines in terms of colour and assimilation and controlled who they might marry, with a view to breeding out colour (Haebich 1988).

These 40 years of a golden age ended abruptly in the 1890s with a depression centred on Melbourne, which had gained most from the prosperity of the preceding years (Serle 1980). Below the Tropic of Capricorn, the Aboriginal population had been moved to the margin of popular concern by force and by previously unknown diseases (Anderson 2002). British patriotism prevailed, but British culture and allegiance were less central than before. The dominance of Sydney had diminished and was replaced for a few years by Melbourne.

Mass assisted migration to Queensland laid the foundations for future growth and prosperity along its thousand-mile coast (Bolton 1970). The 1880s saw more arrivals there than in any decade before or since. Much Queensland labour was recruited from Pacific Islanders for the sugar industry, drawn mainly from the New Hebrides (Vanuatu) and Solomon Islands. This created a plantation society that some equated with slavery, although legally this was not the case (Saunders 1982). Pacific Islanders were recruited on indentures. (Corris 1973; Evans et al. 1993). As most could neither read, write nor speak English these documents meant very little to them. About one in three Islanders died of basic diseases, despite a special hospital for them. Queensland also opened assisted immigration to Germans and Scandinavians, which other colonies did not. It soon became the most multicultural of all the six colonies. Its people were loyal to Britain, but its society was quite unlike anything in the United Kingdom (Reynolds 1987). In particular, it became notorious for its armed assaults on the Aborigines and for frequent riots against Chinese (Evans et al. 1993). By 1891 Queensland experienced armed confrontation between shearers and employers, and the foundation was laid for the Australian Shearers Union and Australian Labor Party (Merritt 1986; Murphy 1975). To an even greater extent than in South Eastern Australia, Queensland was a male-dominated society. The unions and labour parties reflected this until well into the next two generations (Murphy 1975). Queensland had 40 years of Labor government before lapsing rather suddenly into conservatism in the 1950s.

This rapid growth created a large provincial working class of miners, pastoral workers, railwaymen and construction workers, which soon became unionized and politically active. Unlike in Britain, most of these classes had the vote (if male and white) and were not concentrated in large industrial cities. Britain was already an urban and manufacturing society, but Australia was not. Politically its provincial and rural working classes were organized around trade unionism and labour politics to a greater degree than in Britain. One major result of the strikes was for the new Commonwealth to gain the power to intervene in industrial disputes across State borders (Australian Constitution ss.51 xxxv.) This brought the recently unruly trade unions within the arbitration system, hailed at the time as solving previous militancy, continuing to be used for reconciling major disputes as the unions grew in strength and, as they declined into the present century, overseeing their affairs. The violent disputes of the past faded away with the exception of the waterfronts and the mines. Policies adopted after federation thus dealt with many disputed areas, including race and immigration, but left Aborigines to the states until sixty years later.

Organized workers were strongly concentrated in Queensland and New South Wales and were soon electing representatives to their colonial parliaments. The idea of working-class representation had been debated in England since the 1800s. It was not achieved on this scale until the 1920s. The British franchise remained limited until 1918. Australian culture at the end of the 'golden age' was about labour representation, unionism and using politics to defend and advance the working class. This marked a unique Australian input into the colonial political culture, an input that was soon to create governments and long-term loyalties. Australian nationalists presented the new society as the 'Working Man's Paradise', if sometimes sarcastically. The 'Legend of the Nineties' was created, to be commemorated by Australian socialists and unionists for the next 75 years (Ward 1965: Ross 1980). For all of that time it ran parallel with the White Australia policy – a combination that was rarely questioned and had no direct British counterpart.

This was not a socialist movement, so much as a labour one (Gollan 1960). Socialists and liberal radicals had most influence in Victoria, where the trade unions were fragmented and the Labor Party electorally weak (Burgmann 1985). At the trade union centre was opposition to the immigration of non-British labour, which was strongest in New South Wales and Queensland. This was sharpened by the unemployment caused by the depression of the 1890s and the accompanying wage cuts and dismissals. It followed in certain British traditions and was often led by British immigrants like William Lane, Billy Hughes or Andrew Fisher. It was uniquely Australian in avoiding absorption into the major Liberal parties, in not developing elaborate socialist theories, in organizing manual, rural and provincial labour, and in its hostility to non-British immigration (Childe 1923/1964).

Labor was less influenced from Methodism and other reforming religious sects than in Britain, although many of its early leaders were church-going Christians. Unlike the emerging British labour movement, it did not share hostility towards the Irish in its early days. This allowed the Scots and the Irish to take a leading role. However, outside New South Wales, Irish Catholic influence remained limited until World War I, despite the sympathy of Cardinal Patrick Moran, the Archbishop of Sydney. He, like most other Catholic priests, was suspicious of socialism, which they equated with the secular and anti-clerical traditions of Europe (Ayres 2007; Ford 1966). Catholic theologians developed the concept of social justice rather than class struggle. In this they agreed with Protestant liberals and many craft unionists (Gollan 1960; Nairn 1975). Marxism had a modest impact, as in Britain. The American radicalism of Daniel de Leon and the Industrial Workers of the World was more important. British Fabianism was largely confined to Melbourne, visited in 1898 by the Fabian founders Sidney and Beatrice Webb (Austin 1965). She was not impressed.

The history of a uniquely Australian labour movement in the 1890s has tended to be buried in recent years beneath the notion that the Gallipoli military landing of 1915 'saw Australia come of age'. From another angle, the 1890s are seen as the decade led to the Australian colonies finally coming together in the Commonwealth in 1901 (Birrell 2001). This was certainly a climactic response to the huge changes wrought by the 'golden age'. But the creation by widely dispersed, poorly educated and recently arrived working men of a mass political movement, which held office nationally and in all the former colonies by 1915, was at least as important in shaping Australian culture as other 'legends' (Burgmann 1985). The Australian Labor Party had celebrated 120 years of continuous history by 2011. No other Australian party can make such a claim, nor can the British or New Zealand labour parties. Despite many amalgamations, some trade unions trace their origins over that period or longer. In contrast to Britain, the early labour strength lay outside the major cities and especially in Queensland. It adopted the White Australia policy from its beginning in 1891 and hung on to it until 1965 (Tavan 2005; London 1970). The policy was cemented in the *Commonwealth Immigration Restriction Act of 1901*), replaced by the *Migration Act* in 1958.

The commitment to parliamentary politics by the working-class organizations did not entirely eliminate the more radical and violent tactics common on the goldfields and the shearing sheds. Much violence on the goldfields was directed against the Chinese, after the political gains of Eureka had satisfied the majority of enfranchised miners. In the shearing sheds during the depression of the 1890s shearers organized against employers who were determined not to recognize unions or maintain wages. Chinese, Pacific Islander and Aboriginal labour had already been excluded from the shearing sheds, except as cooks, by decision of the Shearers Union. The shearers unions, later amalgamated into the Australian Workers Union, for a century Australia's largest (Merritt 1986) and still a major force.

The Queensland employers tried to enforce a new agreement in 1890, one which would have reduced union influence. In 1891 the use of non-union labour precipitated armed conflict and the closing down of shearing at a crucial time (Svensen 1989). Queensland state troopers were called in to support the employers. Violence, police and militia intervention, the burning of shearing sheds and the formation of armed camps, marked the strikes of 1891 and were reminiscent of similar tactics used by English labourers a century before. The strikes were eventually defeated and the leaders in Clermont arrested, charged with conspiracy and found guilty at Rockhampton in May 1891. They were sentenced to three years in an island prison. The 1891 strike compares with Eureka as one of the few potentially revolutionary episodes in Australian history. Armed intervention against strikes fulfilled the two major objectives of the state – the defence of social cohesion and the advance of the capitalist economy. Social cohesion was thus defined as in the interest of employers.

For eighty years Australia's 'settled policy' was to prohibit the immigration of non-Europeans (Willard 1923/1967; Yarwood 1964). With one individual exception, the three parties represented in the first Commonwealth parliament – Free Trade, Protection and Labour – voted unanimously for the *1901 Immigration Restriction Act* (Simms 2001). As amended, this remained in force until 1958, when it was replaced by the *Migration Act*. This second act did not end the White Australia policy but, like its predecessor, avoided any reference to race. The legislation placed in the hands of immigration officers the power to decide whether an immigrant was non-European (Palfreeman 1967). Unlike colonial laws passed before Federation, such as the NSW Influx of *Chinese Restriction Act of 1881*, the Chinese were not specifically mentioned. Pacific Islanders were the subject of the *Pacific Island Labourers Act of 1901*, which led to their expulsion from Australia. Unlike the Indians or Africans who made up the majority of the British Empire, they were stateless.

The New Hebrides and the Solomons were only protectorates, British and French for the New Hebrides and British for the Solomons. The Pacific Islanders were multilingual and tribal, which tended to divide them in Australia (Wawn 1973). They were also distinct from the Aborigines in being wage labourers. Known only as Kanakas, they were effectively removed from Australia in 1906, with limited exceptions around Mackay in central Queensland (C. Moore 1978).

The 1901 legislation unfortunately introduced two principles into Australian political culture: that immigration would be based on race; and that as far as possible this would be denied, so as not to annoy Britain or India or Asian neighbours like Japan. (Brawley 1995). The second principle became more important after 1945 and was part of the sustained avoidance and denial that characterized discussions of race and immigration into the 1950s. The first principle became a central objective of the Labor Party and the trade unions and remained so until 1965 (Tavan 2005). Britain never adopted a specifically racial migration policy, but devised regulations and legislation from 1962 that changed the status of British Commonwealth citizens, including Australians.

There was, therefore, no uniformity throughout the British Empire. Racially based immigration policies were normally blocked by the United Kingdom before 1901 (Lake and Reynolds 2008). Until 1905, the United Kingdom did not have an *Aliens Act*, but then it was directed against Russian Jews rather than colonial subjects. British subjects, including Australians, enjoyed free entry to Britain until the 1960s. In this, as in many other ways, federation of the Australian colonies on the basis of race was a major step towards true independence. It was to sustain a white, racially pure, society for the next 75 years, with only fragmentary and declining relics of Aboriginal, Islander and Asian minorities. British authorities, concerned about the reaction in their vast empire, tried to block the policy, but lost the ability to do so after Federation. Japan, a World War I ally, made its objections very clear at the post-war settlement conferences of 1918 and was rudely rebuffed by Prime Minister Billy Hughes. Japan changed its previous alliance with Britain and allied with Germany from 1935 until the end of World War II in 1945.

The Commonwealth Constitution of 1901 made immigration an exclusive Commonwealth power (51xxvii), but this was not fully operative until 1920. The "Aboriginal race" remained with the states until 1967. All other "people of any race for whom it is necessary to make special laws" (and Aborigines) then came within Commonwealth responsibility (51xxvi). Franchise and naturalization Acts, passed within three years of Federation, denied the vote to "aboriginal natives of Australasia, Asia, Africa or the Islands of the Pacific". The same formula was used to deny citizenship by naturalization. Maoris were exempted on the insistence of the New Zealand government, which was considering joining the federation. The later files of the Commonwealth Department of Immigration were based on racial categories. These included the Eurasians, Ceylon Burghers and Anglo-Indians who were seeking to leave Asian societies freed from the British Empire. They were Christian and English-speaking, but of the wrong complexion. Applicants were expected to produce appropriate genealogies. Whatever may have been true in 1901, race and colour were pre-eminent considerations 50 years later (Brawley 1995)

The White Australia policy was justified in political debate largely as protecting the interests of working men, who were becoming unionized by 1901. While there was criticism of intermarriage between races, this was mainly an issue in the outback districts of the north and centre with more relevance to Aborigines than to immigrants. It was not illegal, as in some US states, but could be forbidden for Aborigines confined to settlements or 'wards of the state'. 'Race' in the conventional sense became increasingly important as the policy was consolidated around control of immigration (Calwell 1972). By the 1930s and through to the 1960s, inspection of the physical appearance of intending immigrants was carefully implemented by immigration officers, with instructions provided by the immigration departments. Arrival was normally by ship, and officers would board vessels in the harbour before allowing passengers to land. Well before this, ship booking offices would advise intending passengers of 'non-European' appearance that they would probably be rejected, and would not issue them tickets. Shipping companies were liable for rejections and fined or obliged to return failed entrants at their expense. This remained true for airline companies until the 1960s.

As most ships stopped at Port Said, Aden, Colombo or Bombay, this was a precaution against picking up passengers from those ports. The whole operation was based on colour and appearance. It could be offensive to travellers from southern Europe or the Middle East who were dark skinned or of mixed descent. Arguments in recent years that the policy was only an economic or social protection of standards are not plausible (Windschuttle 2004). Early parliamentary debates took this position, but administrative decisions were increasingly based on physical appearance, as defined and developed by the Immigration Department and its predecessors before 1945. This added another bureaucratic strand to nation-building and cohesiveness.

While the policy was very restrictive, it could not cater for all eventualities or individual exceptions. In 1906 Pacific Islanders had been rounded up and deported back to the New Hebrides or the Solomon Islands under the 1901 legislation. Some managed to remain behind and formed the South Sea Island communities in Queensland (Moore 1978). These were mainly rural labourers without any clearly defined status or recognition until well after White Australia was ended. Chinese residents with solid local connections or locally born were given certificates that allowed them to return should they leave Australia. The same facility was extended to members of the small Afghan communities remaining after the decline of the camel transport industry in the 1920s (Cigler 1986;). The main factor in reducing the Asian populations was a prohibition on family reunion for those without certificates of exemption.

Limited concessions were also extended to Sikhs who had served in the British Army. There were more Indians at Gallipoli than Australians. This was sometimes recognized by the ex-service organizations that were otherwise the strongest supporters of White Australia. A viable Sikh community was established at Woolgoolga (NSW) (de Lepervanche 1984). Its members were not admitted to the local RSL Club wearing their traditional turbans. None of these communities, even the large Chinese remnant, had much opportunity to expand their numbers. The Chinese-born in 1911 totalled 20,994, but had fallen to only 6,404 by 1947.

Exceptions were made for Japanese employed as pearl divers in northern Australia, who were all male. They were interned during World War II and deported to Japan afterwards (Nagata 2000). Merchants and students were usually given temporary facilities to remain in Australia for limited periods. The virtual absence of women among these minorities led to intermarriage with Aborigines or Anglo-Australians. While this was frequently deplored it was not illegal and allowed small communities to continue their limited existence. Several Chinese–Aborigines assumed leading roles in community life in the Northern Territory.

White Australia was essentially a Commonwealth immigration policy based on colour and origins (London 1970). Aboriginal affairs were left with the states, all of which were controlled by politicians who also subscribed to White Australia. Police and prisons were also a state responsibility and were central to implementing the policy locally. Three elements of the population were victims of pressure and prejudice even during the 'golden age' of secularism, solidarity and progress. These were the Aborigines, whose culture was seen as incompatible with modern life; the Irish, whose religion was seen as obscurantist and oppressive; and the Chinese, who were seen as threatening settler stability by their potential numbers and alien culture. All of these were cultural rather than racial attributes, but this made very little difference to their rejection. What was later known as 'Islamophobia' in Europe was not based on colour (Morgan and Poynting 2012). In Australia the majority of Muslims would not have passed the colour test. But neither would most Christians from India, Africa, the Philippines, China or Sri Lanka. By the 1970s immigration policy was not only offensive but also a muddle. It remained true after the policy ended that nobody who was a white Christian was ever interned with asylum seekers, although white convicted criminals have been deported. Muslim Albanians and Bosnians from the Balkans were admitted in small numbers in the 1920s and as displaced persons after 1947. Turks were accepted from 1967 and recruited into the car industry, as in Germany (Tavan 2005). Lebanese Christians had been accepted seventy years before, after arguing that they were not Asians.

Other minorities were often too small to attract much attention. Anti-semitism was present, as in England, but had a small target until the 1920s (Rutland 2001; Medding 1968). Jews were excluded from the fashionable gentlemen's clubs in the major cities, but so were women. Anti-semitic cartoons and articles appeared in the popular press, including that supporting Labor. But in pursuit of the principles of secularism and religious equality, Jews were not excluded from public office, as they were in England into the 1880s for failing to take a loyalty oath on the Bible (Getzler 1970). The majority of Jews were originally from England or Germany, both acceptable as sources. The very small number of Asian Jews from India or Iraq were discriminated against as immigrants and specifically listed in the census. Prejudice grew, again as in England, with the advent of Jewish refugees from the former Russian empire.

While 'non-Europeans' were strictly excluded after 1901, small communities of Italians, Lebanese and Greeks were forming by the 1890s, the Lebanese also being Christians (Maronite and Antiochian). Christianity in itself did not assist such Asian peoples as the Filipinos or Koreans. The Lebanese asserted their non-Asian culture and took a small role in business and later in politics after 1900. This did not prevent criticism of them as Syrians. Other Arabs were excluded, and the only significant Muslim population was derived from the Balkans or from the exempted camel driver Afghans from British India, living in central Australia and arriving before White Australia became law (Cigler 1986).

Much larger German communities had been established in South Australia in the 1830s. Queensland positively encouraged German and Scandinavian immigration with fares and land grants from the 1880s (Jurgensen and Corkhill 1988). This preference for white Protestants was consistent with majority attitudes. By the end of the 'golden age' there was political unanimity that the state should prohibit the open migration that had been allowed in the pioneering days. This was a major factor in supporting federation and the Labor parties. Some went even further by forming an Australian Natives Association confined to those actually born in Australia. (Birrell 1995). It was particularly strong in Victoria, the colony that had gained most from the discovery of gold and subsequent immigration.

The virtual elimination of non-Europeans, and the decline in the Aboriginal population to less than 100,000, reduced the probability of ethnic strife and violence. However, cohesion was not manifest. Violent confrontations still occurred during industrial disputes and strikes. These became common as the mass migrations of the 1880s came into collision with the economic slump of the early 1890s. There was also strong opposition to migration from Yugoslavia into Western Australia in the 1920s and the highly critical Ferry Commission report on Greek and Italian immigration by the Queensland Labor government in 1925.

White Australia certainly reduced the non-European population of Australia to a tiny minority of little more than 1 per cent. But it did not reduce violent confrontations or the persistence of prejudice against foreigners and immigrants. Society was not more cohesive, especially in the years of the depression from 1930 to 1939. Unemployment was higher than before, regardless of the absence of migrant competition for jobs. Aborigines did not step into the vacancies left by the absence of Asians, nor was their social situation improved. It also caused severe problems for those Asians who wished to bring further relatives into the country, especially those escaping from Japanese imperialism in China and later throughout the South Pacific. Above all it was stupid to exclude anyone on the basis of their colour alone, as some supporters of the system had argued from the beginning. Rather it would have been more sensible to gradually introduce controlled numbers of skilled migrants from Asia until public opinion got used to the idea (Tavan 2005).

That is what happened from the 1960s onwards, to be modified by refugee arrivals, often from wars in which Australia had taken a part.

Rioting continued as a threat to law and order, but was not predominantly concerned with political outcomes. During World War I, rioting broke out on several occasions involving Australian servicemen, both in Australia and in Egypt. In 1916 rioting in Liverpool (NSW) was violent enough to lead to the six o'clock hotel closing hours, which remained throughout Australia until the 1970s. In Brisbane in 1918–19 ex-servicemen joined in anti-communist rioting against some of the local Russian community and trade unionists. (Evans 1989). A noteworthy strike and riot was at Rothbury (NSW) on the Hunter coalfield in 1929, where a miner (Norman Brown) was shot dead by the police, the only such event in union history and probably an accident. A major race riot took place in Kalgoorlie (WA) in 1934 against southern Europeans, leading to the flight of the Greek population to Perth, where they remained. None of these compared with the armed confrontations of 1891, however, and did not pass into socialist or trade union history for obvious reasons.

Nevertheless, the Australian working class had a reputation for militancy that was more marked than for the English migrants arriving during the late 1920s to find an economic crisis depriving them of work. It was not a happy time (Bolton 1994, 1972). The collapse of the national Labor and New South Wales governments between 1931 and 1932 and the subsequent breakup of Labor unity did not improve solidarity. A fear of unemployment was entrenched, joining the fear of competition from foreign labour. In most elections, state and Commonwealth, 'jobs' still holds priority over all other slogans. Overall, Australia prospered in the nineteenth century through planned input of immigrants, alienation of indigenous lands, mineral discoveries, political stability and access to overseas (mainly British) markets and capital. Economic trends could not be controlled as easily as immigration, which was normally suspended during depressions.

A limited range of Australian traditions, practices and beliefs stands out and helps explain many other myths, realities and practices. These are the search for social cohesion, the urgency of economic development and the belief that the state has a central responsibility in both areas for planning and control. Otherwise the inheritance from Liberal and Conservative Britain was very different in many ways. Society was seen there as determined over the centuries by hierarchies based on social status and religion – "freedom broadening down from precedent to precedent" as the liberal theorists put it.

This left the London government with limited responsibility, with control by an established ruling class spread across the United Kingdom and often serving in the British Empire or exercising local power. The economy was self-managing through free trade, competition and the fluctuation of prices, but with special protection for the produce of the land. If welfare of the poor were needed, it was provided locally through the Poor Law. British railways, water and sewerage, lighting and gas, were all supplied by private enterprise. Housing was privately let and sold or provided by employers for rental to their workforce. There were virtually no standing police forces outside London and Ireland until the 1840s. Before that the army and the yeomanry were brought in to quell the frequent outbreaks of disorder (Griffin 2014). The prison system was largely reserved for debtors or managed by county authorities. All of this began to be changed in the nineteenth century as social problems became evident in the large industrial cities and in London. Britain contrasted with the militarized authoritarian European empires with their conscript armies, secret police and official religions. Australians, following British example, firmly believed they were free from all that. The creation of the armed Border Control Force in 2015 came as a shock to some.

In Australia there were few time-honoured systems. Everything had to be created from the start. In a convict society, where all land had been declared the property of the Crown, the obvious agent for providing services and regulating business was the colonial authority. Most important was the supply of labour by the state through the recruitment of convicts and assisted immigrants. In the eyes of conservatives the most important state function was to maintain social cohesion. Each of the six colonies built its own single police force, compared with the county and municipal systems in England or the myriad local forces in the United States. British soldiers had a declining role until their withdrawal in the 1870s, but were called out at times of civil disorder as in Britain, most notably in Ballarat in 1854 (FitzSimons 2012). They were replaced by troopers, police and prisons under the control of the colonial and then state bureaucracies. Modern Australia was originally a planned and organized society, ruled through the British Empire by governors appointed from London and recruited from the educated classes as officials throughout the nineteenth century. Ever since the 1830s immigration to Australia has been bound around with increasingly complex laws and restrictions. Originally these were applied to convicts and assisted immigrants, eventually reaching everybody. By 2015 legislation was being considered that would allow one person (the Minister for Immigration) to strip people of their citizenship, without trial, for alleged sympathy with Islamic terrorism: the Australian Citizenship Amendment (Allegiance to Australia).

Free settlers arrived in search of gold in the mid-nineteenth century, and rules had to be designed to maintain social cohesion around loyalty to Britain and its laws. From 1901, under the White Australia policy, settlement was not available to non-Europeans. It was freely available to law-abiding white

British subjects, mainly from Britain, Ireland and New Zealand (Hammerton and Thomson 2005). Many of these were assisted to come to Australia, and this was extended to other Europeans after World War II. Between the 1830s and the 1980s Australia was the only major society to build its population with the consistent use of public funds to assist selected groups, nationalities and occupations. Those non-British Europeans arriving before the two world wars, were mainly Germans, Italians, Greeks and Scandinavians. They mostly paid their own way, with exceptions in Queensland, and from the 1920s were limited by landing permits (Fraser 1940). Two-thirds of the people of the world were excluded because of their colour and inability to assimilate into a 'white' society. For years this exclusive policy had the support of the majority of Australians, the print media and the political parties and trade unions. It did not end until 1972 (London 1970; Tavan 2005). By the end of the twentieth century the majority seeking to settle in Australia were from those races and nations previously excluded.

By the standards of most societies, Australia was already free, prosperous and liberal after the ending of transportation and the radical political changes that brought parliamentary rule from the 1850s (Hirst 2008). None of this was true for the Aboriginal population, which was declining (Rowley 1970). Small groups of individuals continued to be locked away from time to time. These included 'enemy aliens' in both world wars, many of German or Italian descent who had been born or naturalized in Australia (Beaumont 2008; Bevege 1993). All resident Japanese were deported back to Japan in 1945 after wartime internment (Nagata 2000). A much larger confined group were Aborigines, many of whom were organized to live in special reservations, where they were under strict control. These were managed by religious bodies or colonial/state governments. Until 1967 Aboriginal policy was entirely a province of the states, except in the Northern Territory, which was Commonwealth controlled and had the highest proportion of Indigenous people. The most draconian state was Queensland and the most liberal was South Australia, but this varied with different governments.

After 1947 large numbers of European displaced persons were located in provincial camps like Bonegilla and Bathurst (Sluga 1988), while many British-assisted immigrants were housed in Nissen huts in the industrial areas of major cities (Hammerton and Thomson 2005). British and 'alien' migrants were not normally housed in the same places, and there were complaints from the British when this happened. The displaced persons were kept away from the cities as a policy, which broke down once they were released from their two-year labour bond. This policy reflected a public fear of 'ghettoes', based on American examples and still causing anxiety during the mass escape from Syria sixty years later. Unassisted migrants, who were mainly southern

Europeans in the 1950s, ignored these expectations and were not subject to direction.

Immigration policy was transferred from the states to the Commonwealth by 1920 and included registration and restriction for aliens (white non-British). Numbers allowed entry were often modified, as in the gentleman's agreement with Mussolini's Fascist government in 1928, limiting exit visas from Italy. Landing permits were used for non-British migrants to ensure that they had the means and ability to support them. These could be varied in number if too many were coming from undesired origins in south-eastern Europe.

Because of these alien and racial restrictions, the displaced persons, who were recruited from refugee camps in Central Europe from 1947, were the largest number of non-British arrivals at one time since the uncontrolled Chinese entered during the 1850s gold rushes. Displaced persons were obliged to work under Commonwealth instructions for two years, but this was not expected of the assisted British (Kunz 1988). Residence in both city and provincial former army huts was normally limited to two years. They were unpopular with many of their residents. The largest of the camps, at Bonegilla, was criticized by an official inquiry in 1967 with the auditor general advocating its closure (Sluga 1988). Bonegilla was closed in 1971 after processing 320,000 migrants and displaced persons. New centres were modernized or replaced by custom-built hostels from the 1960s to the late 1980s, when they were closed down and sold. They were not guarded or restricted, were used for refugees as well as assisted migrants, were in major city suburbs and designed for families. Settlement services were provided through them. Australia, Canada and the United States were the only societies to have planned resettlement programs on this basis. They were provided by the Commonwealth and the states, in cooperation with charitable and religious agencies. This provision has been limited, and the hostels sold. They could have been useful in the current exodus from war-torn states, as they were mainly allocated to refugees, whom policy advisers wrongly thought were reducing in number (FitzGerald 1988).

Communities tended to form around the hostels as inmates secured jobs and housing nearby. This was most apparent around the Springvale (Melbourne) hostel and in Cabramatta (Sydney), especially with the settlement of Vietnamese refugees in the 1970s. Southern Europeans settled in older inner-city suburbs, while East Europeans preferred newly built outer industrial suburbs (Jupp 1966). German, Dutch and Jewish migrants settled in middle-class suburbs, while the British were widely spread, depending on whether they were industrial or white-collar families. The city hostels were mainly placed in industrial districts. This had an important long-term impact on the ethnic character of the working classes (Lever-Tracy and Quinlan 1988).

From 1991 (and ratified with bipartisan support in 1992), 'mandatory and irrevocable detention' was imposed on those arriving by boat without valid visas. They claimed asylum under the *United Nations Convention Relating to the Status of Refugees* of 1951, to which Australia was an early signatory. In 1967 this was extended by a Protocol to cover the entire world, causing Australia to delay ratification for six years until White Australia had been finally terminated. By 1990 there were no longer regular passenger shipping services to Australia, and entry by air required a visa inspected at the points of departure and arrival. Detention was originally designed to discourage a mass intake from Cambodia, where about one million were massacred by the Khmer Rouge government. Many Vietnamese had been settled without detention after the fall of Saigon to the communists in 1975 and the development of an international orderly departure system. This marked the final end of the White Australia policy. A very large contingent of Chinese students was accepted in 1989 as refugees, following the Beijing repression. Many remained permanently.

Whether 'mandatory and irrevocable detention' was intended to be permanent is not clear. But it became so, and remains a major feature of refugee settlement (McAdam and Chong 2014). This led to the creation of many locked centres in remote areas such as Port Hedland, Woomera and Baxter, most of which have now been closed, while others have been opened on Nauru and Manus Island outside of Australia altogether (McMaster 2001). These were managed by private prison companies like Serco, Transfield or G4S. Baxter was built along model prison lines. To avoid claims that 'prisons' breached UN Convention rules, they were always officially called detention centres. Many thousands of refugees passed through them, almost none being of 'European' origin. This was a more rigorous regime than any since the convict era, if for smaller numbers. It was eventually extended to long-term detention with no guarantee of settlement anywhere (Parliament of the Commonwealth of Australia 1994; 2001; 2009; Joint Standing Committee on Migration 2008). White Australia had prohibited entry and deported non-Europeans. It did not impose indefinite detention.

The current detention policy, sends many unvisaed arrivals by sea away to Manus Island and Nauru in the Pacific, after a temporary rest on Christmas Island, an Australian territory but not defined as such for immigration purposes (Briskman 2008). All of these are much more isolated than Norfolk Island ever was. Nauru is one of the smallest and most remote states in the world. Manus Island lies two hundred miles off the northern coast of Papua New Guinea (Cornall 2014). Management rests with Australia, these two Pacific states and private prison companies. The enormous annual cost of up to two billion dollars rests with Australia, but general management remains with the Nauru or PNG governments. Whether it will become a permanent system, or simply fade away as others have done, will be an interesting study in human management. The theory behind this system is that refugees will be deterred from arriving in Australia by boat and without a visa, crossing Australia's imaginary sovereign sea border. This will confine refugees accepted for permanent settlement to those completely selected and authorized by Australia.

In February 2014 Manus was the scene of a major riot in which a detainee was killed amidst considerable confusion (Cornall 2014, 2015). In contrast to the earlier convicts, these detainees had no clear idea what would happen to them, nor were they charged in court for any offences prior to their detention. Their futures were being bandied about between the Australian, Nauruan and Papua New Guinea governments, none of whom wanted to take full responsibility for the residue of several thousand detained under their control. The boats had been stopped, as desired by the Australian government. But no prior thought had gone into the question of what should happen to the people on those boats. This was a classic case of asking the wrong question to secure the wrong answer. Parties on both sides of politics were equally responsible. This contrasted with the treatment of refugees between the closing of Bonegilla and the end of the 1980s, when a range of settlement assistance was available, citizenship could be gained within two years, and an amnesty for 8,000 visa overstayers was introduced.

Chapter 4

PEACE, ORDER AND GOOD GOVERNMENT

Throughout the British Empire official policy aimed at 'peace, order and good government' – in theory. In practice British rulers and leaders occupied the social and political heights while others were regarded as inferior. During the convict period peace and good order could be maintained by force if necessary. That tradition was also maintained against the Aborigines as settlement moved further out into their lands. As part of the British Empire, Australia also tried to secure support from settlers as they developed into citizens and later became voters. (Davidson 1997). A normal process in colonial lands like India, Malaysia or West Africa, was to use local chieftains and aristocrats to supply their own forces as keepers of the peace in the system known as 'indirect rule'. This was not possible in Australia. The Aboriginal peoples did not have such hierarchical social systems, unlike the New Zealand Maoris or many peoples elsewhere in the vast empire. Moreover, the settlers were overwhelmingly British subjects and claimed the real or traditional rights of subjects in Britain and many other parts of the empire. As such they had growing political claims on the ruling élite and expectations of sharing in the wealth already apparent for their rulers.

The explosion of settler numbers and wealth during the 'golden age' expedited the demands of the predominantly male settlers for political and social influence and benefits. The authorities wished to avoid the American experience of colonial revolt. Two major reforming movements were launched in the period starting with the 1840s and reached its height in the 1890s moving towards federation. These were the extension of the male franchise to a level comparable to that in the United Kingdom and the granting of available land to settlers as 'free selections'. As the franchise was not extended to Aborigines or Asians this cemented the settler social ranks behind their rulers with considerable success. The Eureka interlude of 1854 was not repeated, and parliamentary politics became well established. Public policy developed on the basis of British loyalty to the queen and empire, access to land and the franchise for a wider public of small farmers. The wealthy settlers were kept in power, and some of their descendants are still among the largest landholders and influential classes. Many others endured years of hardship with the onset of economic depressions in the 1890s and the 1920s. Australia was already a class society.

Was suspicion of the 'unwanted' a central and historically determined principle of public policy in Australia, rather than simply a disconnected series of disparate beliefs? In political debate extreme terms like 'concentration camps' or 'prisons' or 'queue jumpers' are still widely used. Similar charges of 'slavery' were made against the transportation system two centuries ago, leading eventually to its abolition after a very long delay of 80 years. While immigrants have not been as unpopular as the convicts, public attitudes have frequently been highly critical. A continuing theme has been fear of Asia, made more acute by the dissolution of the British Empire (Walker 1999; Brawley 1995; Burke 2001; Goldworthy 2002; Price 1974: Souter 1976; Ward 2001). Asians were frequently seen as inferior or dangerous, even if few Australians had met one because of their exclusion.

The broadening of Australia's immigrant intake from 1953 raised again the possibility that some nationalities and social groups might prove less acceptable than others. Attitudes towards immigrants have always been ambivalent. Possibly this reflects the historic memory that a majority immigrating in the founding years were transported felons, followed by labourers and their families paid to come under assisted passage schemes. Refugees and assisted migrants were accepted, but rarely with great enthusiasm. The ideal immigrant was one who paid to come and had secure employment and prospects of economic success. In recent years such immigrants are favoured if they can invest large sums in a viable business. The great majority of these are Chinese.

With the ending of the convict system, the main complaint was about the lack of quality among new arrivals, especially those from workhouses. Female immigrants, while welcome as servants and potential wives, were frequently defamed for their real or imagined immorality (Richards 1995). The most popular arrivals who might be termed refugees, were the German Lutheran settlers of South Australia. These became successful farmers and God-fearing model citizens who stayed away from Adelaide. They were forcibly 'assimilated' during World War I through measures such as closing German-language schools. In Sydney and Melbourne immigrants were always criticized for not settling in the bush – a reaction that was still powerful in the 1950s when Australia was already an urban society. German and Scandinavian settlers in Queensland from the 1870s were welcomed for developing the freely available land provided to new arrivals (Tampke and Doxford 1990). The same welcome was not so warm for Italians and Greeks, who also settled in rural districts in the 1920s. Queensland unions did all they could to reserve favoured jobs in the sugar mills for British immigrants and locally born Australians (Reynolds 2003), leaving cane cutting to the aliens.

Opposition to Asian and Pacific Islander arrivals reached its height in the 1880s and led eventually to White Australia. But British immigrants were not always welcome either. Increasing numbers came from urban, metropolitan and industrial cities and had little interest in settling in rural areas and working at farming. One tragic example of this was the failure of the land settlement schemes in Western Australia in the 1920s (Bolton 1972, 1994). Preference had been given to rural migrants in the past. But Great Britain was no longer a rural society, and Ireland had been drained of people, who ceased to migrate anywhere except to Britain and the United States. In neither of these were there serious obstacles to entry. Many British farm labourers were illiterate until the 1870s. The provision of village schools was in the hands of the landlords and parsons, who had other interests than education. Many rural schools in England did not improve until transferred to the County Councils after 1890. Prejudice against newcomers and a basic level of education and general knowledge of the outside world were established in the pioneering years and are still present today.

Refugees admitted between 1918 and 1960 were Europeans and thus acceptable to Australia. None of them were British, which reduced their acceptability. Moreover, the majority were from cities and were often believed to be Jews. The great Jewish emigration from the rural *stetls* of Ukraine and Poland to North America was already over. Only a small minority had come to Australia by the 1920s. The new emigration was an urban flight from Nazism, which had come to power in 1933 on the platform that 'the Jews are our misfortune'. Few in Germany could foresee that this election marked the end of civilization, as previously understood, from then until the abolition of the German Democratic Republic almost 60 years later in 1990.

Australia was a founding member of the United Nations. Its foreign minister, Dr Herbert Evatt, became UN president in 1948. Before the war. the League of Nations had already committed itself to a modest refugee programme. Although the League had a refugee policy, there was no binding definition of a refugee in international law until after World War II, following the massive settlement of displaced persons in Central Europe and the creation of the United Nations High Commissioner for Refugees (UNHCR). The Convention Relating to the Status of Refugees was signed in 1951 and ratified by Australia in 1954. This referred narrowly to those displaced by the events of the war in Europe. A protocol was developed in 1967, which Australia ratified in 1973, as the White Australia policy was being abolished. This expanded the definition of refugees and the powers of the UNHCR to cover the entire world, including Australia's responsibility for the aftermath of the Vietnam War, which ended in 1975 with a communist victory (Loescher 1993).

The basic principles of the convention and protocol include some adopted from the original League of Nations policies. To summarize, its principles are: non-discrimination: non-penalization: and non refoulement (return to a persecuting homeland). Penalties should not be imposed for illegal entry or stay, including arbitrary detention purely on the basis of seeking asylum. Minimum rights include access to the courts, to primary education, to work and to the provision of identity documentation. Other rights include the right to choose their place of residence and to move freely within the territory. Contracting states should facilitate assimilation and naturalization (McAdam and Chong 2014).

These and other provisions assume that individual asylum seekers need to prove persecution. This is provided by Australia in the form of documents of identification, statements at interviews, security clearances by the Australian Security Intelligence Organisation (ASIO) and an assessment of the safety of the state from which the applicant had fled. These assessments were made by officers or appointees of the Department of Immigration and Citizenship, usually in consultation with the Department of Foreign Affairs or later the Office of National Assessments. While there is a growing body of specific local law, it should already be clear from this summary that Australia is no longer rigidly adhering to the convention, nor even adhering to it at all in some respects. Its full compliance was most effective between 1953 and 1991. While Australia followed the practice of assessing each individual, in reality it accepted that wartime events created a de facto cause for seeking refuge for groups of the persecuted. By accepting the protocol of 1967 in 1973 it finally turned its back on White Australia and accepted refugees from Asia and Africa. Some officials in the Immigration Department were uncomfortable with these trends, reviving the fear of 'opening the floodgates', which had been used for many years in public debates. Officers in Foreign Affairs were usually more relaxed.

Regular passenger shipping no longer services Australia. The only practical approach for intending immigrants is by air, which in theory is tightly supervised to prevent hijacking or fraudulent tickets and credentials. Australia does not have borders in the same sense as the United States or most European countries. It has thousands of nautical miles of sea, which mainly impinge on the equally invisible borders of Indonesia with its thousand inhabited islands. Only at the narrowest point of the Torres Strait can these borders be safely crossed in small, unseaworthy boats. By agreement with Papua New Guinea such crossings are supervised from a small Commonwealth office on Thursday Island. Border control was finally tightened in 2014.

The only other anomaly is in the two island outposts of Australia at Christmas Island and Cocos. These are nearer to Indonesia than to Eastern Australia and are inhabited mainly by Malays, Indonesians and Chinese, who are Australian citizens. Timor Leste is a sovereign state across a currently disputed boundary in the Timor Sea. All of these can be reached from Australia by sea in good weather in relatively small, seaworthy boats, but are dangerous crossings in poor weather. They have provided the main routes for unvisaed asylum seekers to Australia in recent years, but have been closed off by naval patrols since the adoption of Operation Sovereign Borders in September 2013. This operation uses naval patrols to identify boats with asylum seekers and to turn them back to their port of origin or take them to Christmas Island for transport to Nauru if the boat cannot be saved.

These sea routes towards Australia are all hazardous, especially during the southwest monsoon. Indonesian fishermen are familiar with conditions between Australia and Indonesia at least as far as Christmas Island. Their ancestors regularly sailed towards northern Australia many years before Cook. Modern fishermen frequently impinge on Australia's economic zone and are sometimes arrested and imprisoned for a year, having no money to pay a fine. Most navigate without radio, radar or charts. They accompany boatloads of asylum seekers for a payment. However, the main problem is not with these reliable guides, but with the often criminal organizers of trips who make a substantial profit from unseaworthy fishing boats or old ferries. One rationale for Australia's 'stop the boats' campaign has been to put these criminals out of business. Their business is flexible. They can move elsewhere if necessary, taking their money with them, leaving their customers behind in Australian hands or stranded.

The criminal organizers, who do not go to sea themselves, have banked their profits safely and can open other businesses in other parts of Southeast Asia or the Middle East. Some of them are undoubtedly local officials in respectable employment and well protected from police investigation. As with the much-larger exodus from Vietnam, some boats are organized by local families who are careful of their passengers but simply unlucky. In the South China Sea attacks by pirates were common, but this is not a problem between Indonesia and Australia. Family organization is particularly likely when some members have already reached Australia, but been prohibited from bringing close relatives. Taking this into account, and the reality of an unfulfilled demand, the claims by both Labor and Liberal leaders that boat organizers are 'the worst criminals in the world' are overdrawn.

More social damage is caused by drug importers, who have corrupted staff in Australian ports and airports. Former departmental officers were claiming in 2014 that much of the documentation required by immigrants was fraudulent.

This was more likely to be available to asylum seekers arriving by plane. Such documents might even have been produced overseas by departmental staff or migration agents. Uncontrolled access to Australia no longer legally exists, even for New Zealanders. This has ended two centuries of planned immigration that encouraged British subjects. Emigration from the United Kingdom has dropped off with better British conditions and security. New Zealanders move between the two countries, without necessarily seeking permanence in Australia.

Throughout modern Australian history public authority has been extended to assure 'peace, order and good government'. These objectives were echoed throughout the British Empire, justifying what were usually commercial and strategic aims. Australia was and remains a managed society. It was planned in London by public servants in the late eighteenth and early nineteenth centuries, seeking solutions to social, economic and strategic problems. British power had already conquered Scotland and Ireland and had colonies in North America and the Caribbean and expanding interests in India. Its major setback was the loss of the American colonies in 1781. Britain was steadily defeating its main rival, France, culminating in the battles of Trafalgar and Waterloo in 1805 and 1815. Both victories were still celebrated in Australia until overshadowed by Gallipoli in 1915. A need to influence the whole known world drove the exploration voyages of Lieutenant James Cook, who discovered a large and hitherto unmapped continent in the South Pacific, on which he planted the British flag in 1770. After that Australia was not planned by accident. Its population, workforce, land and primary production assets were all consciously developed by combining public and private enterprise to an extent greater than in either the United States or in Britain, the sources of much of its capital investment.

While British governments in the eighteenth century were corrupt and incompetent in many ways, their leading figures were well-educated and economically secure. They did not need employment other than public service. Also, the representatives they sent out to conquer and settle the growing empire were not as obsessed with accumulating wealth as were many who exploited India in earlier years. As members of a self-conscious ruling class they were often concerned with problems needing solutions, both at home and overseas. Among these were the social chaos caused by industrialization; rapid urban growth and consequent rises in criminality and disorder; the persistence of rural poverty and ignorance (often on their own estates); the restlessness of Ireland, North America and India; the continuing tensions with France; and the need to secure trade routes, imported produce and export markets. They were rational problem solvers, but not necessarily inspired by the Enlightenment (Gascoigne 2002). Some wanted to spread Christianity and

European culture. This was not as dominant an objective as for their Spanish and Portuguese predecessors. Trade and commerce were the primary British interests.

Australia offered the opportunity to compensate for the rich colonies lost in the American War of Independence. One major problem was where to send criminals and unskilled labourers to work the vast areas previously unexplored but needing men (Frost 1980, 2012). The solution, unlike that in India and, later, Africa, was to colonize the new territories with convict labour and with British immigrants. This led to the displacement and steady decline of the existing Indigenous peoples, to the definition of territory as Crown land and to the limitation of settlement to British subjects, whether convict or free. Victorian England was proud of its empire, its navy and its manufacturing, and of its ability to create peace, order and good government. That these were achieved by seizing the homelands and wealth of other people was either written out of the history books or explained in terms of racial superiority.

As new colonies were formed in South Australia, Queensland and Western Australia, these principles were modified, but never abandoned, for over a century. South Australia specifically forbade convict transportation and encouraged German immigration; Western Australia failed to attract much population for a century, until gold was discovered; and Queensland recruited labour from British and European immigrants and indentured labour from the South Pacific indigenous peoples. Victoria was divided from New South Wales just as its population began a major expansion because of the discovery of gold in 1851. The British government had limited control over this process, with Victoria becoming a multicultural society based on immigration from Britain and Ireland and from other colonies, Europe and China. For the next thirty years a single police force, a free and secular education system, a railway and road network, a legal framework for property ownership and business, a banking system, an elected parliament and a civil service were all created for Victoria, a territory as large as Great Britain (Serle 1971, 1980). As all this advanced, the Indigenous Aborigines retreated before it to the outer limits of Gippsland or the Murray and beyond (Rowley 1970). In most colonies they were usually not officially recorded or given the vote. Reliable figures did not exist until the Commonwealth took over the recording in 1967 by a constitutional amendment and referendum. Occasional estimates showed a steady decline, especially below the Tropic of Capricorn. Unofficial counts were not made until World War II, for defence purposes, in the Northern Territory. The object of the 1967 amendment was not to make Aborigines citizens or voters (which most were already) but to transfer responsibility for them to the Commonwealth (Chesterman and Galligan 1997), where control over immigration had rested since 1901.

Chapter 5

INDIGENOUS AUSTRALIA AND THE SOUTH PACIFIC

The arrival in New South Wales and Tasmania of thousands of convicts – almost all of them men – accompanied by armed soldiers, presented many problems for the Indigenous peoples (Broome 1994). One was the spread of a variety of diseases prevalent among the European poor but hitherto quite unknown to the Indigenous. Smallpox was widespread, and venereal disease and pneumonia became so very quickly (J. Campbell 2002). The same diseases also struck Islanders further away as missionaries, traders and labour recruiters began to settle from the 1840s. The huge gender discrepancy of the convict settlers added to the problem. Indigenous men did not welcome the arrival of numerous rivals and many conflicts were traceable to fights over women. Many of the male settlers were former convicts, sealers and whalers and other unattached wanderers. Some set up relationships with Indigenous people, while others attacked, raped and killed them.

Official restraint was inoperable in parts of Tasmania for years and led to a rapid decline in the already small Indigenous population. A similar male preponderance existed elsewhere. Social and legal controls were limited, especially in Queensland, Western Australia and the Northern Territory, not occupied until later. Attempts to 'settle' the Aborigines were made, but were ineffective until small towns and official camps were established in remote locations, to which some Aborigines attached themselves and their families, despite the hostility of the migrant newcomers.

The British governors adopted the principle of *terra nullius* or nobody's land, which allowed them to develop agriculture and settlements regardless of prior Indigenous usage (Maddock 1983). This was legally enforced by the principle that all land was vested in the Crown, which could hold it, lease it or sell it. The meaning of the Latin term became hotly debated during the 'history wars' of the 1990s (S. Macintyre and Clark 2003; Windschuttle 2004). The meaning was clear at least as early as the 1830s. Uncultivated land belonged to nobody, a principle also being applied in Britain to village commons and highland pastures. Unfamiliar with domestic animals other than dogs, the local Indigenous saw cattle and sheep as welcome sources of food. Their punishments echoed those by British landlords, who had enclosed commons for their own profitable use (Griffin 2014). These prohibited hunting their animals, birds and fish under the Game Laws, a frequent cause of transportation. Indigenous peoples were thus treated as criminals for their normal economic practices of hunting and gathering on traditional lands. Many were simply shot as a punishment rather than being brought to trial.

The legal basis for land ownership and control was the leasing or sale of Crown land by the colonial governments or the subsequent ratification of land acquired by illegal 'squatting' outside controlled districts of New South Wales. The Indigenous had no rights in this allocation. In later years land ownership was restricted to British subjects. This limited the appeal of immigration for aliens, who much preferred North America. An incentive to migrate was provided by assistance with fares from the sale of land, which was also limited to British subjects. Later in the nineteenth century free selection allowed many to create farms, which would have been impossible in Britain, where all landed property was already in private ownership. Planning remained the basis for building a new society rather than laissez faire, at least in the more settled districts. It usually favoured the larger property owners who had political power, as in England, but gave greater opportunity for small farmers. Some land was freely available, especially in Queensland.

The settlers on Indigenous land made no treaties, unlike the situation in New Zealand or Canada. John Batman's treaty with local chiefs at the site of Melbourne in 1835 was repudiated by the New South Wales government. Settlers saw Indigenous use of the land as trespassing and the killing of domestic animals as theft. Native title was recognized, with serious limitations, throughout the British Empire in Asia and Africa, but not in Australia and Tasmania. The Indigenous responses of raiding homesteads and killing settlers were simply treated as murders worthy of revenge. Aborigines brought before the courts were deemed unable to take the oath, which they could not comprehend. They were British subjects, but without the effective rights the settlers enjoyed. Land was reserved for Aborigines in New South Wales, but was subject to acquisition by the colony for other users. This practice continued for many years and diminished the amount of land for Aboriginal agriculture. Coranderrk in Victoria suffered the same fate.

The Indigenous peoples of Australia and Tasmania were the first in the region to experience British colonialism (Reynolds 2012). Others in New Zealand and the Polynesian Pacific were to do so within a generation. Spanish, Portuguese and Dutch colonizers followed already explored trade routes. Only the Dutch established a complete colonial system in the Indonesian islands, by agreement with the British and some local aristocrats. Only the British attempted to colonize Australia and Tasmania, but the islands of the Pacific were shared amongst Europeans. In all cases the impact was damaging for existing cultures and economic arrangements, as well as for their health. Many Polynesians became converted to Christianity, but the islands attracted only small numbers of Europeans, except for New Zealand and New Caledonia. They were frequently used to supply European and American shipping. Queensland made the greatest use of Melanesian labour, with the expansion of the sugar industry from the 1860s (Evans et al. 1993).

The early British settlers of Australia did not normally employ the Indigenous population, as they already had a convict workforce, and slavery was abolished in the British Empire in 1833. Paid employment had never been traditionally practised. This did not change much until well into the 1870s, when cattle stations found locally resident Aborigines to be highly proficient at herding cattle on horseback. This remained so until the mechanization of the cattle industry in the 1950s (McGrath 1995). Aboriginal women were employed as domestic staff in otherwise male-dominated societies. Most women worked in exchange for food and lodging, rather than wages. From the 1860s rationing systems were developed from which food and blankets were regularly distributed by Christian missions or colonial governments. This was part of an overall policy of bringing Aborigines under control in concentrated locations, where they might be taught religion and agriculture. Many practices from the English workhouse system were applied to Aborigines attracted to the various missions, including segregation by sex, bans on alcohol, control over money, uniform clothing, Christian worship and compulsory basic labour.

Such control became easier as numbers were reduced by disease or declining birth rates. However, it meant that Aborigines were rarely employed in a market economy or taught a competent level of English, which might have made them acceptable employees or even owners. Control by missions or employers prevented Aborigines from accumulating personal wealth. A system of welfare and enforced concentration was created in many districts, but without a consistent legal basis. The Indigenous were nominally British subjects, but became controlled by laws specific to them, which essentially restricted their rights under the heading of 'protection'. Aborigines were not legally defined, unlike the New Zealand Maori, which created problems in later legislation. Aborigines had traditional lands from which they derived nourishment but did not own individually. These lands were subjected to pastoral expansion as European exploration and transport spread out.

The British impact on south-eastern Australia and Tasmania was particularly destructive. The bulk of early settlers were convicts and their guards and the military officers who provided government. Official instructions from Britain favoured protecting the Indigenous populations. These took many months to arrive and were not effectively implemented. The one attempt by deputy governor George Gipps to prosecute settlers for murdering 28 Aborigines at Myall Creek in 1838, produced a massive backlash when he had seven of the murderers hanged. Soon after he was recalled to England. Many settlers had moved outside the legal districts in New South Wales, where law and order limited violence and seizure of land. There were no such limits in Tasmania.

The treatment of the unique Tasmanian Aborigines has been fully documented, both at the time and recently (Reynolds 2012; Ryan 2012). From a population of about 10,000 in 1805 they were reduced to a fragmented minority of a few hundred by 1840, living on offshore islands. A few years later it became customary for the Tasmanian government, media and schools to deny any Aboriginal presence at all. Truganini, who died at Oyster Cove in 1876, and Fanny Cochrane Smith, who died in 1905, were both incorrectly described at the time as 'the last of the Aborigines'. The Royal Society of Tasmania played a dishonourable role in exhuming the bodies of Truganini and her contemporary, William Lanney, whose remains were used for 'scientific' purposes.

Tasmanian history has several conflicting aspects that were also relevant to the fate of mainland Aborigines over the next century (Reynolds 2012). Official policies aimed at protecting the Aboriginal population, while removing it from settled districts, teaching Christianity and limited skills, and hopefully speeding its assimilation. A high death rate from common diseases, previously unknown to the Indigenous peoples, was one factor limiting any success (Anderson 2002). Equally important was the unsettled character of Tasmania during the convict period. The Tasmanian Aborigines fought until 1830 with a motley collection of settlers, including military, sealers and whalers, farmers and time-expired convicts. One estimate of deaths in the so called Black War of 1823–1834 shows 878 Aborigines killed against 201 colonists, a ratio of four to one. The difference was accounted for by the effectiveness of guns against spears. The Aboriginal base was quite small already, and the death rates included women and children.

These battles, and the failure of the Black Line of 1830, which tried to track down all the Aborigines in the settled districts, persuaded deputy governor George Arthur to concentrate the Aborigines. The chief architect of this policy, Augustus Robinson, began a process that later became universal in the other colonies, of protecting Aborigines in controlled communities where they were taught to be Christians and to assimilate to rural colonial society. Robinson's tireless work included a full exploration of Tasmania and the settlement at Wyballena on Flinders Island of those he had discovered (Reynolds 2012). Like many later schemes elsewhere this segregation failed in

1839, in this case mainly through sickness and death. Those remaining were removed and settled at Oyster Cove on the southern mainland. Eventually, the remaining Aborigines were relocated to Cape Barren Island, adjacent to Flinders Island, where a surviving community exists to the present.

Essentially, the Tasmanians were reduced to a small manageable group, expected to die out or to be assimilated as ordinary members of British Australian Christian society. Living on an isolated island kept them out of sight. In other colonies similar approaches were directed against much larger and more varied populations. The Torres Strait Islanders were kept from some destructive influences. Their islands, under the general supervision of the Anglican Church, were prohibited to casual visitors (Beckett 1987). Other Aborigines enjoying relative isolation included those in Arnhem Land, where large areas were closed to development for many years, and the Tiwi of Melville and Bathurst Islands off the Northern Territory coast. Parts of the Northern Territory have Aboriginal majorities and gained consequent political influence once the franchise was extended to them. However, standards of living, health, education and life expectancy all remain well below the Australian level. Even the more remote communities were not free from intrusions by pastoral and mining activities nor from the assimilating influences of religion, education and modern economies. In 1984 the last isolated Aborigines, the Pintupi, came in from the Western Australian desert in a state of near starvation and now live in small and remote Kiwirrkurra.

Queensland and Western Australia were colonized later than Tasmania, New South Wales and Victoria. Their Aboriginal policies were no more progressive or successful. One of the earliest attacks on the Aborigines in Western Australia was at Pinjarra in 1834, resulting in a massacre. Mining and the pastoral industry moved into large areas that had been occupied by Aborigines for centuries. Many fought back, as the Tasmanians had done, most notably the Kalkadoon in the Mount Isa region. Unlike the comparable situation in the American West, Aborigines rarely had access to guns. The result was the same as previously in Tasmania, if on a larger scale. After spearing attacks on settlers and police, the Kalkadoon were besieged and 200 killed by rifle fire in 1884.

Apart from this battle, which the Kalkadoon still commemorate, Queensland Aborigines were frequent victims of the Native Police, a unique force distinct from the colonial police. Given official status from 1859 but not fully legalized until the *Native Police Act of 1864*, it was described by a government official in 1884 as 'a native police force quite separate from the ordinary police and maintained solely for the purpose of dealing with offences committed by the natives' (Evans 1993; 60). Its officers were white Australians and its members selected from Aborigines. After a reign of terror by the Native Police, lasting until the force's dissolution in 1900, Queensland's Indigenous peoples were placed under control of the 1897 Aborigines Protection and Restrictions on the *Sale of Opium Act* and were confined to reserves. Many of these remain as the core of Aboriginal communities in places like Palm Island, Cherbourg or Hope Vale. Similar settlements, managed by religious organizations, were established in Victoria in 1869, in New South Wales in 1883, in Western Australia in 1905 and South Australia in 1911. These had the legal right to remove Aboriginal children from their parents, to punish dissidents and to control payment for work.

Several different approaches have affected Aborigines since 1788; extinction by shooting; isolation in remote controlled locations; missions run by religious denominations; missions run by state and territorial governments: settlement home stations on Aboriginal land; special housing estates; special welfare, health and education services; institutions such as boarding schools or training colleges; or simple racial segregation in general society. Most of these approaches were designed to keep Aborigines at the margin of society until fully assimilated. The contradiction was that assimilation would be more probable in towns and cities, from which Aborigines were either excluded or discouraged from settling. In recent years Aborigines have become increasingly urbanized, and the largest number live in Sydney. Their population has increased steadily to beyond 450,000, and their political influence has also grown.

In 1964 the first university degrees earned by Aborigines were granted to Charles Perkins and Margaret Valadian. From then onwards an effective community leadership has emerged from teachers, welfare workers and local and national political activists. Political parties and mining and business corporations have become far more sensitive to Aboriginal claims on society, including the control and management of large areas of land. The statistical picture still shows general disadvantages not suffered by any other major social category.

Queensland continued to struggle against its multicultural reality until 1901, when race relations, apart from Aborigines, became a Commonwealth function listed constitutionally as the power to make laws for 'the people of any race other than the aboriginal race in any State'. Aborigines were left to the states until a constitutional amendment in 1967 (s.51xxvi). Immigration powers aimed at removing the Chinese and Pacific Islander populations and preventing them from returning. The Melanesian sugar cane workers were deported to their presumed home islands from 1906 under the *Commonwealth Pacific Islanders Labourers Act of 1901*, having previously been subject to Queensland legislation in 1880 and 1884. The Melanesians were indentured workers tied to their employers and subject to restrictions on movement (Corris

1973). Even their deportation was mishandled, many being sent to islands in the New Hebrides from which they had not originated. Those who remained formed a South Sea Islander community that finally achieved official recognition as a distinct ethnic group in 2000, making them eligible for several welfare provisions. Among their community leaders were Australian-born Faith Bandler, of Ambrym descent, and Noel Fatnowna, of Malaita descent.

The Indigenous peoples of Australia were consistently kept at the margin of majority society and the economy (Rowley 1970). The shift from armed repression to 'protection' in the mid-nineteenth century, while intended to protect them from the ravages of white settlers, also had the effect of preventing them from geographical, economic or social movement outwards into the general community. The missions and settlements managed by religious bodies or the states, operated on the basis of strict controls. Permission was required for leaving the settlement, for getting married, for seeking occupations outside, for consuming alcohol, for refusing an order by the superintendent or for accumulating savings. Any money earned was normally banked by the authorities, and much of it disappeared or could not be claimed. The use of Aboriginal languages was usually prohibited in the schools and many rituals were forbidden.

The effect was to convert the peoples to basic Christianity and to the use of Kriol. Very few languages remain viable except in the Torres Strait, where arrangements were more liberal, in central Australia where forms of Arrernte survive, with the Yolngu speakers of Arnhem Land and on the Tiwi Islands. Mission policies varied, but missionaries of German origin, such as Lutheran or Moravian, made the effort to learn relevant languages and to encourage cultural work and basic education. The best known of these missions was the Lutheran Hermannsburg in the Northern Territory, which produced the school of painters led by Albert Namatjira. State-controlled settlements often contained Aborigines from a variety of languages and allegiances, with consequent social fragmentation and even violence. Palm Island, off the Queensland coast, was a lasting relic of this policy of mixing different Aboriginal groups.

The compulsory segregation of Aborigines obviously did not contribute much to their assimilation into mainstream society, from which they were largely excluded. It simply locked them away from public knowledge in thinly populated and remote districts. It had more effect through the creation of schools and institutions to which children were sent, away from their parents, and trained in English, domestic and labouring employment. This created the 'stolen generation', which became the centre of political controversy in the 1970s after a century of coercive shattering of families (Edwards and Read 1989). This controversy was the latest and most widely supported of a variety of protests against compulsory assimilation through enclosed centres. It was arguably the only Aboriginal protest movement that secured strong support among the Australian majority. Many of its leaders had themselves been forcibly separated from their families.

The first serious movements of protest against the missions began in the 1930s with the Cummeragunja walkout of February 1939. This settlement on the Murray River (NSW) was formed in 1888 and had an agricultural basis on good farming land. However bureaucratic interference interrupted this relatively successful enterprise. The *Aborigines Protection Act* (NSW 1909) gave power to the manager to remove those who were not in his opinion of 'Aboriginal appearance', or who had disobeyed his instructions. Children were removed to a state institution, causing many families to walk off the settlement and cross over to Victoria.

After a long drawn out dispute with the NSW government, in 1983 land rights became available for Aborigines from Cummeragunja, and the reserve was passed over to its former residents in 1984. By then transfer of lands to Aborigines had become common, following a national campaign and the examples of Canada and the United States. The principle of land rights was given public support by Prime Minister Gough Whitlam to Vincent Lingiari, the leader of a long strike at Wave Hill pastoral station, to whom Whitlam in 1975 personally gave a handful of soil symbolizing a major land lease to the Gurindji. An apology for the 'lost generation' was declared in parliament by Whitlam's successor, Kevin Rudd, in 2008. All political leaders followed, except for John Howard, the former Liberal prime minister.

However, these long sagas of trying to give Aborigines the same rights and status as anyone else, are not yet concluded. Citizenship, the vote, eligibility for social services, some specific to the Indigenous, election to Commonwealth and state parliaments, land rights, protection of sacred sites, widespread public sympathy and understanding and protection from racism, had all developed during the 'second golden age' of 1973 to 1995. All of these were provided through the political system and subject to bureaucratic and partisan control. The most important struggle was based on the Torres Strait Islands and the leadership of Eddy Mabo. His campaign against the concept of *terra nullius* was successful shortly after his death, when the High Court resolved that Indigenous land rights existed, and that Torres Strait Islanders had the right to exercise ownership and control (Beckett 1987). Although the islands have a garden system of agriculture similar to Papuans, this decision was judged to apply throughout Australia. It followed policies already adopted in the United States and Canada.

Aborigines are not numerous enough to influence election results, outside the Northern Territory or above the Tropic of Capricorn for Queensland and Western Australia. Most of this handful of electorates, outside the

Northern Territory, are usually held by the Liberal/National coalition. Inside the Northern Territory, local Aboriginal activists are divided politically and personally, although due to compulsory voting there is a substantial vote for Labor consistent with Aboriginal strength. A basic problem is that critics have not been impressed by the gains made in recent years. Labor is conscious that those changes have not greatly diminished the economic disadvantages of Aborigines everywhere and not only in the north. Conservatives have raised social issues such as alcoholism and domestic violence, while Labor has put the emphasis conventionally on the need for better education and jobs. Both are right in many respects, but unlikely to agree on the solutions. To argue that two centuries of repression, subjugation, exclusion, isolation and brute force might have seriously damaged a whole people, whose culture was never designed for the modern world, would undermine the national myth more than most majority Australians can accept.

The principal problem facing the British settlers and controllers of Australia from 1788 onwards was to create a cohesive society from fellow British who would remain loyal to the far distant United Kingdom and not rebel as the Americans had just done. This involved defending a vast and almost empty continent against other countries and peoples and settling it with patriotic British immigrants and their descendants. A high degree of planning and control was required, a population selected from a limited country of origin, an economy linked to that country, a cultural and religious commitment to Christian and British beliefs, control over dissidents and rebels, repression of the Indigenous, external defence and internal cohesion and established relationships with other similar societies. This latter was provided by the British Empire and its navy and army, without which the new Australian colonies would have been extremely vulnerable. All of this was organized by the mid-nineteenth century and then consolidated around the concept of White Australia before federation in 1901. Building this new society depended on immigration and the exclusion of the Indigenous to the remote margins of society. Aborigines became the first, but not the only, marginalized Australians.

The previous decline in Aboriginal population was brought under control in the original south-east colonies. Numbers were approaching half a million by 2011, with the largest number being in Sydney. They were subject to a continuing degree of physical repression and discrimination in Queensland and Western Australia, which had developed later and with less involvement from London.

In Western Australia a state law of 1936 aimed at total control of Indigenous marriage and sexual relations (Haebich 1988). Indigenous numbers in Queensland were substantial, and in both colonies there were moments of open warfare. The disadvantaged status of Aborigines has continued to the present, despite official and voluntary campaigns for reconciliation, land rights, political involvement and improved education. These come under an all-of-government campaign called 'Closing the Gap'. But a recent analysis by the Jesuit Social Services shows that young Aborigines and Torres Strait Islanders are 15 times more likely to be in prison than are non-Indigenous youths. Australian Bureau of Statistics figures record that the Indigenous made up 27.4 per cent of all prisoners in 2013 (Patricia Karvelas, *The Australian*, 26 May 2014).

All official figures show Aborigines to live shorter and less healthy lives, to be in conflict with the law more frequently than others, to be less educated, more likely to rely on welfare payments, and more likely to be employed in manual work, than either native-born or immigrant Australians. Individuals have, however, often conquered these disadvantages in sporting, artistic and creative activities. Aborigines have had increasing, if marginal, access to political power, especially in the Northern Territory where they constitute majorities in several electoral districts. There are many Aboriginal representative bodies, some subsidized by government. Large areas above the Tropic have been gazetted as Aboriginal land, but these are mainly in remote desert areas. Almost half the Northern Territory is now recognized as Aboriginal land under the *Commonwealth Aboriginal Land Rights Act of 1976*, but is yet to be economically developed.

Over two centuries, efforts have been made to control, discipline, assimilate or otherwise improve Aborigines, most with limited success but considerable disruption to Aboriginal life. The expectation that Aborigines were a dying race limited the amount of public assistance they could expect into the 1950s (McGregor 1997). By 1900 the total population had fallen below 9,000, many of them still living in remote districts, missions or cattle stations. They were in limited contact with government, often as the result of police intervention, including the removal of children to orphanages and distant adoptions or schools. Parents were rarely allowed to visit, even if they knew where their children were. By the end of the twentieth century Aborigines were to be found throughout Australia, with the largest numbers being in the major cities, the next largest in country towns, and the traditional core still resident around former missions and cattle stations, on very remote outstations, mostly north of the Tropic, and in isolated areas like Arnhem Land, Groote Eylandt, Melville Island and Cape York, served by air rather than road or rail.

It was on this latter scattered population that most attention and public intervention was focussed. Some of these Aborigines retained languages other than English and maintained a knowledge of traditional beliefs and practices, despite also being influenced by the Christian denominations of the various missions. Many lived on land judged to be Aboriginal-owned, under legal decisions arising from the Mabo case, which recognized native title for the first time (1992 HCA 23; 175 CLR 1992), including huge stretches of the Northern Territory. However, their economic and social existence was limited by the absence of regular employment, the vast distances from hospitals, schools, welfare services and adequate shopping and the consequent shortages and expense of basic foods and health provision. Their incomes were mainly, but not exclusively, derived from social welfare payments. All had the vote after 1962. Because voting was compulsory, special arrangements were made to reach them through mobile ballot boxes.

The most recent attempt to alleviate the problems of remote Aborigines was in the Northern Territory, the only jurisdiction in which they form a political force. Without effective consultations, the Northern Territory Emergency Response ('the Intervention') of 2007 was introduced by the Howard government and subsequently continued by the Rudd and Gillard Labor governments and the Abbott Coalition. Under Abbott the attempt was extended for 20 years. This 'intervention' was specifically inspired by the official report, *Little Children Are Sacred*, produced by the Northern Territory Government in 2007. This revealed the prevalence of sexual abuse of children in Aboriginal settlements in the Cape York peninsula of Queensland. However, its scope was much wider and once implemented it extended into the lives of over 20,000 Aborigines. Essentially it departed from the policy of self-government in Aboriginal settlements, which had been the previous wisdom. While some welcomed this Commonwealth involvement, many others were reminded of the earlier detailed control of Aboriginal lives and the strong assimilationist traditions of the past.

Among the many changes imposed (and in some places supported by the army) were the suspension of the *Race Discrimination Act*, as only Aborigines were targeted. The system of permits to cross Aboriginal land was abolished, having been developed to prevent the introduction of alcohol into dry communities as well as unwanted intrusion by strangers looking for women. Four hours of English teaching daily was to be required for children who did not speak the language. The Community Development Employment Projects – basically 'work for the dole' schemes – were abolished; compulsory health checks were introduced for children, without necessary parental permission; compulsory purchase of land and property was to be permitted for Commonwealth purposes; income management was to be imposed with 'welfare cards' limited to purchasing healthy and desirable products, naturally excluding alcohol (which was already banned in most Cape York settlements by local agreement). These restrictions went well beyond the protection of children and attempted to produce regularly working, well-behaved and independent citizens like those in suburban Australia. It was extended outside the

Northern Territory in 2014 into public housing in other states, where it also focussed on Aborigines. Its overall effects are still controversial, but it retains bipartisan support. Most efforts to incorporate and settle the Indigenous have shifted between assimilation and coercion. By 2015 both federal and state politicians were publicly discussing closing down remote Aboriginal settlements in Western Australia altogether, mainly to save money.

Chapter 6

RURAL SETTLERS, THE IRISH AND THE CHINESE

The largest number of convicts in Australia were drawn from London and other cities. Rural rebels and minor criminals were also more numerous than is sometimes supposed (Griffin 2014). Many were employed in rural occupations in Australia. A study of 'Captain Swing' rebels going to New South Wales on the *Eleanor* in 1831 suggests that their life might have been rather similar to what they had left behind (Kent and Townsend 2002). Many came from farming villages in Hampshire, Wiltshire and Berkshire. They were separated from their families and unable to return to England or to bring their relatives out. Rural convicts were essential to Australian agriculture, as were the assisted migrants who followed them from similar counties. Many of these migrants were less conservative than in hierarchical England, or even radical, and eventually had much better access to their own land.

Serious unrest in Great Britain began to decline from the 1840s, with movement into towns and cities, emigration, trade unions of skilled workers and English patriotism. Politics settled down to parliamentary concentration on a developing two-party system, with many leading positions still in the hands of the landed aristocracy and their relatives. Some of this was copied in Australia into the 1890s, when the party labels were changed into Free Trade and Protection, a division that also influenced Britain. Discontent among the English and Irish rural populations helps to explain the radical liberalism that characterized many parts of rural Australia during the second half of the nineteenth century. It was not revolutionary, because land was often freely available, and former labourers could become farmers. But neither was it conservative and deferential.

Australian rural labourers had the vote between 30 and 50 years before those they had left behind in England and Scotland. While the landed classes and the Anglican Church had influence in the older settlements in New South Wales, Victoria and Tasmania, many rural Australians were Methodists or Presbyterians, owned their own farms and 'touched their hat to no man' as Henry Lawson put it. Moreover, many rural settlers were Irish and had their own churches and radical traditions, as did many Scots (Partington 1994). The literary England of Jane Austen created a misleading picture of passive rural English – a picture that remains dominant to the present. As in Britain, rural Australians looked to parliamentary politics once the vote and free selection were introduced. As the official anthem of British Liberalism put it, 'why should we be beggars with the ballot in our hands? God gave the land to the people'. Australians had already got that message.

Not all rebels against authority were radicals or republicans. As the labour movement became stronger and began to control governments, conservative organizations developed that challenged the democratic parliamentary institutions when they produced the wrong result. These had their most serious impact during the international depression of the early 1930s, which affected Australia severely. The consequent rise of radical labour campaigns was answered by conservative reactions led mainly by businessmen, former military officers, farmers and suburban Anglophiles (A. Moore 1989; Amos 1976). Their core was in Sydney, but New State movements flourished in northern New South Wales and as far away as Western Australia, which declared for severance from the rest of Australia in 1933, but without effect.

The exception to British parliamentary reformism was in Ireland. Radicalism was muted for a time by the mass famines and emigration in the 1840s (Fitzpatrick 1994). These caused the depopulation of what had been a major area of poverty and unrest in Munster, from whence many survivors emigrated to Australia. (Keneally 1998). However, Irish nationalism flourished, and there was much concern about its threat to British stability. Concessions were made by Parliament, including the 1829 emancipation of Catholics from many restrictions placed on them since the seventeenth century. The Irish made up about 20 per cent of Australia's white population by the start of the gold rush in 1851. While the majority were labourers, small farmers and unskilled, a respectable middle class was emerging, including a Catholic minority as well as Anglo-Irish Protestants. There was also a strong anti-Catholic element, partly drawn from Northern Ireland and centred on Presbyterian churches and Orange lodges. Sectarian outbursts became common from the 1860s and lasted through to the 1920s (Hogan 1987; O'Farrell 1987). The Irish-born population of Australia peaked at 228,000 in 1891, of whom 85,000 were in Victoria.

The most numerous of convicts with a political orientation were Irish (Reece 1989). In 1804 those transported after the Wexford revolt of 1798 took part in organizing a rising at Castle Hill near Sydney. There were well-organized and experienced armed forces in Ireland and Australia to defeat such rebels. The name of 'Vinegar Hill' was bestowed on a nearby hillock, in honour of an earlier rebel defeat at Enniscorthy (Wexford) in 1798. The rebels were already convicts, and many were hanged, flogged or sent to the Newcastle coal mines. The slogan ‘Vinegar Hill’ was raised again by the Irish radicals at the Eureka stockade in 1854. One quarter of the Ballarat miners were Irish. Their leader, Peter Lalor, was severely wounded but recovered, going on to an increasingly conservative political career in the Victorian parliament (FitzSimons 2012).

The height of political concern about the Irish radicals was from the 1860s to the 1890s. This centred around the Irish Revolutionary Brotherhood, founded in Ireland in 1858 and strongly supported from the United States, where it was known as the Fenians (Amos 1988). It was given public exposure with the shots fired at Queen Victoria’s son, Alfred the Duke of Edinburgh, in Sydney in 1868. The Fenian revolt in Ireland in 1865 was one in a long line of failures to overthrow British control. It created a large number of convicts, who were the last to be transported to Australia. The duke’s assailant, Henry O’Farrell, was not a Fenian, but the ensuing panic gave credence to the threat of a widespread and dangerous movement. O’Farrell was insane, which did not save him from the gallows. A *Treason Felony Act* was passed in New South Wales, and the premier, Henry Parkes, launched a rumour about a connection between O’Farrell and the Fenians, which was unfounded. Fenians were transported to Western Australia at the end of that colony’s convict phase. Fenian activity was concentrated between the United States and Britain, with abortive attempts to invade Canada from the United States. These had only limited Australian impact, but were well publicized.

In 1868 three Fenians were hanged in Manchester for killing a policeman while rescuing their imprisoned leaders. This execution for the ‘smashing of the van’ inspired the popular song ‘God Save Ireland’. Sixty-two Fenians were transported to Western Australia in 1868, the last shipment of transported convicts to Australia. The story was completed by the escape in 1876 of six convicts from Fremantle, aided by the American ship *Catalpa*. The various events of the period provided a rich heritage of folklore for subsequent Irish nationalists. However, the emphasis shifted towards elections with the creation of the Home Rule Party in 1874 and later of Sinn Féin in 1905. Under the leadership of Charles Stewart Parnell, the large contingent of Irish nationalist Members of Parliament at Westminster began to agitate through parliamentary politics. The Catholic Church in Australia, where the priesthood was predominantly Irish by mid-century, officially adhered to the Vatican tradition of obedience to legitimate authority. However, many of the clergy sympathized with nationalism, as in Ireland.

The important Irish link was with the United States rather than with distant Australia. The 1880s saw a peak of activity in England, including bombings and murders. This died down as the emphasis moved towards parliamentary approval by the Liberal Party of home rule for Ireland. The party was severely split by the issue. Irish nationalists, consistently supported by the large United States diaspora, kept up an unrelenting campaign of bombings and murders throughout the 1880s. The Australian impact and response was limited. The issue of land ownership was far less acute in Australia than in Ireland.

There were later manifestations of Irish nationalism in the last years of World War I. These were of considerable concern to Australia with its large Irish population. Since the convict days, established authority had always looked upon them with some usually unjustified anxiety. As most of Ireland became independent after 1921, Irish Australians began to define themselves as Catholics and Labor into the mid-1950s. Irish loyalties were kept alive by such Catholic clergy as Archbishop Mannix of Melbourne. Irish politicians were more careful. There were few areas outside New South Wales in which there were solid Irish Catholic majorities: mainly country towns surrounded by Protestant farmers, as in Boorowa (NSW) or Koroit (Victoria). Much Irish discontent was modified by the free selection system, which created a class of small farmers.

The issue of military conscription for overseas service had a special meaning for Irish Australians. It was also a major issue in Ireland, the only part of the United Kingdom that did not have conscription during World War I. The government wisely decided not to arm the Irish, many of whom served in the British Army as volunteers, and there was considerable pressure to extend conscription to Ireland. However, conscription was defeated by referendum in Australia, where the entire military was volunteer. The abortive Easter Week rising in Dublin in 1916 sharpened Irish-Australian resistance. Archbishop Mannix was shocked by the summary execution of the leaders of the Dublin rising, who became national heroes and martyrs. Organized around the Irish National Association, a precursor with Sinn Féin of the Irish Republican Army (IRA), events moved rapidly to the final post-war rebellion and eventual creation of the Irish Free State for all but 6 of the 26 counties of Ireland. Sinn Féin swept the Irish polls in the 1918 British general election.

In December 1917 a second referendum on conscription had been defeated in a campaign in which Archbishop Mannix took a central role. In 1918 Prime Minister Billy Hughes, enraged at this resistance in Dublin, authorized the arrest of seven members of the Irish National Association for conspiracy. They were held in Darlinghurst Gaol, Sydney, until the end of the year, when all but one were released. In 1920 Mannix was denied re-entry to Ireland and three British cities on returning by ship from an overseas journey. He was not readmitted until the following year. Mannix remained a major, and often controversial, leader of Victorian Catholics until his death in 1963 at the age of ninety-nine. Among those very briefly arrested for opposition to Australian conscription was James Scullin, a future prime minister. After Australian Labor split over conscription in 1916, the majority of Irish Australians supported and voted for the party right through to the mid-1950s. Militancy declined as most of Ireland finally achieved independence, but not without a civil war, which Australians did not understand.

Irish Australians became politically absorbed into the labour movement in all states between 1913 and 1960. The IRA had little Australian support for its violent British campaigns of 1939 or the 1970s. Irish politics remained split between the moderate Free Staters and the more radical Republicans, which later organized as Fine Gael and Fianna Fail into the present. But this had little relevance for Australia.

British intelligence services retained an interest in Irish affairs right through to World War II, when Ireland remained neutral, and beyond when civil war broke out in Northern Ireland in 1969. Wartime links between the IRA and the German embassy in Dublin, and with the Irish Communist Party, founded in 1934, were also of interest to British intelligence. These events had little impact on Australia when compared with their import to Britain and the United States. By 1950 money collected through the Australian Catholic Church was largely directed to B. A. Santamaria's anti-Communist Movement (Duncan 2001). Both the Irish and the Australian churches had condemned the IRA since the civil war of the 1920s, although Dr Mannix retained a personal friendship with Eamon de Valera, who became president of the Irish Republic in 1959. Irish Australians began to prosper and joined the middle classes and professions. Their loyalty to the ALP declined as a result of the party split in the 1950s (Murray 1970). The Liberal National Commonwealth government, led by Tony Abbott until 2015, had a larger Catholic component than ever before, but not all were of Irish descent.

Violence against the Chinese was more frequent and destructive than against the Catholic Irish. It was ended with the White Australia policy from 1901. Prior to that, rioting against the Chinese on the goldfields was common, although usually put down by military intervention before anyone was killed. Among these were riots at Buckland River (Victoria) in 1857 and Lambing Flat (NSW) in 1860. There were later riots on the Palmer River in north Queensland in 1873, where miners and Chinese met with Aboriginal resistance as well. By 1901 the transportation system was becoming a memory, although one which had lasted for over ninety years. The Chinese had replaced the convicts and the Irish as a potential threat to stability, but they were a small part of the population and generally very docile (Yong 1977). Some became Christians or married out of the male-dominated Chinese communities. Their roles in market gardening, rural labour and cooking was more appreciated than was their gold mining (Rolls 1996, 1992).

A distinctive Chinese population was expected to die out, although, as with the Aborigines, this never fully happened. The China-born peaked at 25,421 in Victoria in 1857, at 13,157 in New South Wales in 1891 and at 11,253 in Queensland in 1881. Their numbers dropped to a national low of 6,404 in 1947. Chinese were excluded from many occupations by unions and legislation in each colony, but concentrated around mining towns, in catering, laundries and woodworking, and in rural tasks like tree felling and managing vegetable plots. They were overwhelmingly male, and their numbers started falling immediately after the White Australia immigration policy was implemented in 1901. Chinese who were established in Australia were issued with Certificates of Exemption allowing them to leave and re-enter. This assisted them in creating trading companies, but not in reuniting their families. Despite facing hostility, discriminatory laws and eventual bans on immigration, Chinese communities were successful from Cairns to Sydney and Melbourne in the years before World War I. As they had no vote they did not participate in Australian politics. But they had an active political system of their own (Fitzgerald 2006).

Chapter 7

RADICALS AND REBELS

In Australia's restricted and provincial interwar society there was considerable anxiety about threats from eccentric political activists and foreign immigrants. Party politics played out between a small number of parties: Free Trade or Protection before 1910 and Labor, conservative or Country Party since 1920. Individuals and groups with unconventional views took up extreme theories in what was essentially a democratic parliamentary system. Many took positions based on ideologies from overseas, such as communism and fascism. Others subscribed to religious views outside the conventional Protestant or Catholic churches. Some looked to foreign alternatives such as Soviet Russia, Nazi Germany or Fascist Italy. Some who did may even have received moral or monetary support from these sources. If so they became of interest to the rather limited security services maintained by state police special branches or the Commonwealth Investigation Branch. In peacetime conditions no such rebel minorities were declared illegal, even if they were openly committed to the overthrow of existing institutions. Among them were 'secret armies' intriguing with conservative leaders (Cathcart 1988; A. Moore 1989) and the more open Australia First movement (Muirden 1968). The best-known reactionary group was the New Guard in the 1930s (Amos 1976).

The New Guard followed on the Old Guard, which was essentially an anti-communist and anti-Labor grouping of businessmen and former military officers from the more fashionable Sydney suburbs. It was opposed to the Labor State government of Jack Lang and worried about a potential communist rising. How this would eventuate, with the leading forces of conservative society mobilized against the tiny Communist Party, was never clear. It assumed trade union support for such a rebellion, which was opposed by the dominant Australian Workers Union. This element of fear and fantasy continued through conservative extremists well into the twenty-first century, when the threat was from Islam and their old opponents were irrelevant.

On the Left both the Old Guard and the New were regarded as fascist, which was not surprising, given the rise of real fascist movements all over Europe and even in England. However, it was all nonsense, leaving a small residue of extremism in some Sydney branches of the conservative party.

The established institutions did not collapse. Despite conservative sympathies neither the police nor the armed forces quit their constitutional duties. The eventual removal of Lang as premier by the state governor took most of the steam out of the threatened civil war (Cathcart 1988). However, 1930 to 1932 was the only period in modern Australian history when significant numbers believed in an impending revolution and organized accordingly. The removal of the Whitlam government by the governor-general in 1975 produced no comparable hysteria or threatened violence.

Communists and radicals were periodically arrested for disturbing the peace or even for sedition under the *Crimes Act*, but not simply for being communists. Recently, organizations are declared illegal in peacetime due to a concern with terrorism. This is a new development, but it echoed concerns with the Industrial Workers of the World (IWW) during World War I (V. Burgmann 1995; Turner 1979). Small counter-espionage agencies were first created during that world war, but were reduced in peacetime or delegated to state police forces. Their main overseas links were with understaffed and barely competent British counterparts, until a rapid restructuring in World War II. The banning of political organizations was judged permissible in wartime, but not in peace.

On that basis the Communist Party of Australia was temporarily declared illegal in 1940 (S. Macintyre 1998). This distinction has now become blurred with the chaos in the Middle East and the use of suicide bombers and assassins. As in the United States and Britain, Australian governments maintain official lists of 'terrorist organizations', not all of which are Islamic or uniformly accepted by all three international partners.

Immigration control has been central in determining the treatment of unpopular individuals or groups. Policy became increasingly bureaucratized as control moved from the states to the Commonwealth after 1920. World War I was an important dividing point, with new powers facilitating the deportation of dissident or unwanted individuals. The *Immigration Restriction Act of 1901* gave the power to prevent landing to immigration officers, appointed by the Commonwealth, at the various ports of entry. Prior to that, entry was a colonial matter and easily avoided. The early Victorian law of 1855, controlling Chinese entry by ship, was simply evaded by landing at Robe (South Australia) and walking into Victoria. About 15,000 used this approach in two years, which is commemorated locally in a monument. The first recorded group of gypsies to arrive in Australia (in 1898) were helped along the way from Robe by public donations and food until they arrived in Melbourne (Sayer 2017). Apart from the strict control over Asians, movement into Australia was relatively free, especially for white British subjects. In wartime, however, things changed.

Prime Minister Billy Hughes had become fanatical about the war effort and opponents of conscription after he had been expelled from the Labor Party on these issues in 1916. His government used the *Unlawful Associations Act* to suppress the Industrial Workers of the World. Twelve of their activists were sentenced to 15 years for conspiracy to commit arson. Under the *War Precautions Act* another IWW member (Paul Freeman) was deported to the United States. Deportation was threatened for the seamen's activist Tom Walsh for leading a prohibited strike. Walsh, who was a British subject of Irish origin, was arrested and held pending deportation in 1925, but was released on appeal.

Immigration control has been central in determining the treatment of unpopular individuals or groups. Policy became increasingly bureaucratized as control moved from the states to the Commonwealth after 1920. World War I was an important dividing point, with new powers facilitating the deportation of dissident or unwanted individuals. The *Immigration Restriction Act of 1901* gave the power to prevent admission to immigration officers, appointed by the Commonwealth at the various ports. In wartime, however, things changed. Deportation could always be used to dispose of illegals and the undesired. It was rationalized once immigration became a Commonwealth power at Federation (Nicholls 2007). In recent years annual deportations of up to 20,000 have become normal. Most are for visa offences rather than political activity.

Hughes's post-war government used the *Unlawful Associations Act* to suppress the Industrial Workers of the World (V. Burgmann 1995). Twelve of their activists were sentenced to 15 years for conspiracy to commit arson. With the Russian revolutions of 1917 and the formation of the Australian Communist Party in 1921, the continuing *War Precautions Act* enabled the government to imprison the Bolshevik representative, Peter Simonoff.

Ex-servicemen broke up a demonstration in Brisbane defending the right to fly a red flag, which had been made illegal (Evans 1989). These battles began the process of seeing communism as a major area of concern for the security services. These were mild compared to the United States reaction, but they established a set of priorities that were to last well beyond World War II. The IWW and the communists were to become targets for J. Edgar Hoover, director of the US Federal Bureau of Investigation (FBI) through the interwar years and beyond (Weiner 2012).

The IWW was declared illegal in Australia as an 'unlawful association' from December 1916. Tom Barker, editor of the IWW newspaper, *Direct Action*, had already been arrested and was eventually deported from Australia to Chile in 1918. The IWW had certainly engaged in militant tactics in the United States, where industrial strife and state repression were far more violent.

Whether such tactics were also used by the Australians remains in doubt (V. Burgmann 1995; Turner 1979). Their main offence was consistent hostility to the world war and conscription for overseas military service. Their influence declined with the creation of the Communist Party in 1921 (Davidson 1969). As anarcho-syndicalists, the IWW rejected the ideological approach of the new Leninist party. The IWW was the most severely suppressed of parties on the Left, but owed no allegiance to any state, unlike the communists who owed allegiance to the Communist International in Moscow. Nevertheless, the IWW remained under surveillance into the 1930s, when their influence on trade unions had become negligible. Tom Barker ended his days as Labour mayor of St Pancras in London. This was typical of the route of many radicals over the past century.

Surveillance and infiltration practices were set up just after World War II as the basic approach of the Australian Security Intelligence Organisation (ASIO). ASIO was founded by the Chifley Labor government in 1949 at the insistence of the United States (Horner 2014; Cain 1983, 2008). The United States made this a condition for sharing secret information gained from the 'Venona' decoded Soviet ciphers, some of it referring to Australia (West 1999; Ball and Horner 1998; Cain 2008; Haynes and Klehr 1999). The United States and ASIO made communism and the Soviet Union their major targets. This was acceptable to the Labor government, which faced an industrial relations crisis largely caused by communist-led unions such as the Miners' Federation. Chifley sent in troops to work the mines in 1949, a most unusual response from a Labor government (Deery 1978). The election of Robert Menzies and the conservatives in 1949 naturally moved ASIO closer to the governing party. Communist influence was at its height between 1945 and 1950, mainly in the trade unions.

Australia had previously had small intelligence organizations associated with the state police special branches and the Commonwealth Investigation Branch (McKnight 1994). The major targets of interest, in sequence, have been the Irish, the communists, and the Muslims, over a century. Priorities have changed, responding to international rather than local situations. Both world wars expanded the scope of intelligence work, with the Irish joined by the union militants of the IWW, followed by the communists after 1920. None of these organizations had any significant membership in the early 1920s except in a few Sydney and Melbourne unions and in Broken Hill. Fascist groups, oriented towards Italy and Germany, attracted some attention between the 1920s and 1940 and enrolled some Italian and German Australians (Cresciani 1980; Menghetti 1981; Gumpl and Kleinig 2007). ASIO also studied Italian 'mafia' organizations from the 1950s, although had limited impact on their success as drug importers or as profiteers from their compatriots. The

Calabrian N'Drangheta has had more influence than the Sicilian Mafia, locally and internationally (Small and Gilling 2016).

Not all deviant groups were based on immigrants. Prominent Australians and ex-servicemen also created similar organizations, most of which were hostile to non-British immigration. Among these were the New Guard (E. Campbell 1965) and the post–World War II Australian League of Rights (A. Campbell 1978). From the founding of the Communist Party in 1921 until the creation of Pauline Hanson's One Nation in 1996 (Leach et al. 2000) there have always been significant organizations outside the mainstream partisan system, most of them conservative. These have tended to appeal to alienated sections of society, such as manual workers for the Communists, rural and provincial people for One Nation and retired military for the New Guard. Only the New Guard and the Riverina Movement either advocated or used violence. One Nation was more the victim of attacks than their originator. Many of its supporters were elderly. The League of Rights was formed in 1946 and was always led by Eric Butler (A. Campbell 1978). It had an elaborate network of front organizations and publications and links with South African and Rhodesian groups. It was consistently anti-Semitic and fanatically loyal to the monarchy, the British Empire and White Australia (A. Campbell 1978; Gott 1965; St John 1972).

The New Guard was largely a product of the world depression and of ex-servicemen alienated from the New South Wales Labor government led by Jack Lang (Amos 1976). The League of Rights led by Eric Butler originated in the Social Credit movement, which in the 1920s and 1930s had a following in rural areas of Australia, New Zealand and Canada. One Nation appealed strongly to rural communities in Queensland and was also alienated from the Labor Party, though drawing considerable support from Labor voters in its hostility towards Asians and Aborigines. Of these parties, only the New Guard and its leader Eric Campbell might reasonably be called 'fascist'. Pauline Hanson's ideology was drawn to a large extent in the 1990s from traditional Queensland Labor's support for White Australia. It emerged again in 2016, focused on Muslims.

The militarized nature of the New Guard and its leaders made it potentially dangerous to civil order. Its leading members included former service officers with wartime experience. The New Guard and organizations like it directed their hostility against Jack Lang (1876–1975), the New South Wales Labor premier, who they regarded, quite incorrectly, as a communist (Amos 1976). After Lang's removal by the state governor in 1932, this obsession decreased in importance. The New Guard leader, Eric Campbell, developed an admiration for Hitler, which was not always shared with his followers. None of the reactionary organizations were declared illegal until the outbreak of World War II.

The main driving force of reactionary and pseudo-fascist organizations in the interwar period was the fear that social harmony would be shattered by militant trade unionism, economic collapse and communism. Threats from Asia were much less important. The White Australia policy had effectively cut Australia off from any contacts or interest in that vast and mainly colonized region. The Australia First movement established close links with Japan, which eventually sealed their fate. (Muirden 1968).

The Australia First movement was illegalized on the outbreak of the Pacific war in 1941 because of the sympathy of its leaders for Japan. Its supporters were middle-class eccentrics, including Adela Pankhurst. One of the English suffragette Pankhurst family, she became a foundation member of the Communist Party of Australia in 1921. She endured periods of imprisonment in the true Pankhurst tradition and detention on Garden Island (Sydney), while awaiting deportation with her communist husband, Tom Walsh, president of the Seamen's Union. An appeal allowed them to remain in Australia, where they gradually moved away to the political right and affinity with Japan, passing through the Australian Women's Guild of Empire and the Australia First Movement of the writer P. R. Stephensen. It was the Japanese link that interested the security organization in 1942. Stephensen was arrested and held without trial from 1942 until 1945.

The conventional reactionary groups had an exaggerated view of the power of local communism, of the trade unions and of the ALP. These reached their height during and following the world depression, which peaked in 1932, driving almost one quarter of the Australian workforce into unemployment. Eric Campbell was attracted to fascism and courted support from both Hitler and Mussolini. Like his British counterpart, Sir Oswald Mosley, his first enthusiasm was for Mussolini, but he later moved towards Nazism (E. Campbell 1978). Otherwise Nazism was admired by a small number of German Australians, mainly in South Australia (Gumpl and Kleinig 2007). These organizations were anti-Semitic, often associating Jews with communism. None presented a serious threat to society once the depression was resolved. However, like the communists, some were associated with a foreign power through the Italian or German, and later, Soviet embassies. Reactionary organizations tended to split into mutually hostile groups. Later, One Nation would suffer this fate (Leach et al. 2000), which previously affected the Old and New Guards (Amos 1976; Cathcart 1988; Connell and Gould 1967). Currently, the many reactionary groups are also seriously fragmented, united only by their hatred of Muslims, multiculturalism and each other. Some maintain links with more influential organizations in the United States, from whom most of the racist material sent to Australia and Britain originates.

Chapter 8

COMMUNISTS AND THEIR ALLIES

From the end of the war in 1945, communists and industrial militants were once again the main government targets (Horner 2014; Cain 2008; McKnight 1994; Ball and Horner 1998; Blaxland 2015; Blaxland and Crawley 2016; 2016). This continued for over forty years, until the collapse of the Soviet system in 1991 finally shattered the international and local cohesion of the communist parties. The unfamiliar objectives of Islamism required a complete reorientation of ASIO's often basic skills and practices (Blaxland 2015). However the 'five hands' (or 'eyes')' collaboration among ASIO, the CIA, MI6 and the New Zealand and Canadian Security Intelligence Services, gave Australia access to a wealth of contacts and information (Richelson and Ball 1985; Ball and Horner 1998). One great asset, if highly secret, was ownership of the 'Venona' decoded Russian messages which, among many other items, revealed details of a Soviet spy circle within the Australian Department of External Affairs (West 1999; Haynes and Klehr 1999). US influence, from the Federal Bureau of Investigation (FBI) and Central Intelligence Agency (CIA), ensured a major obsession with communism, which was not always justified in the Australian context. The FBI leadership of J. Edgar Hoover sustained this dedicated hostility for almost fifty years into the 1970s (Weiner 2012).

Unlike Australia and New Zealand, Canada, Britain and the United States have extensive experience of terrorism, as well as wide-ranging networks of informants. Australia's pre-war dependence on British intelligence was diminished by the discovery in 1963 that a leading officer of MI6 (the Secret Intelligence Service), Kim Philby, had been a Soviet agent for many years (B. Macintyre 2014). He eventually retired to Moscow, where he received a medal from the Soviet government and lived out the rest of his life. Like Philby, the most effective spies were not publicly revealed communists.

Dissident political movements in democracies are normally distinguished as being either Right or Left. In Australia this implies a relative closeness either to the Liberals and conservatives or to the Labor and socialist political positions. Many activists have moved between Left and Right loyalties. A few have even moved back again. Nor can anti-Semitism be taken as a benchmark for 'rightism'. Radical Labor leaders like Jack Lang were also anti-Semitic. Some Labor politicians were xenophobic towards all foreigners, which reflected the views of many of their supporters. English immigrants were not welcomed in the 1920s, when there was a shortage of jobs (Bolton 1972), but were subsidized and sought in the 1950s and 1960s as an alternative to continental Europeans (Appleyard 1988). Aboriginal representatives became the main customers of the Race Discrimination complaints system (Anderson 2002).

It was not until after World War I that clear divisions between Right and Left began to emerge. Labor was committed to a socialist objective similar to that adopted in Britain. This Right–Left division was largely due to the Russian revolution of 1917 and the subsequent creation by the Bolsheviks of the Communist International in 1919 (Farrell 1982; Gollan 1975). This divided the official Labor movement and its trade unions. Democratic socialists, the mainstream tradition in Australia and Britain, were abused as traitors by the communists until 1934, when a united front between the two was being urged against fascism. Labor and communist unionists struggled for control from the 1920, long before the anti-communist 'movement' was established by B. A. Santamaria in 1942. Major unions like the Australian Workers Union took the leading role in resisting communist infiltration of the ALP. This did not prevent the New South Wales Labor party adopting in 1939 a pro-Soviet position (Gollan 1975), which promptly led to a split by more conventional party members and affiliated unions. In 1940 the ALP Federal Executive withdrew recognition from the NSW branch for its policies and opposition to the war effort.

Communist influence in Australia rose from the mid-1930s, lapsed briefly while opposing the war between 1939 and 1941, and then took off to its greatest strength between 1945 and the 1950s (Davidson, 1969; Gollan 1975; S. Macintyre, 1998). The irony was that the Communist Party began to grow rapidly when it was illegal, between 1940 and 1942. The Liberal and Country parties and ASIO all regarded communism as a dangerous movement. This tended to alienate ASIO from the labour movement and vice versa. Despite their failure to control Labor, the communists continued to influence ALP supporters and affiliated trade unions. This was, indeed, almost all they could do, as their electoral appeal was very limited. Only one official communist, Fred Paterson, in Queensland, was ever elected to an Australian parliament.

Between the 1940s and the 1960s communists also had a following among intellectuals and academics, especially in Melbourne (Gollan 1975). This gave ASIO an interest in checking on several well-known academics and literary figures, consequently annoying them and their influential friends (Capp 1993). No Soviet spies were discovered amongst them, but the concept of 'agent of influence' was invented to describe their friendly attitude towards the Soviet Union and links with its embassy in Canberra. This term was applied in 1983 to David Combe, a Labor Party secretary and friend of a Soviet embassy officer (Marr 1984).

Invigilation had its limitations, as subjects soon became aware. Infiltration of suspect organizations was rarely as dangerous as its undercover criminal counterpart. Being an agent in the Soviet bloc was far more hazardous. For a time, during the wartime ban on the Communist Party, many communists joined the ALP, which increased the likelihood of supervision annoying the governing party at a time when admiration of the Soviet Union was at its height. In the relatively limited and inbred world around the trades halls of the major cities, most activists already had a fair idea of who were communist or security infiltrators. The most consistent invigilation was for personnel of the Soviet embassy in Canberra and those Australians with apparent links to them. The most useful function of ASIO was checking the communications of the Soviet embassy. Infiltrating spies into the Communist Party was arguably much less fruitful. (Blaxland 2015). Of all the dissident groups, the communists had the closest links with a foreign power, to whom they pledged loyalty (Lovell and Windle 2008). In the end this sealed their fate (Manne 1994).

Communist influence increased and spread to some universities in the early post-war period. Some conservatives found it hard to distinguish between socialists and communists. A selection of 28, mainly former communists with ASIO files, suggests a high degree of political ignorance and lack of imagination in the ASIO invigilators (M. Burgmann, 1995). This raises the question whether there was any point in the expenditure of time and money in trailing innocent people because of their presumed views. The ASIO defence must be that everything is now different, which is indeed true. Electronic invigilation saves many long days standing on cold corners.

While the Industrial Workers of the World (IWW) had been declared an unlawful association under wartime powers in 1916, and the Communist Party during World War II, peacetime attempts to prohibit the Communist Party were frustrated by the courts and by a constitutional referendum. The Liberal Party had promised before its victorious 1949 election campaign that 'the Communist Party will be declared subversive and unlawful and dissolved'. The Communist Party Dissolution Bill was introduced in Parliament in 1950, duly passed with Labor support, and was then declared outside the powers of the Commonwealth by a High Court decision of five to one. The objection was that the defence power could not operate this way in peacetime, which must now seem redundant as wars are seldom actually declared. The only solution was to amend the constitution by referendum (Webb 1954). Opinion polling showed a strong margin for dissolving the Communist Party in 1951.

But, as often happens, the opinion polls were wrong. The referendum was lost by a very narrow margin of 52,082 votes out of 4,687,936 cast. It also marked the start of a major split in the ALP, which had many members in favour of the bill (Murray 1970). After the referendum to amend the Constitution, the Royal Commission on Espionage, arising from the defection of a Soviet Ministry of Internal Affairs (MVD) officer, Vladimir Petrov, from the Soviet embassy, followed (Manne 1987; 1994).

In contrast to later terrorists, the Australian communists never seriously supported local violence or revolution, whatever their party literature might have suggested. They were only a menace to Australian cohesion because of their activity in unions, which were militant both before and after the 70-year activity of the party. Their close links were with foreign states with which Australia was never officially at war, including the Soviet Union and the People's Republic of China. The different paths of these two states hastened the collapse of the party altogether in the 1960s.

The Communist Party tactic of influencing the Labor Party through the affiliated unions naturally focussed ASIO's investigations on the ALP rather than the Liberal and National parties. For the dissident conservative factions these squabbles on the Left were irrelevant. Anyone who favoured socialism, state ownership of utilities or just a national welfare system, was suspect. Extreme conservatism was not of much interest to the security agencies either before or after the creation of ASIO in 1949, although they kept an interest in any that were violent or Nazi. As elsewhere ASIO tended towards the Right and focussed on the Left. The release of 30-year-old files, despite ASIO objections, has allowed a much closer inspection of the ideology and limitations of this agency. ASIO was unable to prevent release, but reserved the right to censor individual names of their agents and informants and anything encroaching on cabinet secrecy. These files have been used for producing an official history of ASIO. The first excellent volume, extending to 1963, was published in 2014 (Horner 2014), the second in 2015 (Blaxland 2015) covering the years to 1975 and the final volume in 2016 covering the years to 1989.

Of more interest than ideology was the extent to which anyone was linked to a hostile foreign power or was organizing violence and social disruption. This could only be effectively ascertained by infiltrating suspect organizations or intercepting Soviet coded messages. These practices became very widespread. The amount of time and public money involved were revealed by the memoirs of former communist leader Mark Aarons in his review of his family's vast ASIO file (Aarons 2010). This had a large number of snapshots of men in grubby raincoats entering the communist headquarters in Sydney in broad daylight.

Australian communists were publicly known, did not engage in terrorism and only became involved with violence during strikes and demonstrations. Contacts with the Soviet embassy were disrupted by its departure from Canberra between 1954 and 1959, following the defection of Petrov. His was by far the most important defection in Australia and brought over a great deal of information. (Horner 2014: 317–78) The major weakness in counter-intelligence was not in Australia, but in the leading role of Kim Philby as a Soviet agent in Britain's MI6 (B. Macintyre 2014). However, the official history of ASIO (Vol. 3) accepts that there was penetration by Soviet or communist agents (Blaxland and Crawley 2016; Sassoon 2015).

ASIO operated in secret and by infiltration and, like the police, through informers. Both the Americans and former ASIO employees believed that it was infiltrated. It does not seem to have been compromised to the same extent as its British counterparts MI5 and MI6. The highly placed Philby almost became MI6 director. He made his escape to Moscow in 1963, where he joined two other major defectors and friends, Guy Burgess and Donald Maclean. Philby had the public school and class connections that were typical of MI6 but were less so for ASIO. Among these were a Middle Eastern background through his distinguished father, St John Philby. Another double agent in the British service was George Blake, who was sentenced to 42 years imprisonment by the British courts.

These crises damaged relations between the British and US intelligence communities, but Australia was free from their dramatic impact. A major function of double agents was to reveal the names and locations of Western agents to the Soviet KGB, which normally had hostile agents killed if they were in the Soviet Union or its allied countries. Australia experienced the opposite trend with the information handed over by Petrov on his defection: closing the Soviet embassy and sending its agents home if that is what they wanted and were not Australian or British subjects.

ASIO concentrated most of its efforts on Australian communists, unionists and intellectuals and on the staff of the Soviet embassy. Later it had to retrain and enrol staff with an insight into Islamic and Arab affairs, which it had previously lacked. As all of its activities are governed by strict secrecy it is hard to know how many successes ASIO has scored to justify its rapidly expanding staff and budget. The defection of Petrov in 1954 was claimed as a triumph. A Polish ASIO agent, Michael Bialoguski, had been cultivating Petrov for some time (Bialoguski 1955). However, defection was almost certainly due to the crisis in the Soviet MVD, caused by the overthrow and hasty execution of its leader, Lavrentiy Beria, in December 1953. Petrov remained in Australia for the rest of his life, supported by a pension from the security budget. Had he returned to the Soviet Union he might have suffered the same fate as Beria and other MVD officers. Petrov had direct access to much useful information, especially in the field of ciphers and codes.

The decoding of information from Soviet-oriented governments was part of a complex game of deceit, double agents, burglaries and bribery, pioneered by the FBI under long-term director J. Edgar Hoover. The decoding operation nicknamed 'Venona' was central to breaking Soviet codes, revealing among much else, the existence of Soviet agents within the Commonwealth bureaucracy (Ball and Horner (1998; Blaxland 2015). These professional anti-Soviet activities were undoubtedly more useful to Australia than the much-criticized invigilation of civilians or even of Communist Party members. Infiltration of the Communist Party was widely practiced, but not to the American extreme of reducing the party to a nullity. Infiltration was countered with similar activity by the Soviet KGB/MVD (Internal Security) and GRU (Military Security). The final collapse of Australian and British communism was caused by the collapse of the Soviet system in the 1990s.

ASIO came under hostile criticism from the 1950s. It was disliked within official and professional occupations because of its major function of informing employers about the political leanings of future appointees (M. Burgmann 2014). It was disliked and later actively hated by Labor Party members for its suspected role in the split of 1956, which kept Labor out of office nationally until 1972 (Murray 1970). It was suspected again by the same people for the alleged role of ASIO's partner, the American CIA, in the 1975 dismissal of the Whitlam government. It engaged in foolish tactics, such as publicly collecting car registration numbers from meetings of people not under any reasonable suspicion, a strategy copied from the FBI. It triumphed over H. V. "Doc" Evatt, the Labor leader, whose own foolish involvement in the Petrov crisis became a factor in his downfall (Bialoguski 1955; Manne 1987). Its close association with the Liberal leadership and the Democratic Labor Party, and its penetration of communist and union activities, rarely found anything of vital importance, but annoyed those who were well aware of what was happening. The regular briefings in the 1950s between the labour attaché at the Melbourne US consulate and the four unions affiliated to the Democratic Labor Party, particularly annoyed those who saw the hand of the CIA in everything. Whitlam, for one, always denied any CIA involvement in his overthrow.

Relations between ASIO and the ALP reached a crisis point on the election of the Whitlam government in 1972 (Blaxland 2015). One Labor minister, Jim Cairns, had been the leader of the moratorium movement against the Vietnam War, which raised huge rallies in Melbourne. He was certainly a 'person of interest'. The attorney general, Lionel Murphy, who was the minister responsible for ASIO, created a serious rift in 1973 by demanding to see ASIO files on Croatian terrorism. ASIO refused to show him these when he arrived at their Melbourne office. An eyewitness account details total chaos. (Sasson 2015). Prime Minister Gough Whitlam was less than impressed. This incident earned the media title of a 'raid' and emphasized that ASIO was outside political control. The principle was subsequently established in law that the director of ASIO was not answerable to the attorney general, who was nominally responsible for his organization.

Of all the displaced persons who had migrated to Australia after 1945, only the Croatians had acquired a serious reputation for organized and violent political activity (Blaxland 2015: Chapter 5). The pre-war Croatian community had mainly been organized by the communists, and most returned to Croatia after the war. The newcomers' enemy was the communist government of Yugoslavia and its Australian supporters. Their local political friends were in the Liberal Party and the Catholic Church, along with some other East Europeans. They had no terrorist targets in Australia other than unfriendly compatriots and the Yugoslav embassy and consuls, but plenty of enemies within the Labor movement, including Senator Murphy, Jim Cairns and Mark Aarons (2001). This minority of Croatian nationalists was the only politically violent group of immigrants, but their target was in far distant Yugoslavia, which ceased to exist in 1991. Their hero, the Ustashe leader Ante Paveliç, was safely settled in South America, having evaded post-war capture. He died peacefully in Spain aged 70. The 1990s presented a quite different task for security organizations, with the dissolution of the Soviet Union, the communist states of Europe and Croatian independence.

The 70 years of surveillance of communists and their allies in Australia between 1920 and 1990 were mainly useful in monitoring Soviet intelligence (Ball and Horner 1998; Blaxland 2015). It does not seem to have uncovered much else that was startling or seriously dangerous to social stability and peace, except for electoral fraud in some unions and communist strength in several strategic industries, including mining, the metal trades and the waterfront. Communists had been warned by Stalin, in his early days as party secretary, against terrorism (which he had practised when younger). Whatever may have happened elsewhere, this prohibition was accepted by the Australian party and by the British communists, under whose general guidance they were placed by the Communist International. The IWW soon faded away after 1918 due to serious repression in the United States, retaining a distant influence from America and an undeserved reputation for anarchism. Communist control of unions and, through affiliation, influence on the ALP, was quite serious from the 1940s to the 1960s, being largely blocked by the movement of Santamaria and the solid resistance of the Australian Workers Union (AWU), the New South Wales ALP and most Labor politicians (Santamaria 1981). However, the split in the ALP in Victoria, which created the Democratic

Labor Party, had the unproductive effect of increasing communist sympathies in the remaining Victorian State Labor Party and its affiliated unions in the 1960s (Murray 1970).

The major areas of communist influence were on the coalfields and the waterfront, where a threat to national security was feared during the war. What was potentially serious was the close link between the Australian party and the Soviet Union. This was limited by the expulsion of the Soviet embassy from Canberra between 1954 and 1959. Even the tiny Trotskyist groups centred on Balmain (Sydney) were of interest to ASIO, which maintained a watch on the leader, Nick Origlass (Greenland 1998). As the communist cause started to fragment from 1956 a significant number of activists moved over briefly to the Trotskyists, on the way, eventually, to positions in the conventional Labor movement (Blaxland 2015). Most important among these in turning against their old comrades was Laurie Short of the Federated Ironworkers Union (Short 1992).

Extremist conservative organizations were cultivated by the German, Japanese and Italian embassies in the 1930s. There were few equivalents on the Left. The splinter Communist Party (Marxist–Leninist) led by Ted Hill in the 1960s, maintained close links with the Chinese government. These links faded away as the Chinese Communist Party ended its interest in international allies with little credibility. The Socialist Party of Australia had a similar link with the restored Soviet embassy, replacing the 'revisionist' Communist Party of Australia. It too faded away with a small group colonizing the Sydney Greens. The more recent Socialist Alliance has relationships with small Trotskyist groups in Britain and Sri Lanka and with the embassy of Venezuela, but these are scarcely of much intelligence value. It influences issues through well-organized demonstrations and a weekly newspaper.

The record of actual spying for the Soviet Union through the Communist Party was limited by the Soviet practice of avoiding known party members for espionage and by the system instituted from 1945 of security checks on public servants in sensitive positions. The main individual consistently associated with passing information on to the Soviet embassy was Wally Clayton alias Klod. Clayton had been responsible for building the party's underground organisation between 1939 and 1942 while it was illegal because of its opposition to the war. He avoided arrest and imprisonment, although well known to security organisations as linked to the Soviet People's Commissariat for Internal Affairs (NKVD). His passport was eventually withdrawn. Among his collaborators was a senior foreign affairs officer, Ian Milner, who defected to Czechoslovakia in 1950.

State action against communists followed in the tradition set in World War I by the arrest of leaders of the IWW.

The IWW was of American origin and strength. Individual arrests were often caused by disturbances at meetings or during industrial disputes. In the United States there was substantial fear and repression of the IWW for its anarchist beliefs and alleged actions. Violent industrial relations, bombings and assassination were not uncommon in the United States, including the violent deaths of four presidents since the 1860s. This echoed hollowly in Australia, where the IWW was both much smaller and much less likely to commit terrorism than its American inspirer. The IWW was founded in 1905 and, only two years later, an Australian branch was established (V. Burgmann 1995). It worked with other unions, most fruitfully with the meat workers. Their union, the Australian Meat Industrial Union (MIEU), was still under communist control in the 1960s, long after the IWW had been reduced to a tiny minority. The Communist Party dissolved in 1991, leaving a residue of schismatic Marxist organizations (Blaxland 2015).

Hostility to communists had a variety of allies. The largest elements were the conservative parties, employers of militant unionists and patriotic organizations like the Returned Services League, which banned communists from holding office, even despite their war service. Large segments of the labour movement were also actively opposed, including the AWU, Australia's largest, and a majority of Labor national and state politicians. The Catholic Church campaigned against communism on ideological grounds, especially through Santamaria's Movement and its paper, *News Weekly* (Santamaria 1981) (ECJJ). But this created a rift between Victoria and New South Wales and eventually led to a Vatican intervention when the Movement began to involve itself in Labor Party internal politics. The communists did not help their own cause by their virulence against all these opponents. But they did not adopt any really violent or revolutionary tactics that might have justified ASIOs invigilation over the years. Fixing union ballots was the closest to outright illegality, other than feeding information to the Soviet embassy. The communists were assumed to represent a 'hostile power' and were in breach of the Criminal Code, accordingly, although never in a state of warfare with Australia.

Action against individual alien supporters of communism included denial of visas or deportation. These were not normally used against Australian or British subjects, especially before 1949, when the *Australian Citizenship Act* created a distinct nationality within the power of the Commonwealth government to grant or deny. Under the White Australia policy it was usual to deny citizenship to non-Europeans for any reason.

Action against political radicals included the Kisch case of 1934 and the Burchett case of 1955. Egon Kisch was a Czech communist and Wilfred Burchett an Australian-born citizen who always denied that he was a communist (Burchett 2005). The attorney general, Robert Menzies, refused landing to Kisch in 1934 on the grounds of his "close association with Communist International activities" and information from London that he was denied entry to the United Kingdom. Kisch lied about his connections with the Communist International, which the Australian authorities were too ill-informed to check. He was widely known in Europe for this affiliation and for his writing, organizing and public speaking in German.

Kisch was undoubtedly a Comintern agent and not simply a peace activist and socialist, as he is often described in friendly accounts (Kisch 1937/1969). His visit to Australia was to address the peace movement on the Nazi threat in Europe, from which he was a refugee. This was precisely what the Australian government wanted to prevent by keeping him on board ship and returning him to Europe. His dramatic jump from the *Strathaird*, breaking his leg, made him a hero. He challenged his exclusion through the courts and addressed many successful meetings. His account of his adventure, *Eintritt Verboten!*, was published in 1939 and was not flattering (in English as *Australian Landfall*, 1969). Apart from being a hero of the Left, Kisch might be remembered as one of the last arrivals to submit to the dictation test normally used to exclude Asians. The High Court ruled that Gaelic, in which he was examined, was not a 'modern European language', causing much indignation among Scottish Australians. This decision destroyed the government's case and Kisch left Australia after a stay of one month. He was much better at public relations than was the Australian government (Zogbaum 2004).

As an alien he had no right to be in Australia, but both public opinion and a foolish official attempt to exclude him by using the obsolete dictation test, saved his campaign.

Wilfred Burchett was Australian born and bred and, by his own often-questioned account, never a communist (Burchett 2005). An experienced journalist, Burchett was the first one to reach Hiroshima after the atom bomb was dropped, and he was profoundly affected. His varied career included residence in Vietnam, China, North Korea, Burma and Cambodia. He claimed to have been present at one of Kisch's Australian meetings and to have been consulted on the Vietnam War by Henry Kissinger. A remarkable record, but one that kept him an exile from Australia for 17 years. His problem arose from his consistent sympathy for the communist case on Asian affairs, which ran counter to American and Australian policy. A renewal of his lost passport was denied in 1955. This was only overturned by Gough Whitlam in person, as an early act by his government in 1972. This made it clear that an Australian passport remains the property of the Commonwealth and that birth in Australia does not, in itself, qualify everyone to seek Australian protection. Without a passport Burchett would have been unable to leave Australia. He was rescued by friendly communist states such as Bulgaria, Cuba and Vietnam, which issued him with valid travel documents.

Returning to Australia, Burchett foolishly sued for defamation against leaders of the Democratic Labor Party. Unable to meet the massive costs, he left Australia again. Burchett's case raised the question of the value of Australian citizenship for those consistently allied with national enemies, and the legal status of wars never officially declared by Australia, as in Vietnam or Korea. Burchett's interrogation of Australians captured by the North Koreans was condemned as constituting 'aid and comfort to Australia's enemies'. The same principle was applied 50 years later to Australians fighting for the Islamic 'caliphate' in the Middle East. These conflicts were not formally declared as wars.

Undeclared wars had become common for Australia with the rise of Asian communist regimes. They were to continue with the battles against Muslim forces, which escalated after Burchett's death. The civil wars in Syria, Afghanistan and Iraq attracted about 200 young Islamic jihadists and converts from Australia who, it was feared, might return to Australia fully trained and experienced. Unlike Burchett none were likely to be communists. By 2014 they ran the risk of losing their passports and being imprisoned should they return to Australia. Deprivation of a passport was rare, but increasing. The youth going to support jihad were usually Australian citizens by birth, like Burchett. Automatic loss of citizenship was legislated for in 2015, but was never applied to Burchett. The law in his time would not have allowed it without a formal trial.

The end of World War II saw a direct link between the Soviet allegiances of the communists and the pressures on the local party. The *Crimes Act* legitimized prosecution of 'agents of a foreign power'. Political practice soon ventured as far as advocating illegalizing the Communist Party on that basis. Australian law does not have constitutional protection for freedom of speech or of organization. However, much of the repressive policy between 1949 and 1970 was inspired by the United States, which had earlier suspended this freedom for radical groups under the post-war *Sedition Act of 1918–1920*. Britain made communists and their newspaper, *The Daily Worker*, illegal during wartime, but this was relaxed once the Soviet Union became an ally in 1941. Post-war Australia followed the peacetime British course until 1949, when there was strong support for illegalizing the party with a change of Commonwealth government from Labor to Liberal. (S. Macintyre 1998). The High Court and the Constitution saved the communists, which might not have been the intent of the founding fathers had there been any communists in the 1890s.

Communists could still be arrested for the ancient crime of sedition. In 1949 the communist secretary, Lance Sharkey, was imprisoned for three years for sedition under the *Crimes Act*, followed by several others. All had declared that, if Australia were at war, the workers would welcome Soviet forces. This followed similar remarks from European communists, but was typically absurd coming from Australia. On appeal, Sharkey's term was reduced by a half and he was released in 1951. By then the Victorian Liberal government had introduced legislation aimed at banning the party. They relied on a defector, Cecil Sharpley. The Victorian Royal Commission reported in 1950 under the *Royal Commission (Communist Party) Act 1949* and was chaired by Sir Charles Lowe (Gollan 1975). It exonerated the party from serving a foreign power, union ballot rigging and raising its funds from outside Australia. This judgement avoided the question of whether a state government had the right to ban a political party, and passed such a decision over to the Commonwealth. In retrospect it seems rather naïve. While the IWW had been declared an unlawful association under wartime powers in 1916, and the Communist Party during World War II, peacetime attempts to prohibit the Communist Party were frustrated by the courts and by the constitutional referendum.

The effectiveness of communist links with the Soviet Union was limited by the extent to which these were well known to the security organisations infiltrating the party and monitoring party and embassy communications. Serious crime and risk of civil disorder became more relevant to national security and cohesion than the openly 'revolutionary' parties. The 'old Left' strategy of organizing the working class for the overthrow of capitalism was almost laughable by the turn of the new century. The communists had served the Soviet system so loyally that they lost credibility as it gradually disintegrated (Lovell and Windle 2008). Several of the communist-controlled unions, like the Builders Labourers Federation, amalgamated into the Construction, Forestry, Mining and Energy Union (CFMEU), which remained militant, but without identifying with foreign powers. Other once-communist-controlled unions were merged into the Maritime Union of Australia. Both unions were later subjected to a rigorous Royal Commission in 2015 and had negotiated an amalgamation by 2016, making it one of Australia's largest and most militant unions.

The final attempt to illegalize the Communist Party in 1951 followed immediately upon the election of the Menzies national government. Controversy did not centre on communist ideology or politics, but on the constitutional right of the Commonwealth to prohibit a specific organization and its related allies, in the interest of national defence (Davidson 1969; Gollan 1975). These included trade unions, front organizations and any newly created body, including former communists. These could be nominated as coming within the act and therefore eligible for a declaration of illegality. Individuals could also be named as suspected communists. The party would have undoubtedly gone undercover, as it had during the war. The Constitution could be altered to justify this wide range, but would need to be amended by a majority of the total referendum vote in a majority (four) of the states. The High Court had decided that use of the defence power to override these requirements was illegitimate, as Australia was not at war. A bare majority of Australians agreed (Webb 1954).

By extending arbitrary powers to such an extent and relying on the newly created ASIO to get it right, the Menzies government went too far. The Labor Party, led by constitutional lawyer "Doc" Evatt, the trade unions, reforming and religious bodies and liberal opinion were all effectively mobilized. The referendum result was narrow but decisive. No further attempt to prohibit a formal political organization was made. Specifically, Islamic organizations with terrorist links soon filled the gap, with an entirely different clientele. They were international and could be listed on advice by the CIA to ASIO, which accepted most, but not all.

Chapter 9

THE AUSTRALIAN SECURITY INTELLIGENCE ORGANISATION

The establishment and expansion of security and intelligence agencies in Australia owed a great deal to the fear of communism and its influence in the trade union and labour movements (Horner 2014; Blaxland 2015; Toohey and Pinwill 1989; Hocking 1993). Previous threatening movements, such as Irish nationalism, were mainly dealt with by old-fashioned police forces using old-fashioned invigilation techniques and a special branch. Each colonial or state police force acted on its own, with limited rights of interstate extradition validated by a judge. With varying degrees of corruption or criminal influence from place to place and time to time, the chance of controlling professional criminals was limited, let alone the search for agents of a foreign power. Prior to World War II most foreign countries were only represented in Australia by consuls. The two major fascist powers, Italy and Germany, sought consciously to recruit support from their diasporas (Cresciani 1980; Gumpl and Kleinig 2007). Now there are over a hundred fully staffed embassies in Canberra. Some represent countries that are at war with each other, either formally or in effect, and who may be spying on each other.

The failed attempt to outlaw the Communist Party began the founding of the Australian Security Intelligence Organisation (ASIO), the main organization concerned with communist activities (Horner 2014). The abortive Victorian Royal Commission on the party reached few significant conclusions. Although the Communist Party was quite small in 1950 it had a complex web of organizations and influences well beyond that of most state police forces. None of its members attempted terrorist violence. Its support for the Soviet Union and its satellite states led to a consistent loss of support after 1945. Communists were among those passing information on to the Soviet Union, but they were not alone (McKnight 1994). ASIO was founded because of American concern that the Commonwealth was infiltrated by Soviet agents and sympathizers. This led to direct pressure from the United States for a remedy (Horner 2014; Cain 1983, 2008). A major American concern was with the communication systems in the South Pacific, based on Western

Australia and the Northern Territory. US influence was persistent. However, the security problems faced by Australia were relatively modest. Protection of US communications was undoubtedly important.

Neither the jihadists nor the Tamil Tigers have ever attempted suicide bombings in Australia, although both did so overseas and had Australian supporters. Subsequent developments in the Islamic 'caliphate' (ISIL; *Daesh*), formed from parts of Syria and Iraq in 2014, show clearly the link between those charged under the Pendennis prosecution of 2012 and their close associates and friends from Sydney and Melbourne. Pendennis was a major anti-terrorist operation and marks a much more developed relationship between ASIO and the Australian Federal Police and much better intelligence work than during the anti-communist era (Chulov 2006). That long and unproductive phase might now be seen as expensive practice for the real battle. ASIO unfortunately confused the relevance of sympathizing with the Soviet Union, organizing on the left of the ALP and unions, and being a serious danger to the integrity and cohesion of Australia. It identified ASIO too closely with two partisan organizations – the Liberal Party and the Democratic Labor Party. It relied too strongly on a handful of displaced persons continuing their never-ending struggle against the Soviet Union or Yugoslavia. Had Soviet embassy staffer Vladimir Petrov not defected in 1954, there is very little that ASIO could have done to justify its existence. Its decoding work was highly secret and never revealed. Some recently discovered terrorist plots have also remained secret.

The identification of potential terrorists within the large and complex Muslim communities of western Sydney and northern Melbourne requires, without making errors and risking community hostility, a higher level of training and sophistication than was available in the past. Just as there were hostile voices demanding a ban on the communists, so there are hysterical demands to end Muslim immigration and to extend permanent vigilance to all Muslims. This overlooks that the Muslim world of almost two billion and its Australian communities of half a million, are very complex. Most warfare, from Libya to Somalia and to Syria and Iraq, is between Muslims and other Muslims. The original jihadists in al-Qaeda are at war with the new jihadists in ISIL. Others seek to overthrow the Alawite government of Syria, led by Assad, which Russia seeks to preserve. Australia and its allies were responsible for destroying the governments of Libya, Iraq and Afghanistan, leaving almost nothing in their place. Extremist converts to Islam enslave and publicly execute females and males from deviant tribes and religions, selling off the women they have captured and the ancient relics they have plundered. What unites this variety is an unswerving rejection of Western civilization. Welcome to the real world! Meanwhile Australian conservatives organize to ban female head covering, *halal* food rules and the building of mosques. The gap between relevant knowledge and public opinion is vastly greater than before. Defence and security organizations need to operate within a completely changed environment, while members of the political parties, major religions and the media continue with the beliefs and prejudices with which they grew up (Coulsaet 2011; Blaxland 2015).

Apart from a shortage of useful contacts, languages and ideological knowledge, Australian intelligence organizations suffered from the common problem of modern bureaucracies of poor shared knowledge and cooperation. This has been most openly analysed in published work on rivalry between the CIA and the FBI in the United States and between MI5 and MI6 in the United Kingdom (Weiner 2012; Jeffery 2010). This was complicated in Australia by the need to work with the state and federal police forces and in Britain with the metropolitan and county police forces. Even in Russia the massive reach and powers of the two national intelligence forces, MVD (civilian) and GRU (military), were not enough to prevent terrorist attacks by Chechens. The Russian state resorted to destructive military action causing many Chechens to join with al-Qaeda or the Islamic State. The relationship between Australia, the United States and the radical forces of Islam is potentially very complex. The ASIO report to Parliament of 2012–13 includes among its other functions 'investigating several hundred advocates of a violent Islamist ideology' and 'providing intelligence on people smugglers' (Australian Security Intelligence Organisation 2013). But it still retained the time-consuming vetting of passport applicants, asylum seekers and public employees.

Chapter 10

REFUGEES BEFORE THE UN CONVENTION AND ENEMY ALIENS

All wars, however modest their impact, produce flight from the battlefields by civilians. All revolutions, however well intentioned, also produce flight from internal struggles and frequently involve suppression of dissent. The medieval tendency to massacre inhabitants of resisting cities gradually died out in Europe. It continued into modern times in the Ottoman empire and by warring Arabic forces, despite Islamic injunctions against it. This made it imperative that citizens who could escape would move away from battlegrounds and besieged cities and seek a new life elsewhere. Many regions were so devastated by warfare that movement away became unavoidable. The mass movement from Syria through Europe in 2015 was an unexpected recent example, of which Australia had no previous experience.

Such refugee experiences did not directly affect Australia. Effective military control was established over the whole continent by the 1840s, and the Indigenous resistance was soon conquered or driven away from the settled districts. Nor were immigrants from the British Isles fleeing from military conquest. The whole United Kingdom was effectively pacified before 1788, except in marginal areas of Ireland. Those emigrating were predominantly British subjects, with access to countries closer than Australia, such as Canada or the United States, which raised no barriers against them. Australia could draw on these fugitives from rural poverty by organized migration based on funds provided from the new colonies. Unlike migration to the United States, non-British were ineligible for these inducements and assistance. Nor were many British fleeing from political or religious persecution. This kind of flight was largely absent by 1780 and confined to Jacobites moving to France, or a few radicals moving to the United States.

Thus, the concept of the *refugee*, which had first been developed in response to the French Revolution of 1789, had no legal status in British law or financial status in British immigration policy. Refugees were, by definition, escaping from warfare, political and religious persecution in foreign, mainly European, states that had recently experienced all of these. The nearest approximation was among the Irish, fleeing from starvation during the potato famine of the 1840s or from the restrictions on their ownership of land and their practice of Catholicism. The great majority preferred the United States. As British subjects they were entitled to apply for support and funds within the United Kingdom migration schemes to Australia and other British colonies. Many did so, but did not think of themselves as refugees.

The first foreign group escaping religious persecution were German Old Lutherans brought to South Australia in 1838. They objected to the Prussian reform of their liturgy and practices imposed by their government, and were subject to imprisonment for failing to conform. Led by Pastor August Kavel of Klemzig, they made an agreement with George Fife Angas, an English businessman and Baptist, to finance a collective emigration to the newly established colony of South Australia, where land was readily available (Tampke and Doxford 1990).

Out of this grew a flourishing German colony the success of which was only challenged by the outbreak of World War I in 1914. The growth of the villages of Hahndorf, Klemzig and Lobethal and the Barossa Valley encouraged further Lutheran migration (Tampke and Doxford 1990). German refugees can rightly be described as the pioneers of South Australia, as they arrived within two years of the foundation of the colony. Continuing migration from Germany enlarged the community and led to movements into western Victoria. South Australia subscribed to Asian exclusion, but allowed this above the current border of the Northern Territory, which was within its jurisdiction until 1910 and included Chinese and 'Afghan' communities. Apart from missionaries, few Germans went there.

Group settlement by refugees became rare after these exceptions, and individual arrivals became more common. Revolutions in Europe in 1848 and gold in Victoria brought a small number of Hungarians between 1851 and 1867, many of them Jewish (Kunz 1988). At this time there were few immigration restrictions, except briefly for the Chinese. Early Jewish migration, which included London convicts, was not based on refugees and came mainly from England and Germany. A significant number were attracted to Victoria during the gold rush. Jews enjoyed full civil rights in Australia and were later eligible for grants in support of their religion, which was not true over most of Europe or in Britain (Getzler 1970). The trend towards Jews seeking refuge in large numbers began in 1881 following the assassination of Russian Tsar Alexander II and consequent anti-Semitic pogroms throughout the Russian Empire. Most migration went to the United States, passing through Britain, where many remained in East London. Some moved on to Sydney and Melbourne, but not as refugees. Jews became well established in Australian society, building businesses and being elected to public office. Leading citizens included governor-general Sir Isaac Isaacs and military leader Sir John Monash (Rubinstein 1991; Rutland 1997).

Jewish refugee numbers from Eastern Europe began to increase in the 1920s with the independence of Poland and the imposition of limitations on immigration by the United States in 1924. Britain had already passed an *Aliens Act* in 1905, aimed at limiting foreign settlement. Many Russians fleeing the 1917 Communist revolution settled in London or Paris, but were not predominantly Jewish. Few of these came to Australia, but significant numbers of Russian Orthodox Christian refugees came to Brisbane, arriving through Shanghai. Many Jews arriving in Melbourne in the 1920s were Yiddish-speakers from Poland, assisted by one of the first refugee settlement organizations (Benjamin 1998). The notion that Jews were 'aliens' was based largely on this intake when new arrivals came, following the Nazi victory in Germany in 1933.

From then on, the urgency of seeking refugee status meant that Australian public opinion tended to equate being a refugee with being Jewish. The League of Nations had established a system for refugees who mainly came from Russia or from the exchange of populations following the defeat of the Ottoman Empire in World War 1 (Marrus 1985). Jewish refugees operated through specifically Jewish or Zionist organizations. Australian Jewish Welfare was set up in 1937 and has continued to work for Jewish refugees ever since and to negotiate with governments on their behalf. Jewish communities have recently added a strong component of well-educated South Africans, who did not arrive as refugees (Tatz, Arnold and Heller 2007).

The main concern of the League of Nations was not with Jewish refugees but with the major disturbances caused by the breakdown of the Russian and Ottoman empires due to their defeats and revolts in World War I. These saw the Russian monarchy and autocracy replaced by the militant Bolshevik regime dedicated to state control of the economy, the ending of the power of the Orthodox Church and the suppression of pre-existing liberal, conservative and democratic forces. Refugees from Russia in the past had often been Jewish, but those fleeing the Bolsheviks were usually from the property-owning and Orthodox Christian classes. Refugees from the Ottoman Empire were predominantly Christians of Greek and Armenian origin, suffering severely from forcible removals.

These disruptions of major societies gave the League of Nations an opportunity to develop a reform agenda in which the modification of military disputes and the settlement of displaced people were central. Unfortunately, the post-war disruptions also encouraged the rise of reactionary and revolutionary forces, which further disturbed Europe. Most powerful and effective by 1930 were the German Nazis. There were comparable movements in Italy, Spain, Hungary, Romania and throughout the Balkans. Most of these movements were strongly racist and anti-Semitic. On gaining power the German Nazis put their ideology into action. Even before the outbreak of war in 1939 their persecution was generating a refugee exodus from Germany, which the League of Nations took on as its responsibility. There was considerable resistance by the major democracies to taking any strong action that challenged Germany and its allies. Remote from Europe, Australia joined in this hesitation (Bartrop 1994; Blakeney 1985).

At the international Evian conference of 1938, held to respond to increased and violent anti-Semitism in Nazi Germany, Australia refused to increase its alien immigration quotas based on specific nationalities (Bartrop 1994). After a deterioration in the German situation this was amended and a quota of 15,000 refugees was allocated to be spread over three years. The outbreak of war in September 1939 led to only 7,500 being accepted by Australia. The Evian refusal was justified on the grounds of 'not having a racial problem and not wanting to introduce one' (Blakeney 1985). However even the very conservative Lyons government was persuaded that Nazism was a unique phenomenon requiring a positive response.

Those coming to Australia in the quota included Austrians and Czechs. Hitler had already annexed those countries before the war began and started persecution that would soon expand to the entire Jewish population of Europe, numbering 9.5 million. The two major creators of refugees in this period were European states engaged in warfare and repression. It was an entirely new situation, which has now spread throughout the world.

'Enemy Aliens', although not refugees, were also governed by law but were not immune from detention during wartime. Even if naturalized citizens, they were liable to internment, as many found during both world wars when they could not benefit from consular protection. The great majority of Australians before 1950 were British subjects. Australian citizenship was not created until 1949 and is determined by the Australian Citizenship Acts of 1948 and 1973 as amended. Exceptions were aliens who owed allegiance elsewhere and had not been naturalized. British, colonial, state or Commonwealth oaths included declaring loyalty to the British monarch. Dual citizenship was not available to Australians born before 2002, but could be held by others who had already acquired it from their birthplace. There were advantages to taking British–Australian citizenship, including access to many occupations, rights to own land, freedom from deportation and the right to vote and to hold public office. The disadvantages often included loss of citizenship in the country of birth. This might involve losses overseas of rights that were available in Australia, such as the right to own property or to vote and hold office (Fraser 1940).

These complications were largely modified in 2002 by Australia, but may still be true in foreign jurisdictions. Difficulties arise when Australian-born go away to join forces in a state engaged in warfare, even where formal wars are not declared, as in the Spanish Civil War of the 1930s (Inglis 1987). The *Foreign Fighters Act*, passed in 2014, regulated this with the power to remove passports from involved Australians. It is aimed at participants in the Islamic 'caliphate' or similar organizations and is based on earlier United States law. It was strengthened in the following year by the *Australia Citizenship Amendment (Allegiance to Australia) Act*, which applied only to dual citizens. The reason for loss of Australian citizenship is now participation in terrorist or related armed activity, not the legal criterion of taking up arms for a declared military opponent of Australia. The numbers in Australia with dual citizenship have escalated to several millions, of whom the largest proportion are likely to be subjects of Queen Elizabeth (the Queen of Australia and of the United Kingdom). In many families the withdrawal of citizenship from younger members, Australian by birth, could separate them from their immigrant parents, who are citizens by naturalization. Citizenship by birth thus loses its permanence. A single politician, the Minister for Immigration, has been given the right to remove citizenship.

During peacetime aliens may have limited rights until they adopt citizenship in the society in which they are living (Elkner et al. 2005). In wartime this becomes more urgent as they may be interned or deported as 'enemy aliens', whether they are naturalized or even locally born. (Fischer 1982). This was the experience of many unfortunates in Britain and Australia during the two World Wars, 1914–18 and 1939–45 (Beaumont 2008). It was also used extensively against Japanese civilians in both the United States and Canada after 1941, for which both states recently apologized. Japanese were interned in Australia in 1941 and all were deported to Japan from 1945. The various 'Geneva conventions' from 1865 provided detailed protection of prisoners-of-war captured in a wartime situation. But these did not effectively protect civilians in the 1940s, nor do they today.

Complications arise when states change sides during a war. In Australia Germans, Austrians, and Ottoman subjects were enemy aliens in World War I. Italians were allies in World War I, enemy aliens in World War II from 1941 to 1943, and friendly aliens until 1945. Russians were friendly allies in both World Wars but lost that status with the Bolshevik revolution in 1917. Japanese were allies in World War I, neutrals in World War II until 1941, and then the most directly menacing enemy aliens until 1945. The Irish were British subjects throughout World War I, but citizens of the Irish Republic were neutrals in World War II. Individual complications arise from such changes, especially where families are of more than a single nationality. Difficulties arose when Australia was engaged in warfare without a formal declaration of war. This became increasingly common with civil war replacing international wars. Enemy aliens became a particular focus with the outbreak of internecine wars in the Arab world. Legislation introduced in 2015 threatened Australians with losing their citizenship if they became involved in these wars in any way, on the decision of a Minister for Immigration, advised by ASIO. They may also, as a consequence, lose their right to remain in Australia or to apply for Australian citizenship ever again. Under international agreement their only protection is that they should not be made stateless.

Australian immigration policy effectively prohibited non-European immigration from the 1880s to the 1970s. Consequently, there were few Asian enemy aliens presenting problems in either of the World Wars. Most Asian societies outside China, Japan and Thailand were colonial possessions until the 1940s. Japan was an ally of Britain in World War I, which did not affect the implementation of White Australia. Japanese representatives at the post-war Versailles conference in 1919 were rudely rebuffed by the Australian representative, Billy Hughes when they objected to White Australia. Chinese Kuomintang allies were rebuffed in the same way after 1945. Indians fought as British Empire soldiers in both wars, but were usually forbidden from immigrating. Thus, nearly all 'enemy aliens' in these two massive conflicts were Europeans (Lamidey 1974).

Race was a factor in peace, but nationality was more important in wartime. (Fischer 1989). Under the principles laid down by US president Woodrow Wilson, the great European empires of Austria-Hungary and Ottoman Turkey, were divided up among their various peoples into independent states based on ethnicity and self-determination. The same policy was followed for the dismembered Ottoman empire in the Middle East, for the benefit of the Arab sheiks and the owners of profitable oil fields.

Although Australia was represented at the post-war negotiations after 1918, it had only a limited involvement with enemy aliens or ethnic minorities during the war. Its soldiers had fought in the Middle East, but the main policy concern was with control of the Suez Canal on the maritime route to the East and to Australia and New Zealand. Everything else was determined between Britain, France and the Arab sheiks. Apart from some Christian Lebanese there were no Arabs in Australia and very few Turks. Many Ottoman subjects, who had to register with the state police as enemy aliens, were actually Greeks from the large and ancient settlements of Pontian Greeks such as Smyrna (Izmir). Other Greeks came from islands only recently liberated from the Ottomans, such as Crete or Castellorizo. These were still Ottoman subjects in many cases. The Pontians had been driven out of Smyrna by the Turks with considerable violence after the war and forced into exile, mainly in Athens and Macedonia, thus changing their nationality but not their identity.

Greeks became unpopular during the Great War because they remained neutral under a monarch who was closely linked to the German royal families of Europe (as was the British royal family). Several riots against Greek shops had to be endured, but Greeks were not normally interned. The largest post-war riot was in Kalgoorlie, which had a reputation for rioting right through to the 1930s. These were mainly directed against southern Europeans, as in the major riot of 1934, when most Greeks left for Perth, leaving the large Croatian workforce behind. These were Yugoslav subjects, but many did not wish to return there until 1945.

The complexity of the Austrian detainees was due to a large proportion being Croatians from the Dalmatian coast and islands (Splivalo 1982). These had been established in Victoria and Western Australia since the 1860s and were hostile to the Austrian empire occupying Croatian territory. 'German Austrians' were barred from migrating to Australia from 1918 until 1923. But they might have become citizens of Austria, Poland, Yugoslavia, Italy, Hungary or Czechoslovakia by then.

Policy towards enemy aliens included the prohibition of German or Austrian immigration for five years after 1918, which was replicated again after 1945 for Germans, inadequately in both cases. Wartime policy, however, was directed against quite substantial communities of Germans and German-descended Australians as well as Austrian subjects. Policy against 'Germans' was more rigorous in South Australia than in Queensland against Italians. There were many complications in the blanket use of ethnic terms to describe people with varied attitudes and experience. The Pontian Greeks and Dalmatian Croatians were the largest Australian examples in the 1920s.

The German internees in 1914–18 were numerous, assimilated and entrenched in the rural societies of South Australia and Queensland. This did not save them from being interned for the four years of war, even when they were Australian born (Price 1946). No account was taken of their political views or religion or their social role as elected politicians or local councillors. The major difference in their treatment was between the conservative government of South Australia, which was very rigorous, and the new Labor government of T. J. Ryan in Queensland, which was very tolerant. The Croatians, who had mainly settled in Kalgoorlie and Broken Hill, were not so fortunate. Most ended up in the large Holsworthy camp on the edge of Sydney. German Australians and prisoners-of-war were also interned in World War II (Neumann 2006; Winter 1986; Saunders and Daniels 2000). Japanese were detained from 1941 and then all returned to Japan as prohibited residents under White Australia (Nagata 2000; Oliver 2004).

Many Slav and Germanic immigrants and locally born were interned on islands in 1914, a practice that goes back to the convict days but was not nearly so brutal. These were at Rottnest (WA) and Torrens Island (SA). Eventually the Holsworthy camp was built near Liverpool (NSW) and was officially known as a 'concentration camp'. This did not have the meaning given later to those built by the Nazis, but was a reference to South African internments in which many civilians died during the Boer War of 1899 to 1902. Internment lasted until well after the war was over and was authorized by the Aliens Restriction Order of 1915. Restrictive rules banned the teaching of German and corrected the German names of villages to British and Australian military heroes of the war. The long-established German–Australian community of South Australia was decimated by deportations and voluntary repatriation. The media played its usual hysterical role by claiming that there were 3,000 German spies operating throughout Australia.

It took about 20 years for some of this forced assimilation to be corrected. The rise of the Nazis and the work of the Adelaide consul for Nazi Germany undid most of what good had been done (Gumpl and Kleinig 2007). South Australia had undertaken the only serious attempt to wipe out a well-established European minority community, with its bans on German language, clubs, schools and place names. It had interned Australian-born citizens, including many distinguished public figures. It had sent many of its own citizens to a custom-built concentration camp for anything up to four years. It had finally said goodbye to many long-established families and supported a ban on any replacements from Germany for five years. Just as these policies started to be remedied, the active Nazi consul in Adelaide began to divide the remaining community into Nazis and democrats.

The reaction in 1939 was less extreme than in 1914, but also destructive. Johannes Becker created a Nazi nucleus in the Barossa Valley, but was arrested immediately when war broke out in 1939 (Gumpl and Kleinig 2007). Interned for seven years, he escaped in 1947, was deported to Germany and never allowed to return to Australia. The Germans in 1914 were not Nazis, nor were they responsible for the later Nazi murder of millions of civilians merely because of their ethnicity. In both wars interning Australians on the basis of their nationality was understandable, but likely to be unfair. By 1947 Australia was actively recruiting migrants from some parts of Europe that had willingly participated in these events as Nazi collaborators. The Australian record of tracking down European war criminals was much less rigorous than in some other democracies. It was strongly influenced by the belief that European Communist states would not guarantee a fair trial. Some of those wanted for extradition to Germany or Eastern Europe lived out their Australian lives into their nineties (Aarons 1989).

The best-documented account of unfair policy in wartime was the deportation from Britain of a whole boatload of 'enemy aliens' who had been interned since war began in 1939 (Patkin 1979; Pearl 1983; Bartrop 1990). This is a shameful British story from which Australia emerges with some credit. The British ship *Dunera* was filled with 2,730 German and Austrian subjects from detention on the Isle of Man, and sent to Fremantle, Melbourne and Sydney in September 1940. There it was unloaded and the passengers sent by train to a camp in remote Hay (NSW). During the voyage the ship's crew and military guards bullied and robbed the passengers, with the connivance of the officers. A later inquiry condemned this. The blame was correctly put on the British troops. Even Prime Minister Winston Churchill condemned this 'regrettable mistake'.

Apart from the treatment on the *Dunera* (Patkin 1979; Pearl 1983; Bartrop 1990), the other aspects of this event were due to Australian lack of understanding of the Nazi system and lack of sympathy for enemy aliens, especially Germans. However, this broad category was too undifferentiated, as it had previously been in World War I. The core of the prisoners were Jews, who had been deprived of their German citizenship by the Nazi Nuremberg laws of 1935. To these were added Austrians who had been forcibly subjugated by Germany in 1938 and Sudeten Germans from Czechoslovakia, who had suffered the same fate in 1939. Some Italians were also included. Jews, Austrians, Nazis and Sudeten Germans were all allocated common huts, which led to serious conflict until segregation by ethnicity was introduced. Removal of the prisoners to Tatura (Victoria) in 1940 solved this problem. However, links with the outside world were largely forbidden, as was release into the Australian community in the early years.

Anti-Semitism was common in Australia in the 1940s. It had been evident in public debate about Jewish refugees before the start of the war. This made some official Australian Jewish organizations cautious about contacting the Hay or Tatura inmates. Eventually those internees who could establish their support for the Allies were released into the community. As most were well-educated and skilled, this was an asset for Australia, both during the war and afterwards. Many went on to hold distinguished positions in post-war society, especially in universities. Regular reunions were held.

The largest group of enemy aliens interned in World War II were Italians, especially in Queensland. (A. Fitzgerald 1981). Italy entered the war as an ally of Germany in 1940 and left it as an ally of the United States, Britain and Australia in 1943. Thus, the status of Italian aliens changed before the war was over. As with German Australians, the Italians had been cultivated by their embassy. A mainly middle-class minority formed an effective fascist party (Cresciani 1980). There were also some communist and fascist supporters among the predominantly working class and small-farmer settlers in North Queensland (Douglass 1995; Menghetti 1981). Almost 15,000 Italian prisoners-of-war were also interned. As with the Germans in 1914, there were many civilian enemy aliens. Italian settlement in Queensland had started in 1881 and had grown to over 8,000 by 1933. Many had replaced the South Sea Islanders expelled in 1906 and had become sugar cane growers. They were not highly politicized, but the fascist Italian government had a representative in Townsville whose job was to maintain the support of his compatriots and oppose communist influence.

Fascist Party branches began to be founded in Australia in 1925 with the support of the Italian consul-general (Cresciani 1980). The limited Italian-language press also endorsed fascism. The main organized opposition were the communists, whose party was illegal in Italy. Italians were mostly located in rural areas and were not unionized. By the 1930s local fascist branches had tenuous links with the British fascists and the Nazis, both of which were of interest to Australian intelligence agents. Diplomatic appointments from Rome were filled by fascists. Some individual Catholic clergy also endorsed fascism, especially during the Spanish Civil War, which began in 1936. Links with Japanese consular officials attracted intelligence interest in 1935–37, after the founding of the German–Italian–Japanese Axis.

Italy declared war on Britain and Australia in June 1940 and Italian aliens began to be interned and moved away from Queensland to South Australia and New South Wales prison camps (Cresciani 1980). However, internment was selective, and many remained in the community under supervision, working for the Civilian Alien Corps or on selected farms. Alien internment was justified by the notion that Italians might assist an expected Japanese invasion of North Queensland. Consequently, the level of their alien internment became the highest in Australia. Because of serious labour shortages many Italian prisoners were allowed to work in the sugar cane fields of Queensland without guards and to fraternize with locals. About 20,000 Italian prisoners-of-war from North Africa were mainly located at Cowra camp (NSW).

The often-arbitrary arrests had damaging effects on the supply of labour to the cane fields. Fortunately, the surrender of Italy in September 1943 began the slow release of Italian 'enemy aliens' who had now become Allies. As with the Germans in 1914, the media, in the form of *Smith's Weekly*, stirred up hatred, in which they were joined by the Returned Servicemen's League and other patriotic organizations. Community relations on the cane fields recovered only slowly, while the former fascists of middle-class Melbourne were more readily integrated.

The most horrendous result of wartime internment affected Japanese prisoners-of-war, military men who were nominally protected by the Geneva conventions (Nagata 2000). This was the breakout from the prison camp at Cowra in central New South Wales in August 1944. This was filled with

Japanese prisoners-of-war, rather than civilians, interned when Japan attacked the United States at the end of 1941. Thus, they were not 'enemy aliens' but were protected under the Geneva conventions for the conduct of war, to which Japan was not a signatory. Other prisoners were mainly Italians, Koreans and Indonesians. Most were prisoners-of-war rather than enemy aliens. The Koreans had been subject to Japanese imperialism since 1910 and were at best unwilling soldiers. The Italians also had a very ambivalent attitude. Many were civilians, and Italy had already changed sides with the overthrow of Mussolini.

The only very large group with a desire to rebel were the Japanese. Over one thousand attempted to escape after careful planning, and 359 prisoners-of-war succeeded. After ten days the escapees were rounded up, with 231 Japanese killed and 108 wounded, for only four Australians killed. The Australian guards had been armed with machine guns and rifles. This breakout had very little chance of success and was explained as reflecting Japanese culture. Many of the dead appeared to have committed suicide, according to the official report. Whether deaths would have been so high if the escapees had not been Asians was not queried at the time. The prisoners at Cowra were not finally released until 1947. In a gesture of reconciliation, a Japanese garden and graveyard were created at Cowra and became a major tourist site.

The status of 'enemy alien' operates in wartime and may be extended after that, as it was for Germans in the 1920s and the 1940s. But it is controversial during undeclared wars, which have become increasingly common. Australia has been involved in wars in Vietnam, Afghanistan, Iraq and Somalia and when dealing with subjects of states like Yemen or Syria. In all these cases and potentially many others, some Australian citizens may be allied with Australia while others are actively engaged against Australian troops and allies. This is of importance when considering the refugee status of those seeking asylum. The practice of returning unsuccessful and unwilling asylum applicants to their former states is contrary to the Refugee Convention as *refoulement*. Australia has actively done this on many recent occasions and actually had agreements to do so with China, Iran and Sri Lanka. The Iranians normally refused to take their refugees back.

In the period 2013 to 2015 Operation Sovereign Borders returned 663 'potential illegal arrivals' in 20 boats while they were still at sea (Official Immigration Ministerial Statement of 6 August 2015). The official claim that those returned face no problems is hard to believe, especially as many have breached laws forbidding undocumented departure from their state of origin. However, if asylum seekers can be shown to have committed war crimes or been engaged in ethnic cleansing they can be legitimately returned for trial in their homeland. This has often been difficult to prove or disprove. A rare case was the return of Serbian general Dragan Vasiljkovic for trial in Croatia in 2015, arising from the Bosnian 'ethnic cleansing' 20 years before. As a rule, alleged war criminals from World War II were never returned by Australia, even on request from their former home countries (Aarons 1989). Vasiljkovic was found guilty of the charges against him by a Croatian court in 2017.

Chapter 11

CRIME, CORRUPTION AND TERRORISM

As with its predecessors, after 1949 ASIO was primarily concerned with communism and espionage. Yet Australian society was changing rapidly, developing different crimes and criminals and extending their links internationally. Corruption had always existed but paled into insignificance with the rise of a drug culture that knew no international boundaries or restrictions. Some emerging criminals were connected to the developing multicultural populations, while others had roots in pre-existing Australian crime families and youth gangs. None were a major concern of ASIO unless they overlapped with security issues or espionage. One issue Australia had committed to in 1945 was detection and punishment of war criminals. Most suspects in Australia were from communist-controlled countries in Eastern Europe. Some had local political influence and protection in churches and parties.

Ethnic politics often involved disagreement on homeland issues, for example between Croats and Serbs, Russians and Ukrainians and Greeks and Macedonians. These were of only limited interest to the security services, apart from communist influences. Occasionally, they led to violence or even arson. The closing report of the Special Investigations Unit on war criminals complained that its work could not be completed. The report listed a large number of cases that had been drawn to its attention but rejected. These mostly concerned former enemy subjects from Croatia, Ukraine, Latvia, Lithuania, Belarus, Hungary, Serbia, Romania and Slovenia, all then under communist control. Australia, like other Western states, was reluctant to accept representations from any of them. Most suspects died peacefully in their beds as aged relics of horrors that most Australians wanted to forget, but a minority never could (Commonwealth of Australia 1993). As we saw in the last chapter, only one person was returned, Serbian general Dragan Vasiljkovic – remanded to Croatia in 2016 after years of delay. Nobody had ever been returned for war crimes in World War II. A concern with 'migrant crime' was widespread in the 1950s with the arrival of non-British immigrants in large numbers, especially those from Southern and Eastern Europe. This became an ASIO concern where communists were involved. Immigrant frustration at unemployment led to a threat to move the army up to Bonegilla migrant camp near Albury in 1952. Again in 1961, Italians and Yugoslavs held a riotous meeting about their isolation from the labour market in their remote location away from the large cities (Sluga 1988). This mobilized support from the growing Italian organizations in Melbourne and a handful of Labor politicians and communists. However, threatened criminal charges were not proceeded with and the army had only been alerted but not mobilized. The disputes helped to sustain the notion that foreigners were excitable and liable to violence. Fifty years later asylum seekers were rioting in remote detention centres against much worse conditions than endured at Bonegilla and with much less prospect of resolution. Reliable research on immigrant crime was frustrated by differing recording policies on the part of state police and prison administrations (Francis 1981). This has largely been remedied, with trial and prison records showing lower than average crime rates among Southern Europeans (Hazlehurst 1987). The myth that immigrants increase the crime rate lingers on and is revived whenever a new contingent arrives. This was particularly true for the large intakes of Vietnamese and Lebanese in 1975. As recently as 2010 a professional survey found that 43.4 per cent of respondents believed 'immigrants increase the crime rate', a slight drop from 1996 when a bare majority of 51.8 per cent also agreed (McAllister and Pietsch 2011: 58, 106).

Media focus and public interest moved from communism and migrant crime towards concern with Islam. But there was also a continuing revelation of the degree of corruption at the state level of politics. This affected major public figures from business and politics, some of whom spent periods in prison, including three state premiers. The misuse of public office for private profit was a common Australian practice that originated from Britain. The fortunes earned from British India in the eighteenth century became so massive as to lead eventually to impeachment and imprisonment of some politicians. In the nepotistic and hierarchical British system most political and social leaders were protected by social networks, which soon developed in Australia.

State and local governments were frequently characterized by corruption at various levels, from the politicians to the police. As ownership of land was ultimately vested in the Crown there was much scope for increased wealth for ruling politicians, especially where minerals lay beneath the surface. More recently, land speculation grew at the core of state and local corruption, especially in Western Australia, Queensland and New South Wales. The drug industry was at the heart of organized crime, but was usually avoided by established politicians and public servants. Despite occasional bursts of cleansing reform, media revelations and public indignation, Australians have grown used to the idea that power often protects and advances wealth. Faith in the police remains high, but faith in politicians is much lower, according to professional polls. Attempts to create distinct organizations such as the New South Wales Independent Commission Against Corruption ran into continuing trouble. A comparable fate met the Queensland attempt to control biker gangs by the *Vicious Lawless Association Disestablishment Act*.

Federation in 1901 had done little to change this situation. There was no national police force until the creation of the Australian Federal Police in 1979, largely in response to the growing inter-state and international drug trade. The seven state and territory police forces remained in existence in the absence of local police forces, as in Britain or the United States. In subsequent years all of them have been subject to rigorous reform responding to public scandals and dismissals. Had the police forces been more localized the situation could well have been worse. Officials as distinguished as state premiers or commissioners of police were investigated and in some cases imprisoned. Politicians of all three major parties were involved (Prasser et al. 1990; McClymont and Besser 2014; Beresford 2008).

Most identified corruption has involved state politicians. However, even at the Commonwealth level of Customs and Excise, criminal activity at the Sydney airport has been uncovered. Anti-corruption bodies were created in all states, with the strongest being the New South Wales Independent Commission Against Corruption (ICAC) in 1988. These have the power to investigate, but their findings depend on further action by the state Director of Public Prosecutions. The rationale for their continuation is based on the proposition that corruption undermines lawful business practices, affects political parties and governments and diminishes public faith in institutions. The most searching enquiries into corruption in the past 20 years have been in Western Australia, Queensland and New South Wales. Recently, party political motives have extended enquiries into the funding of parties and the practices of trade unions, both subject to royal commissions. A minor concern in 2015 was the exceeding of politicians' privileged support for travel and hospitality. The main object was to condemn the radical Construction, Forestry, Mining and Energy Union (CFMEU), for its allegedly violent behaviour on building sites.

Corruption has many contested meanings. Legal definitions change over time and from place to place, or defamation laws advantage the powerful over whistle blowers and researchers. Partisan interests are engaged, and group solidarity protects those in office. Corruption in the British tradition has been defined as the use of public office to benefit unduly from that position and the willingness of private interests to encourage this. Public appointments are often made on nepotistic, patronage or partisan bases. This is much more difficult to condemn than the simple exchange of monetary or commercial benefits. In recent years public policy has moved in opposite directions. More and more public–private funding arrangements have developed, while stricter rules for political donations and parliamentary allowances have also been introduced. Most detectable and prosecuted corruption occurs at the state government level, but may affect private companies, trade unions, political parties, local government, educational institutes or sport, among other activities.

In the light of this complexity only blatant examples that come into the public and media arenas can be safely publicized. Three major examples have been what the media termed WA Inc., which saw two premiers, Ray O'Connor and Brian Burke, sent to prison for a spell (Beresford 2008); the Bjelke-Petersen era in Queensland (Prasser et al. 1990), and the NSW Independent Commission Against Corruption (ICAC), the investigations of which in 2014 centred around land speculation (McClymont and Besser 2014). All these involved elected politicians from the three major parties. Corruption in land speculation was rife along the whole coast from Wollongong to Newcastle. The limitation on controlling corruption has been that the state Director of Public Prosecutions has the final decision on whether to prosecute. This requires convincing evidence that would stand up in court. The complex ICAC investigation around the affairs of members of the New South Wales ALP government, exemplifies the difficulties involved in bringing to completion so many cases involving major public figures (McClymont and Besser 2014).

Organized crime at a lower social level has presented serious problems for major cities; the growth of motor bike gangs and their fortified clubs, control of neighbourhoods, massive illegal profits from drugs, murders other than 'domestics', and an increased use of guns. None of this is directly the concern of the two national security organizations ASIO and ASIS. ASIO's full official history has only reached 1989, a few years behind Britain's MI5 and MI6. Archives are released after 20 years, but severely 'redacted' (an ancient legal term now meaning censored for security reasons). Thus, it is difficult to say what precisely these major Commonwealth agencies do to justify their large and growing budgets and staffing and the huge office building, erected in 2014 on a commanding site as the largest in Canberra. Most of the work done to control crime rests with state police forces, the Australian Federal Police, formed in 1979, and the Commonwealth Customs. Supervision, invigilation and individual reports still make up a lot of the ASIO workload. The control of asylum seekers linked to overseas criminal smugglers and the control of international commerce through Customs and Excise, will call on ASIO involvement in the new Border Protection Service, created from the Immigration and Customs Departments. Of considerable concern to ASIO and the Australian

Federal Police are relations between criminal elements and actual or potential terrorism where the use of weapons may form a link. In the major cities there is an overlap between criminal and terrorist groups, and individual and personal links are established in prisons. However serious, group terrorism is very rare in Australia compared with Britain or Europe and was more likely to be from the Irish Republican Army than Islamist organizations until recently.

ASIS and the Office of National Assessments deal with overseas intelligence (Toohey and Pinwill 1989), and there is also the Defence Signals Directorate, which listens in on the world. ASIO and other intelligence agencies are part of the 'five eyes' cooperation with similar bodies in Britain, the United States, Canada and New Zealand. Within the Commonwealth government there are close links with the Department of Immigration and Border Protection and the Attorney General's Department. These agencies do not, however, always work together or make uniform assessments. A major responsibility is the detection and frustration of Islamist terrorism. The distinction between traditional crime and terrorism has become rather artificial in Sydney and Melbourne. In both cities there are links between criminals in the drug trade, corruption in the building industry, and jihadists who came to terrorism through earlier involvement in traditional crimes. This requires interagency collaboration between different layers of government. The earlier obsession with communists and their allies pales into insignificance when compared with the threat to a stable society presented by terrorism, corruption and organized crime in the new century. One limited solution was to withdraw the Australian passport from Alex Vella, president of the Rebels motorbike club, leaving him stranded in his native Malta. Queensland nominated specific organizations as illegal, including motorbike gangs. This was bitterly opposed by those clubs not involved in crime.

Withdrawal of passports was entirely within Commonwealth powers. Withdrawal of citizenship for those born in Australia was more controversial, but under serious consideration by 2015. This punishment was limited to dual citizens, by an international agreement. There were no records of the number of dual citizens, but it was expected to total several million, the majority being Australian–British subjects. This reflected the lack of distinction between Australian and British subjects prior to the 1970s. Both still owe technical allegiance to Queen Elizabeth. Complex amendments produced the Australian Citizenship Amendment (Allegiance to Australia) Bill of 2015 and the Advisory Report of the Parliamentary Joint Committee on Intelligence and Security of September 2015.

Until 2014 there was no official history of Australia's large and growing security services. Its affairs are not publicly revealed until 20 years after the event and then in heavily censored (redacted) form. There have been two individual terrorist attacks in Australia – in Martin Place, Sydney, in 2014, causing the death of two hostages and the assailant, and in Parramatta in 2015 with two deaths. However, following the destruction of New York's Twin Towers in 2001, intelligence agencies worldwide have become very concerned about their ability to check militant Islam. The transformation of ASIO from an intelligence to a security organization advanced consistently from 2001, as did the expanded powers of the Australian Federal Police. The Commonwealth and states agreed to greatly extended laws to arrest, search and detain. These included limited detention without trial, restrictions on legal representation, electronic tagging of suspects, penalties for membership of a named terrorist organization, and new penalties for advocating terror or inciting racial hatred. Many of these powers do not need parliamentary approval. ASIO had been created and built up to deal with communists (Horner 2014). It maintained close ties with its counterparts whose tasks were similar in the United States, Britain, Canada and New Zealand. But the rise of Islamic militancy raised new issues for which the long experience of watching and reporting on communist and socialist activities was neither well-equipped nor relevant (Chulov 2006; Blaxland 2015).

Jenny Hocking, in her major work, *Terror Laws*, traces the steady increase in security and police powers up to 2004 (Hocking 2004). Her conclusion at that date was that

> the perception expressed throughout the current legislative developments in counter terrorism – that issues of national security should not be dealt with by the courts; that it is for ministers not judges to determine what the interests of national security require – is a critical issue in any attempt to reconcile national security needs with democratic principles. (Hocking 2004: 247)

This conclusion is validated by events over the following decade. Operation Sovereign Borders, authorizing naval operations against asylum seekers' boats, brought in a new dimension by allowing information to be treated as though it were a wartime secret. Decisions made 'on the water' then become arbitrary and without need for further justification. Instances of crossing into Indonesian waters can be dismissed as navigational errors. Towing boats back towards Indonesia can be denied, as they are contrary to declared Indonesian government policy. If unavoidable, a subsequent apology is offered. The Australian Department of Foreign Affairs and Trade and its minister have the task of mollifying consequent Indonesian annoyance. As a regional agreement on asylum seekers needs Indonesian support, this is not a very helpful situation. Sri Lanka has been less sensitive, actively helping with the return of boats to its ports. This may not be the policy of the new government, elected early in 2015 and critical of Australian support for the former president, Mahinda Wijesekera.

Terrorism is now officially defined as

> an act or threat intended to advance a political, ideological or religious cause by coercing an Australian or foreign government or the public, by causing serious harm to people or property, creating a serious risk of health and safety to the public, disrupting trade, critical infrastructure or electronic systems. (Criminal Code, 1995)

If by terrorism is meant the deliberate use of violence for political purposes outside the system of states and leading to death or destruction, Australia has had a very limited experience. By this definition, major terrorism has been confined to the Bali bombing of 2002. The Indonesian suicide bombers who organized this attack had been preparing it for some time, encouraged by the teachings of Abu Bakar Bashir, an elderly Indonesian who kept well away from the action. He was eventually jailed for fifteen years for another conspiracy.

The deaths of 88 Australians in Bali in 2002 could not be prevented, either by Australian or Indonesian intelligence. This was religious terrorism pure and simple, not tied to any secular objectives or a foreign government. It did inspire a much faster escalation by Australia of anti-terrorist organization and legislation. Like the attack on the New York Twin Towers in the preceding year, it had been unexpected. The Indonesian government also took a more serious interest and was willing to cooperate with Australia. The Australian embassy in Jakarta was also subjected to a bombing attack in 2004. In both cases surviving bombers and organizers were prosecuted through the Indonesian courts. The Bali suicide bombers were followers of the Jemaah Islamiya extremist Islamist group, and the arrest and trial of those who survived were the responsibility of the Indonesian state.

Otherwise the record includes frustrated plans for an attack on the Sydney Hilton during a visit of the Indian prime minister in 1978, which had nothing to do with Islam, and a hostage occupation in central Sydney in December 2014, leading to the deaths of a single Muslim and two innocent bystanders. The Hilton bombing was traced to the pseudo-Hindu sect, Ananda Marga, and ended with the wrongful arrest and imprisonment of its local leader, Tim Anderson. This rather limited case prompted the Australian intelligence community to expand and improve its organizations. Publicized statements by Islamist spokesmen have named Australia as a target and ally of the United States, but most uncovered plots so far have not materialized. The Martin Place, Sydney, hostage-taking on 16 December 2014 was potentially serious.

It affected the whole centre of the city. The terrorist, eventually killed, showed an Islamic flag and had a criminal record including alleged murder. He was a refugee from Iran and mentally deranged.

Defining 'terrorism' has occupied the time and energy of many societies since 1945 and led to the creation of new laws and institutions that would not have been acceptable in more peaceful times. Essentially, 'terrorists' are defined as acting outside the international conventions established for the conduct of formalized warfare ever since the mid-nineteenth century. These cover the treatment of prisoners-of-war, the declaration of war and peace, the use of unconventional weapons, refugees and the status of enemy aliens. Many were developed by the League of Nations in Geneva following World War I. They rarely cover the fate of civilians caught between warring forces, which has become the major cause of refugee flight and human destruction since 1945. The laws of warfare prohibit the use of unconventional weapons like gas. They did not cover the use of atomic bombs against Japan. The Nazi treatment of prisoners-of-war was differently applied to the Western allies and the Eastern Soviets. The treatment of civilians by Nazi Germany and its allies was so horrendous as to create the mass slaughter still known as the Holocaust. These wartime acts were classified as war crimes.

Redefining 'terrorism' did not cease in 1945. The surviving leaders of Nazi Germany were tried and executed for war crimes at the Nuremberg trials between 1945 and 1949. Among their judges was the Soviet leader Andrei Vyshinsky the chief prosecutor at the Moscow trials of August 1936. These began the years of trials and executions of thousands of leading Soviet communists and the expansion of the gulag system of prison camps, in which many millions were imprisoned. International laws and conventions did not survive well in the twentieth century. As many terrorists have also been patriots and martyrs there is always the risk of a plausible defence and public approval of many of their deeds. Martyrs and warriors may have appealed to the same young men as once followed communism or fascism. Martyrs have a special status in Shia Islam, but the majority of effective terrorist organizations are Sunni, including those responsible for the attacks on New York and Bali. Terrorist organizations often compete with each other, while others are state supported.

Terrorism is not confined to armed attacks on civilians by enemy forces. It may also include similar attacks on their own subjects by heavily armed defence and security organizations. The bloodthirsty conclusion of the Sri Lankan civil war in 2009 was a widely debated example. Australia, in the interest of keeping Sri Lankan support for its asylum policy, decided that no Sri Lankan asylum seekers would be accepted as 'genuine' refugees and sent back those it was holding. Leaders of African 'religious' terror movements, like the Boko Haram in Nigeria or the Lord's Resistance Army in Uganda, are outside any normal human understanding. The same could be said of activists forming an Islamic state in Syria and Iraq. As is often the case in wars and revolutions, judgement depends on which side you prefer and who wins. This is very unpredictable in any case.

Another aspect of state-organized terror has been the use of weapons of war to pacify or destroy civilian opponents of the state or non-combatants of another state. The Middle East has been a classic venue for this, using the enormous armoury of sophisticated weapons poured in by developed states as a form of 'aid'. As this impinges on formal warfare it is not usually classified as terror at all. Civilians are normally the victims and towns and services often the targets. Somalia has been a major victim of this random destruction, but Iraq, Afghanistan, Syria, Libya, Sudan, the former Yugoslavia, Yemen, Cambodia, Kuwait, Sri Lanka and several other African states, have all suffered internal and international bombardment with sophisticated weapons for domestic political purposes. Somalia has almost been totally destroyed in the process.

These battles are major producers of refugee flows. The Australian response to the mass refugee flows from Syria in 2015 was to send in bombers allied with the United States. The logic of this escaped many. It seemed inconsistent with an offering of 12,000 refugee places for Syrian women, children and members of persecuted minorities. No action was suggested against Syria's Assad government, which has been responsible for massive human-rights crimes. It was seen as the protector of Catholic and Orthodox Christians and favoured by Russia.

The claims made by apologists for these raids was that they were targeted on known terrorists and their locations, which is implausible.

The contribution of Australia has been to join in as a peacekeeper, with very limited results, and often to accept small numbers of refugees from the ensuing disasters. A preliminary concession of 4,000 in the Special Humanitarian programme was extended to refugees from Syria in 2015. It was expected to apply to local Christians and possibly the minority Yazidi. Such concessions could be a valuable instrument in reducing levels of detention and expanding refugee intakes from the small and narrowly defined humanitarian programme. Such assistance was rendered in the past, but is now inhibited by the obsession of 'stopping the boats'. Excising such numbers from an existing program could penalize those already approved. Emergency visas do not normally include a right to Australian permanent residence although this might eventuate over time as the massive refugee waves continue from Syria into Central Europe.

Who in all this is the 'terrorist' and who the 'victim' can be a matter of opinion or preference, as argued by Jenny Hocking in her groundbreaking study *Terror Laws* (Hocking 1993; 2004). As Australia normally follows the preferences of the United States this originally meant joining serious warfare with North Korea, North Vietnam and the Vietcong, Saddam Hussein in Iraq and the Taliban in Afghanistan. It has also meant a growing popular suspicion of the activities, beliefs and politics of Muslims in general. Once the Vietnam War had ended in defeat the main suspect changed dramatically. Australia followed on behind the United States in defence of freedom and democracy, insofar as consistent believers in these creeds could be found. It was acknowledged reluctantly that the obsession with communism had been overplayed. Friendly and business-like relations with China and Vietnam were soon established. Chinese students flocked into Australian universities, and their parents into high-income suburbs of Sydney and Melbourne. Special business visas expedited these processes.

Australia had already committed to a modest refugee programme before the war, grudgingly confined to Jewish refugees from Hitler. This was not a generous response in comparison with what was to come between 1950 and 1953. There was no binding definition of a refugee in international law until after World War II, following the massive settlement of displaced persons from Central Europe and the creation of the United Nations High Commissioner for Refugees, under the Convention Relating to the Status of Refugees.

Australia does not have borders in the same sense as the United States or most European countries. It has thousands of nautical miles of sea, which mainly border on the equally invisible borders of Indonesia, with its thousand inhabited islands. Only at the narrowest point of the Torres Strait can these borders be safely crossed in small, unseaworthy craft. Timor Leste is a sovereign state across a currently divided boundary in the Timor Sea. Cocos and Christmas Islands are Australian territories, but were declared not to be part of the Australian migration zone. All of these can be reached from Australia by sea in good weather in relatively small, seaworthy boats, but are dangerous crossings in poor weather or the Southeast monsoon. They have provided the main routes for unvisaed asylum seekers to Australia in recent years, but have been closed off by naval patrols since the adoption of Operation Sovereign Borders in September 2013.

A new departure in 2014, which was shrouded in official secrecy, was the use of Australian naval vessels to transfer Sri Lankan passengers aboard two ships in the open seas to Sri Lankan boats. This was welcomed by the Sri Lankan government and defended by Australia on the basis that the asylum seekers, who had been living in India, which is not a Convention signatory, would be safe back in Sri Lanka. Critics argued that this was a clear case of *refoulement*, which Australian officials denied. It was an aspect of agreement between the two states to cooperate in preventing Sri Lankans from seeking asylum elsewhere. The argument went to the High Court in 2014, which ruled by four to three that Australia was within its rights to detain suspected refugees on the high seas.

Within Australia those claiming to be Muslims numbered 470,000 (or 2.2%) in 2011. One-third were born in Australia and the second largest proportion in Lebanon. Muslim immigrants came from a wide variety of other states, including: Turkey, Albania and Bosnia in Europe; Pakistan and India in South Asia; Somalia, Egypt, Sudan in Africa; Iran and Afghanistan in Central Asia; Syria and Iraq in the Middle East; and Indonesia and Malaysia in Southeast Asia. The Census does not record sectarian loyalties, but the great majority were Sunni, with Shia concentrated in Arncliffe (Sydney). By far the largest concentration of Arabic Muslims is in the adjacent cities of Canterbury, Bankstown and Auburn (Sydney). Centres of Muslim settlement in Sydney and Melbourne have a network of Islamic mosques and schools and there are national organizations such as the Australian Federation of Islamic Councils and the Australian National Council of Imams, both conservative and constitutional (Saeed 2003; Kabir 2005).

With such a variety of origins and beliefs, and homelands engaged in internecine warfare, Muslims present a problem to security organizations (Chulov 2006). To monitor the small minority actively or potentially with terrorist affiliations requires a much wider knowledge of appropriate languages, cultures, beliefs and politics than was ever needed for the communists or any other perceived threat to stability. The risk of alienating a substantial element of Sydney and Melbourne society by unfounded allegations is always present. Current concerns include the movement of a few young, Australian-born men to wars in the Middle East and the possibility that they might return very experienced in guerrilla or subversive techniques (Coolsaet 2011). Given the mass slaughters in Syria and Iraq it is quite probable that they will not return at all.

Even so the potential movement of over a hundred young jihadists, raises legitimate concern and some policy issues. As native-born Australians with dual citizenship, most are eligible at present for Australian passports, freeing them from the usual immigration controls on aliens. This has led the Australian government to withdraw passports, making it difficult for them to enter or leave Australia and making them prime targets for ASIO supervision within Australia. Under the *Crimes (Incursions and Recruitment) Act* dual citizens may join another state's armies. Under the *Security Legislation Amendment (Terrorism) Act of 2002*, eighteen organizations were listed as illegitimate terrorist groups, membership to and help for which brings severe penalties, including loss of citizenship or passports. A basic problem in depriving citizenship is that it divides families between dual citizens of Australia and other states (the immigrants) and Australian citizens by birth (the militant younger generation).

After the overthrow of individual leaders such as Muammar Gaddafi and Saddam Hussein, most fighting in the Muslim world has been between Muslims. One objective is to change the boundaries set up originally by Britain and France in 1920 and to create a model Islamic state or caliphate ruled under *shariah* law. This idea had its origins in India and Egypt and was endorsed by the Egyptian Salafist writer Sayeed Qutb (1906–1966). The caliphate was to exclude all other religions, including other Muslim sects such as Shia, Alawites, Ismailis and Ahmadiyas. An Australian movement, Hizb-ut-Tahrir, advocates a caliphate, but has so far escaped being banned as a terrorist organization, despite some sympathy with the murderous Islamic 'caliphate'. The differences between such ideologies, and rival clans in the deserts fuel heavily armed conflict in Syria and Iraq. Ideally, Australians should remain aloof from such struggles and learn the lessons of the lost wars in Afghanistan and Vietnam. However, jihadists can recruit a limited number of Muslims from the developed societies, including converts, and attack targets in non-Muslim societies. Australia, like many other Western democracies, has been nominated as worth attacking by spokesmen of the Syrian 'caliphate'.

Apart from two one-man incidents in Sydney, terrorists and communists have never taken a life in Australia so far, whatever their revolutionary or reactionary propaganda might have threatened. Australians and Australian diplomatic targets were much more at risk overseas. The major losses were in Bali in 2002 and with the shooting down of a Malaysian airliner over the Ukraine in July 2014. The second had nothing to do with Islam. Individual journalists and tourists have often been arrested or even executed, but not specifically as Australians. However, they were also assets who could be sold back, a practice common in Afghanistan and Yemen. Public execution, as practised by the Syrian 'caliphate', shocked liberal democratic opinion, but was regularly imposed by Australia's political friends in Saudi Arabia without a word of official complaint.

Organized terrorism had become defined as Australia's main threat by the advent of the twenty-first century (Neighbour 2004). Yet neither Australia nor New Zealand has ever directly experienced a major terrorist attack. The reliable and expert *Global Terrorism Index* for 2017 shows quite clearly that large-scale Islamic terrorism is largely confined to five countries: Iraq, Afghanistan, Pakistan, Nigeria and Syria. The number of individuals killed in these five states was 19,229 in 2016. Terrorism was not confined to them or to Islamic organizations, with India affected by Maoists and Sri Lanka by Tamils. Salafists, Deobandi and Wahabis are all powerful Muslim minorities that reject liberalism and Western beliefs. But they are not in a position to challenge Australia or change its ideas and practices. What they may do is to convert small numbers of Australian youth and persuade them to adventures from which they are unlikely to survive. Over a hundred have responded and a third have already been killed. Those fortunate to return to Australia were liable to loss of passport and criminal punishment. From 2015 they were also likely to lose Australian citizenship, whether by birth or naturalization.

A growing fear, as in other countries, is of the return of battle-trained young citizens. Their movements have been closely followed, both overseas and upon their return. As Australia was not officially at war in several Middle Eastern battle sites this raised the question of what crimes they might have committed, or might possibly commit on their return to Australia. 'Working with or giving comfort to a proscribed terrorist organization' was the most obvious. Detailed invigilation of such suspects was suggested, but estimated to cost $8 million per person per annum. Impounding their passports was more practical, provided there was effective control at airports to check on false documents.

By 2015 cancelling the citizenship of Australian-born jihadists became law. The only limitation, due to an international agreement, was that nobody would be made stateless. This left room for the Australian-born to lose their citizenship if 'eligible' for a citizenship elsewhere. The potential population liable under this 2015 proposal probably exceeds six million.

A further bill that sought to remove citizenship from the Australia-born, is the Australian Citizenship Amendment (Allegiance to Australia) Bill 2015, introduced in June 2015. The assumption underlying this legislation is that Australians by birth had a contractual agreement to accept Australian loyalties and values. Relevant support for terrorism would automatically trigger loss of citizenship and be announced by the Minister for Immigration.

The Minister for Immigration, Peter Dutton, argued at the second reading in 2015 that 'relevant conduct' would include engaging in a terrorist act and engaging in foreign incursions and recruitment (Peter Dutton: Press Release 19 June 2015). The implications of this legislation cut across individual freedoms and the separation of powers and provoked considerable controversy. It incorporated the novel notion that a newborn baby had entered a lifelong contract with the Australian state and society. This apparently insane view might reflect the fact that many detected terrorists were born in Australia rather than the Middle East.

An alternative policy to invigilation was to compel the retention of all electronic messaging (metadata) for two years, with an assurance that the innocent had no need to worry about its use. Social media has been a novel weapon both for and against terrorists, one that had not been readily available to the communists. Storing all these messages could be both a challenging and expensive burden, requiring translators and invigilators. The defence was that networks could be constructed from message exchanges. This is obviously true for a range of backgrounds, from love affairs to betting on horses. It can be avoided by meeting in open spaces, a tactic widely used by Soviet agents, but now much less effective with long-range listening devices. One aspect of the metadata packet that disturbed the media was a limitation on the use of information by journalists arising from security operations. This was revised in 2015. One cause for serious concern is that the law should apply equally to all. In practice these extensions of state power will focus on a Muslim minority of less than 3 per cent, as well as the criminal fraternity, who expect to have their phones tapped.

Chapter 12

THE MULTICULTURAL ERA

The 'multicultural era' was short, roughly between 1975 and 2000. But it had a long-term impact (Bongiorno 2015). Its national leaders were Gough Whitlam, Malcolm Fraser, Bob Hawke and Paul Keating. All these party leaders were eventually defeated at the polls, except for Hawke who was pushed aside by his own party. The era came to a deliberate end as national policy with the election of the John Howard Liberal/National governments in 1996 and 1998 (Bean et al. 1997; Simms and Warhurst 2000) and Howard's dedication to reversing much that had gone before. Perhaps more importantly, this was also a period of dramatic change in prosperity, lifestyle and public controversy around national identity.

Between the original report of 1978 (Galbally 1978) and the Bicentennial celebrations of 1988, support for multiculturalism broadened rapidly as the logical replacement for White Australia. But it remained a welfare, educational and settlement programme for immigrants, not a nationwide attempt to change society, as its friends and enemies claimed. It did not include Aboriginal activists, at their own request. Its origins in immigration cut across Indigenous claims by the First Australians. The focus of multiculturalism was in the Immigration Department and aimed largely at immigrants. This excited conservatives and traditionalists, who found their voice in One Nation and the more conservative wing developing in the Liberal Party under the influence of John Howard. Rural and provincial Australia still had only a limited experience of immigrants and a long tradition of suspicion towards them tinged with racism lingering from White Australia.

The newly founded One Nation was the first party to challenge multiculturalism, which its leader, Pauline Hanson, believed should be abolished. Despite massive media attention and strong electoral returns in Queensland, One Nation did not originally last for very long. But while it did it changed the clock back towards White Australia, created room for conservatives to reduce the liberal element in the Liberal Party and to frighten timid elements in the Labor Party. Howard mobilized this support around traditional Australian values and in defiance of the reality that Australia had become a multicultural society since he was a boy. In the end he lost his Sydney seat in 2007 after a strong swing against him by the local Chinese and Korean communities. As prime minister he was able to abolish the Office of Multicultural Affairs and the Bureau of Immigration Research, thus returning the Immigration Department to its previous monopoly over research and information. In the meantime, both the Liberal opposition and the Labor government had endorsed the policy of mandatory detention for asylum seekers arriving by boat. This began the era of winding down Australia's relatively generous response to the refugee demand created by the collapse of civil order in the Middle East and Afghanistan.

Australia was officially committed to multiculturalism (Castles 1998; Jakubowicz and Ho 2013). As a public policy endorsed by all Australian governments – Commonwealth and state, Labor and Liberal – it moved away from a major aspect of Australian culture, the search for ethnic uniformity. It argued in favour of enjoying the skills and cultural variety immigration had brought. As Asia was opened for Australian migration, trade and political contacts flourished. This concrete reality and the shift in immigration from Britain and Europe towards Southeast Asia, China and India, did not impress opponents. Conservatives saw it as repudiating the British origins of Australia, while others were influenced by the virulent opposition coming from the United States (but not from Canada). It is worth remembering that multicultural policy was originally developed within the Immigration Department on the basis of the major report by Melbourne lawyer Frank Galbally (1978). This report concentrated on the common-sense argument that as many 'new Australians' were not English speaking they were likely to be inadequately served by services to which they were legally entitled. The most detailed analysis of how the policy came to be accepted (Lopez, *The Origins of Multiculturalism*) has been quoted as showing that the policy was fixed up by a small coterie of Labor supporters in Melbourne. This level of attack was common among conservative critics. It ignores the creation of networks of ethnic organizations in the major cities and the development of hundreds of vocal and well-informed immigrants built up from the post-war mass migrations.

Multicultural changes were encouraged by Liberal Prime Minister Malcolm Fraser and his ministers of Immigration, Michael MacKellar and Ian Macphee, and developed by another Liberal, Petro Georgiou. Despite its origins in the Commonwealth, the new policy was welcomed by state and municipal leaders as well as by the growing number of ethnic organizations. That the post-war generation of migrants supported it was shown by the rallies against amalgamating the Australian Broadcasting Corporation (ABC) and Special Broadcasting Service (SBS), the multicultural broadcaster, an issue that was being canvassed again in 2016. Modest Commonwealth funding encouraged the formation of multicultural organizations like the Federation of Ethnic Communities' Councils (FECCA) and its local branches. State politicians were willing to be engaged, as they were often less remote from the issues than the Commonwealth officials and politicians.

Between the original Galbally report of 1978 and the Bicentennial celebrations of 1988, support for multiculturalism broadened rapidly as the logical replacement for White Australia. But it remained a welfare, educational and settlement programme for immigrants, not a nation-wide attempt to change society, as its enemies claimed. Neither did the multicultural program incorporate Aboriginal activists; its home in the Immigration Department cut across Indigenous claims to be the First Australians.

Australia was officially committed to multiculturalism from 1978. This was never wholly true of Britain and owed a great deal more to Canada, Scandinavia and, with limitations, to the United States. As we have seen, as a public policy endorsed by all Australian governments it moved away from a major aspect of Australian culture, the quest for ethnic uniformity.

This was too extreme for the more conservative elements in the Liberal and National Parties, who, as we have seen, began to limit such approaches once elected to national government in 1996. In doing so they moved along a track developed by Pauline Hanson's One Nation, the first party to challenge the changes of the previous decades. One Nation collapsed, but revived in 2016. Meanwhile, both the Liberals and the Labor Party recognized that there were votes to be won in the space created by Pauline Hanson. Labor had been shifting from one leader to another, was faction-ridden and governed by the opinion polls. The 1990s ended in ignominy and a refugee policy that reversed the welcoming attitudes of Hawke, Fraser and Whitlam.

The Vietnam War and subsequent mass refugee intakes had cast a shadow over significant progress. The world of Southeast Asia was coming closer, as it had already done briefly in World War II between 1941 and 1945. It would be unduly critical of all parties in this period to overlook genuine anxieties about the victory of communism in Indochina and the mass refugee movements this set off. The collapse of Lebanon into civil war and the Vietcong entry into Saigon, coincided to produce the largest refugee explosion since 1945. The Lebanese and Syrian-born population increased by 23,000 between 1976 and 1986, and the Vietnam-born by 80,000. The response of the Fraser Liberal government was to work actively for a regional solution to the Vietnam exodus and to accept from Vietnam the largest intake of Asians since the Chinese arrivals over a century before (Viviani 1996). Suddenly, by the mid-1970s, there were 151,000 Vietnamese and 70,000 Lebanese in Australia, where previously there had been few of either people. While many of these were Catholics, others were either Muslims or Buddhists. Race and religion had ceased to have any direct relevance to intake policy. They lingered in the public conscience and anxieties (Tavan 2005) and were taken up by One Nation and sections of the media.

The short but rather frenetic 'multicultural era' endured much political chaos. The intervention of the governor-general, Sir John Kerr, with the support of the leader of the Opposition (Malcolm Fraser), saw the removal of the Labor prime minister, Gough Whitlam, in 1975. This raised a whole series of constitutional questions and long-term criticism. It revived agitation for the adoption of a republic, but without ultimate success. The links with Britain were sustained by the victorious Liberal and National parties. Political analysts noted the decline of trade unions and the Australian Labor Party as a long-term trend.

They were wrong, as the victories of Bob Hawke and Paul Keating proved. But not so wrong, as the victories of John Howard emphasized. There were no long-term trends in national politics, only the alternation of the two forces that had dominated politics since World War I, and the temporary rise of small parties such as One Nation, the Australian Democrats and later the Greens. Yet public debate centred around such abstractions as 'Who are we?', 'What do we stand for?', 'Where are we going?', 'Who are our friends and enemies?'. This all seemed to assume a uniform society ('who') moving ahead in an agreed direction. The 'rage' advocated by Whitlam on his dismissal did not materialize. Yet anxiety remained and was eventually reinforced by the rise of Islamist militancy. Multiculturalism had been widely accepted during the Bicentennial celebrations despite substantial disagreement on what this meant and consistent opposition from the conservative side of politics.

Thus, when the 'multicultural era' came to an abrupt end with the victory of the Liberal/National coalition in 1996, the era bequeathed a wide range of reforms and reorientations, but a fragmented and leaderless radicalism. It also witnessed the declining following of the established political parties and the trade union movement. White Australia had disappeared from public debate, but not some of the anxieties that had always accompanied it. While the Bicentennial of 1988 focussed on variety, many saw this as a threat to the hard-won acceptance of cohesion. The past was being inadequately celebrated, while the future was not defined. The Bicentennial was a muddle, which correctly reflected popular ambivalence about the history, nature and future of Australia. This was best epitomized by the arrival of the 'tall ships' into Sydney Harbour, decorated with a Coca Cola sail and, more seriously, by organized Aboriginal groups denouncing the 1788 invasion.

Chapter 13

ISLAM AS THE NEW THREAT

By 2001 ASIO no longer had a local target. The Yugoslav ambassadors and staff all went home to their six respective states to await relocation. The war in Vietnam had led to American defeat and withdrawal. Communism and the Soviet bloc disintegrated. But asylum seekers arriving by boat increased to 4,000, most being Afghans. In 2001 the Norwegian container ship *Tampa* picked up 400 mainly Muslim refugees, was denied access to Christmas Island and boarded by armed Australian border guards. After detention and processing, the majority secured residence in Australia, but not before official efforts to send them elsewhere (Brennan 2003; Marr and Wilkinson 2003).

From 2001 security emphasis shifted towards Islamist terrorism, which was not organized in the same way as either the communists or the European nationalists. There were no undisputed national or local Muslim leaders in a potential Australian base approaching half a million (Chulov 2006). International contacts were varied and splintered, especially between Saudi, Pakistani and Yemeni Sunni and Iranian and Iraqui Shia, and their followers. Islamic affairs, whether terrorist, religious or business, were conducted in Arabic. This language is taught in few Australian institutions, but is the fourth most common Australian language after English. (Kabir 2005). The new enemy actually killed people (including themselves) and bombed civilians, which the Australian communists never did. This did not seriously apply in Australia, with less than a dozen deaths, including Muslims. It certainly applied to Australian jihadists in the Middle East. A handful of individual murders were enough to create serious concern in Australia. The greatest loss of Australian life was in Bali among holidaymakers.

The Islamist threat might have been overlooked until the 2001 World Trade disaster of 9/11 and Australian involvement in the war in Afghanistan. The replacement of the communist target by Islamist terrorists presented major challenges to ASIO, despite the expansion of a new legal system designed to enhance its work. Cooperation was strengthened between ASIO and the Federal Police as well as the state police. ASIO powers started to expand from the ASIO Legislative Amendment (Terrorism) Bill of 2002.

'Operation Pendennis' from 2005 to 2008 continued under these new laws and arrangements, focussing on local Muslims. Eventually 18 arrests were made and 15 successful convictions won for advocating and planning, but not implementing, terrorism (Chulov 2006). Evidence was provided of the collection of chemicals that had explosive potential if expertly mixed. The main agencies for this success were the Australian Federal Police, ASIO and the Victoria Police. The exercise named 'Pendennis' was the most successful so far revealed.

The principal member of the arrested group was Abdul Nasser Benbrika, an established Islamic teacher in Melbourne, born in Algeria, who was sentenced to 12 years. A major Sydney participant, Mohamed Elomar, was sentenced to 21 years. He and another accused had trained in Pakistan with Lashkar-e-Taiba, a terrorist organization banned in Australia and many other countries. Most of the information had been gathered by electronic interception. Later Faheem Khalid Lodhi, was sentenced in 2006, accused of planning the bombing of a prominent building. Three Sydney Muslims were also jailed for 13 years under 'Operation Neath' in 2012 for planning a suicide attack on the Holsworthy barracks. Relatives of Elomar later turned up in the 'caliphate'.

All of these and many others were under justifiable surveillance and communications checks, but none had yet committed a violent terrorist act. Of those charged through Operation Pendennis, fourteen were born in Australia, four in Lebanon and one each in Bosnia, Nigeria and Bangladesh. The three condemned for the Neath conspiracy of 2009 to attack Holsworthy Barracks were born in Australia, Lebanon and Somalia. These distinct events underline the extent to which locally born, second-generation Muslims, rather than immigrants, are at the core of active terrorism. Pendennis and Neath also suggested the wide extent of sympathy for militant jihad. Seven different birthplaces were represented out of twenty-one people involved.

The social backgrounds of the Pendennis and Neath accused offer a good available measure of those attracted to terrorism (SMH 4 May 2012). The great majority had been born in Australia and lived there for most of their lives, with periods of training in Pakistan or Afghanistan. Of these, one was an Australian convert and ten others were also Australian-born. They were in their late twenties or early thirties by 2012 and descended from the Muslim refugee and migrant intakes of 1975 to 1985. They had their education and work experience in Melbourne and, in a few cases, Sydney. Most were semiskilled manual workers, several with serious mental problems. Overseas training included Lashkar e-Taiba in Pakistan and al Shabbab in Somalia, both organizations banned in Australia. There are serious social problems among this youthful population, and a few have sought the answer in terrorism. The opportunity to die for Islam was expanded by the civil war in Syria and the announcement of the Islamic 'caliphate' embracing parts of Syria and Iraq and advancing towards Baghdad. The use of social media was highly effective and well understood by this young cohort.

There is considerable movement between the large Muslim communities in Sydney and Melbourne and Southeast Asia and the Middle East. A regular visitor to Australia, making at least nine trips in a decade, was Abu Bakar Bashir, spiritual leader and inspiration of Jemaah Islamiah. Precisely what he was doing in Australia is presumably locked in the secret files of ASIO or ASIS. His Indonesian organization was responsible for the Bali bombing of 2002. Bashir was eventually tried for a different conspiracy in Indonesia in 2011 and sentenced to 15 years in prison.

Converts play an important role in Islamist terrorism and the Australian-born generation is at its heart locally. When any social class is marginal to society its resentment is likely to lead to crime, anti-social behaviour, violence or even terrorism. Those parts of western Sydney and Melbourne that have been affected by de-industrialization and contain marginalized ethnic minorities have within them many young, locally born Muslims. At present individual grievances may be more important than social factors, but some jihadists seem to have been well socialized and integrated.

Operations Pendennis and Neath were the high points in detecting possible Islamist Australian conspiracies. Whether they would ever have got beyond the discussion stage was, fortunately, not tested. Their crimes were not the implementation of terrorism, but its planning and membership or recruitment of an organization dedicated to violent jihad. At the same time a number of Tamils were arrested in Melbourne on similar charges for materially assisting the Tamil Tiger revolt in Sri Lanka. However, this case could not be pursued. The LTTE (the Liberation Tigers of Tamil Elam) were not a listed terrorist organization in Australia, although they were in the United States, Britain and most of the European Union. Moreover, Sri Lankan Tamils are not usually Muslims, nor do they enjoy the patronage of a major power. They were part of an effective international network with strong followings in Canada, Britain and Europe. Thus at least two substantial minorities in Australia, Arabic and Tamil speakers, found themselves the subject of suspicion and supervision. There was no evidence that the Tamil Tigers threatened Australian targets, unlike the jihadists. They came from a more established community in different parts of Melbourne or Sydney and had no quarrel with Australia.

Dealing with potential Asian and Middle Eastern terrorism is complex and highly specialized (Saeed and Akbarzadeh 2001). It requires a knowledge of several languages, scripts and cultures. Potential terrorists come from many different countries. It needs sociological understanding of such institutions as the Somali clans or the Pakistani *biraderi* system of monetary relationships.

It may require supervision of native-born Australian converts to Islam, who are often more dedicated than immigrants (Yusuf 2009). It also requires a background on the highly fractionalized world of political and religious Islam, which has set brother against brother in the vast Muslim *ummah*, or world. The restructuring of the Immigration Department in 2015 may improve the control of fraud. Staff have been overburdened with 'stopping the boats', when the main leakage in the system occurs with airline passengers, the great majority of arrivals. The minister denied this possibility, which is not surprising.

Failing to understand such complexities can lead to serious errors of judgement or discrimination against whole communities. A particular problem is the lack of trust produced by the regular criticism of Islamic religious practices by the media and public figures. Mischievous organizations like the Q Society of Australia, the Australia First Party, the Salt Shakers, Rise Up Australia, Reclaim Australia, the United Patriots Front and the Stable Population Party go out of their way to keep hostility to Islam alive. They have invited Geert Wilders from the Netherlands to speak, a man barred from entering Britain to preserve communal harmony. These groups work with committed American critics like Bat Ye'or and Robert Spencer, and refer frequently to the situations in Britain and Europe. They are free to do so, but are not helpful (*News Weekly* 14 February 2015).

Attempts to unify these scattered anti-Muslim groups were launched in 2015 by the Australian Liberty Alliance. Its professional website included an elaborate outline of a new political party designed to 'stop the Islamization of Australia, the divisiveness of multiculturalism and the deconstruction of Western civilization'.

Islamism was defined as 'a totalitarian ideology with global aspirations'. On closer inspection the proposed Alliance aimed to ban face coverings in public, sharia law, Muslim immigration for ten years, dual citizenship, affirmative action, same-sex marriage, republican change and the UN Convention on Refugees. It endorsed the Q Society hostility to all Muslims, received a welcoming letter from Geert Wilders (the Dutch enemy of Islam) and promotion from the conservative broadcaster Andrew Bolt. It avoided any charges of 'fascism' by endorsing Israel as the only democracy in the Middle East. This reflected its ideological commitment to the Judeo-Christian and Humanist heritages. In the unlikely event of its organization flourishing it could fill the gap left by the decline of One Nation, but with a bolder denunciation of Islam and broader scope, appealing to fundamental Christians.

At the other extreme, Hizb-ut-Tahrir is a youthful international organization, founded in 1953 and dedicated to the restoration of the caliphate, abolished in 1924. It is not banned in Australia nor are its objectives violent, if somewhat utopian: 'We reject both integration and isolation and advocate positive interaction for Muslims in society based solely on Islam' (Statement of November 2013). They claim 'the Australian government has developed and implemented a broad range of counter-terrorism policies that target the Muslim community'. Their basic argument is that 'this counter extremism work, which adopts and promotes moderate Islam, expressly promotes secularism, democracy, and liberal values and seeks an enlightenment in Islam on the model of Christianity. The outcome sought is a secular, politically impotent, localized version of Islam: an Australian Islam for Australian Muslims'. This is a direct attack on public policy towards Muslims, but not illegal or a call to terrorism. It is also not particularly helpful. Prime Minister Tony Abbott suggested that it weakened social cohesion, but he did not illegalize it. While a basic understanding of Islam would possibly assist in modifying terrorism, it could be argued that neither Christianity nor Islam can justify the crimes and massacres that have characterized the 'civilized' world since 1914 and were largely the work of religious leaders, politicians and generals.

This brief but direct statement by Hizb-ut-Tahrir suggests basic problems presented by law-abiding but fundamental Muslims in a multicultural society. They do not normally advocate violence or terrorism, especially not attacks on civilians. They do express a great deal of resentment at criticism and a desire not to be influenced by democratic and liberal ideas. Fundamentalism leaves little room for compromise. It is, however, the work of young idealists and not of experienced religious leaders or criminals. A broader Islamic tradition is for adjustment to the society in which you reside, provided it respects your religion. It is lack of respect that inflames Muslims. In their turn, some Muslim advocates tend to arrogance about other religions and the democratic process, which undermines any degree of acceptance by the Australian majority. Those critics who wrongly accuse Muslims of trying to force their ways on the majority are often responding to such attitudes. The belief that the Qur'an was the direct word of Allah as transmitted to Mohamed, gives Islam a powerful but very conservative appeal, freed from the many changes and reforms of most other world religions, including Christianity.

Muslim leaders in Australia mostly wish to preserve those aspects of *shariah* law which do not conflict with majority practices, for example female hair covering, interest-free loans, *halal* food and parental control of children. Female circumcision and polygamy are illegal and uncommon in Australia. *Halal* butchery is similar to *kosher* Jewish practice. In general Australia has not taken the rigid approach of states like France, due to its official endorsement of multiculturalism. This includes public subsidy of Islamic schools on the same basis as for other denominations. Protests against building mosques or other religious buildings are universal, often on the ground of parking or traffic congestion, but usually fail. The arguments used in Australia are similar to those used in other majority Christian countries, but the Australian solution is more liberal.

A central problem in negotiating with Muslim Australia is the absence of an authoritative structure and leadership within the religious followings. There simply are no national 'leaders', only prominent individuals who have earned respect from their own followers, who may or may not advocate militant tactics. That many of the most respected religious *imams* do not effectively speak English and come from conservative backgrounds in the Middle East also presents problems not encountered in other communities. Organizations like the Islamic Federation of Australia, or the Lakemba-based Lebanese Muslim Association, do not speak for all Muslims and nobody can. The Mufti of Australia is a respected teacher but not a political leader. Shia Muslims do not work closely with the Sunni majority. Religious leaders may issue *fatwas,* but these are usually opinions rather than instructions (Aly 2007).

One of the most professional analyses of this variety is from sociologist Riaz Hassan (Hassan 2008: 308). His essentially liberal conclusion, based on cross-national research, needs qualifying for the many Australian Muslims whose parents came from the deserts and mountains of Afghanistan, Lebanon, Iraq, Somalia, Syria, Pakistan, Bosnia or Kosovo, seeking a better life. They found themselves in Lakemba, Auburn, Broadmeadows or Thomastown, attacked by Radio 2GB, or the *Daily Telegraph*, and watching factories closing around them. Their responses are protective rather than aggressive. Some sons of migrants turned to militancy, others to crime. Most study to improve their language skills, business understanding or sporting ability.

More effective and selective settlement services might have been developed for the mass entries of 1975–1985, instead of concentrating on their occupational value to industries, which were starting to contract and move away to Asia. They arrived just when policy was shifting from settlement towards employability, as urged by the influential report of 1988 (FitzGerald 1988). The valuable networks of education and social services available to immigrants, and especially refugees, were run down or defunded. Eventually they were dispersed away from the Immigration Department altogether in 2015, or left to states and municipalities. The driving force behind this neglect was mainly in the political parties. Most welfare and religious agencies and many schools were more constructive.

This fragmented and highly diffuse Islamic community of less than 3 per cent of the population, is sensitive to criticism and investigation. Because of its complexity, serious errors can be made. One outstanding example was the treatment of a South Indian Muslim, Mohamed Haneef, a doctor at the Gold Coast Hospital in Queensland. Haneef was related to one of the two suicide bombers who attacked Glasgow airport on the other side of the world in June

2007. The link between the two was a transferred mobile phone card, which Haneef gave to his cousin when leaving England for Australia. Here ASIO must be forgiven, as it advised from early in the investigations of July 2007 that Haneef was not likely to be involved in terrorist activity, despite having a relative who was. As Geoffrey Robertson QC puts it, he 'was an innocent man presumed guilty by overzealous police and prosecutors, and over-excited politicians and pressmen' (Ewart 2009: 6).

The 'over-excited politician' was Kevin Andrews, Minister for Immigration in the Abbott Liberal government, which was radically changing asylum-seeker policy and the powers of the security services. To have caught a live Muslim terrorist would have enhanced his career. But this did not happen, and he was transferred from Immigration to Social Services soon afterwards, and later to Defence and then from a ministerial post altogether. The Queensland police interviewed Haneef at length. The available transcript suggests their complete lack of any understanding of Islam, terrorism or of the world outside Queensland. The Australian Federal Police and ASIO were anxious to distance themselves from this increasingly unlikely suspect.

Haneef became an Indian folk hero, underlining the long-held Indian belief that Australia was a racist country. Andrews intervened at the last moment to suspend Haneef's residence visa, which would have made him an unlawful immigrant and prevent him from leaving Australia or returning to it. After a concerted intervention by some of Australia's best lawyers, Haneef was completely cleared, left the country and ended up with a position in the Gulf Emirates. Queensland had lost a good doctor. Haneef himself agreed that his relationship with one of the Glasgow terrorists looked suspicious, but that he was completely innocent and not interested in Islamic politics (Ewart 2009).

The Haneef case and the resentment of many Muslims at the atmosphere of suspicion created by a growing intelligence machine, presented difficulties in integrating Muslims into society, including the one-third who were born in Australia and were growing in number more rapidly than the immigrant communities. Converts like David Hicks and Jack Thomas and citizens like Mamdouh Habib were problematic for Australian diplomacy, as they became the centre of campaigns for their release from arrest in Pakistan or Afghanistan.

Mamdouh Habib, who was a naturalized Australian citizen of Egyptian origin, was locked away in the American detention camp at Guantánamo (Cuba) between 2001 and 2005, having been of interest to ASIO in Sydney since 1993 (Thom 2011). Both Hicks and Habib made charges of torture by CIA officers, contributing to a growing concern about CIA treatment of alleged terrorists and the lack of Australian intervention in the interests of their own citizens. An inquiry into Australian government treatment of this issue was delivered by the Inspector-General of Intelligence and Security in December 2011, seven years after Habib's release and following a decision in the Federal Court favouring some recompense. At the end of 2014 a United States Senatorial Committee detailed the extensive use of torture against CIA detainees. This was endorsed by President Obama but attacked by the CIA and its friends in the Republican Party, including president-elect Trump on one occasion.

The case against Habib, who was sold to the Americans by one of the private armies supporting the US in Afghanistan, was that he 'may have had prior knowledge of the September 11 terrorist attacks'. His case against Australia was that he had inadequate support from the Australian embassies in Egypt and Pakistan. The general picture that emerges from a subsequent official inquiry is that Australian authorities did very little for Habib and put no obstacles in the way of his being moved between Pakistan, Egypt, Afghanistan and Guantánamo. As with Haneef, ASIO had advised as early as 2002 that there was no evidence of Habib planning future terrorism. This was not taken seriously by other Australian officials. There is a contrast here between the enormous effort to free the Australian David Hicks, an admitted armed militant, and Habib, a mere Egyptian in the wrong place (Habib and Collingwood 2008; Hicks 2010).

Throughout Australian history there has been a tendency to choose minorities as targets for the fears and suspicions of the majority, as in many societies. The dominant traditions taught in England and Australia a century ago stressed the influence of militarized and efficient Rome, rather than the imaginary Judeo-Christian inheritance. It was through this imperial history that generations of Australians were taught about the world in which they lived, and which no longer exists. This selective history, which was passed on to Australia, concentrated on British victories over inferior foreigners and the glorious days of the empire and the world wars. That the British Empire has followed the downward path of all other empires is a constant cause of puzzle and resentment in England, but more easily accepted in Australia. It burst out in 2016 with the wide vote to remove Britain from the European Union, which caused only a mild Australian response.

A particular gloss was put on this record of victories by the popular schoolboy stories *Deeds That Won the Empire*. These yarns by W. H. Fitchett were published in Melbourne in 1897 and became popular reading throughout the entire British world. When Australia became a nation in 1901, the empire spanned the globe. The only continent without large British colonies was Europe, controlled by five great empires – Germany, France, Russia, Austria and Ottoman – four destroyed in World War I. Great empires were lost, including the Muslim caliphate in Istanbul. A century later that British Empire is confined to a few tiny islands in remote Oceanic isolation, while the Muslim world is growing.

Most imperial deeds were in conflicts with non-European peoples. Racism had a theoretical origin in mid-Victorian misinterpretations of Charles Darwin's analysis of evolution and associated notions of the survival of the fittest attributed to Herbert Spencer. Racism had a strong popular and patriotic basis in the victories and eventual decline of the empire. Australia also had a strong response to the victories creating this massive empire. Trafalgar Day was regularly commemorated until overtaken by Gallipoli in 1915. A century later the bicentenary of the Battle of Waterloo was also cause for celebration, officially endorsed by the Commonwealth government (and no doubt politely acknowledged by the French ambassador). In Britain, rather than Australia, the 'finest hour' of the 1940s air battles is annually commemorated, with Gallipoli rarely mentioned. In contrast, the celebration of Gallipoli has become a centrepiece of Australian nationalism, although it was a military defeat by Asian Turks (with German support).

Colonial peoples in the former empire, including Arabs, Chinese, Pacific Islanders, Africans and Indians were all regarded as conquered peoples and thus inferior. This helps to explain the popular support for White Australia for over a century. The historical and cultural dimensions cannot be ignored. They have been effectively maintained throughout the British element of the Commonwealth, of which Australia, Canada and New Zealand are among the largest examples other than Great Britain. These constitute the core of the world of defence, security and counter-intelligence, along with the United States, inheritor of earlier British influence.

The reaction to this ideological relic of the Victorian Age has been strongest in the Arabic and Asian inheritors of the now disbanded empire. These societies were either occupied or effectively controlled by the British Empire for the economic benefit of the United Kingdom. Their economic resources, which were substantial, were sacrificed or taken over. Societies that had been both independent and rich, such as Bengal, were reduced to the impoverished level of Calcutta or Bangladesh. Racist exclusion completed the picture, with clubs, sports and colleges often closed to the former élites. Islam and Hinduism were consistently denigrated or ridiculed in favour of Christianity and modern liberalism.

The sense of a great civilization lost to crusading Christianity adds fervour to the Salafist movements inspired by the Muslim Brotherhood, or the Indian *khilifat* movement, and more recent ideologues like the Taliban, al–Qaeda and the Islamic State. They breed on traditions of repression, violence and loss of power and prestige, which stretch back for centuries. These lead to statements and actions that are closer to fascism than to communism or traditional nationalism, but have yet to create a strong fascist state or party, a single leader or a secular ideology. Coming from a harsh desert environment like that of Egypt, Somalia, Afghanistan, Iraq or Syria, only sharpens the weapons and increases the brutality. The swamping of the Arab world with sophisticated armaments by the manufacturing powers makes their conflicts more destructive and vicious. As the historic centre of the Muslim world, the Arabic influence spreads conflicting messages into states and regions in which the Judeo-Christian message has little appeal. The suburban mass culture of Australia is inadequately equipped to deal with this. Its public policies seem to be based, however unfairly, on racial prejudice and hostility to the neighbouring world and one of its most powerful cultures. Multiculturalism offers some guidance here, but has been consistently denigrated by conservatives for the past 40 years.

Australia's attempt to create a liberal, democratic and multicultural society has been relatively benign compared, for example, with the United States. Australia was not founded by revolution, nor cemented by civil war. It did not conquer its indigenous people or neighbours by military might, but by marginalization. It did not rely on slavery, nor crush the labour movement. It aimed at equality rather than personal riches. It was a small and distant society, protected by its 'powerful friends' and able to build its population by careful selection and limited intakes of similar peoples. After 1945 it came increasingly into contact with a dangerous and disturbing world, which was constantly at war somewhere. It started to dismantle many of its old myths and to worry unduly about its future. From 1945 to 1991 it steadily opened its doors to the world. From then on it began to close them again for the less fortunate and to reassert national solidarity, by law if needed.

Throughout the two centuries of modern Australian history there have always been official concerns about the frailty of the society, its lack of cohesion and of threats from internal and external enemies. While sometimes very serious, these have eventually proved illusory or exaggerated. Political and social concessions ensured a degree of national cohesion. Society was organized and homogenized as it had been from the colonial past. Adequate incomes and employment, universal education and welfare, political compromise and distance from trouble were basic foundations for cohesion, rather than the Enlightenment or the Judeo-Christian ethic. A reserve force of coercion, mainly police and security, directed against unpopular minorities, helped to discourage any serious threats.

A century ago the threat from Germany impinged on Australia because patriotism drove many thousands to fight and die for the empire on the other side of the world. By far the most serious threat in modern times came from the Japanese, who conquered nearly all of the colonial societies in the Asia–Pacific, with the exception of Australia and New Zealand. Communism was painted as a comparable threat. On close examination it was what the

Chinese derided as a 'paper tiger', which finally lost its influence in the labour movement when the Soviet system collapsed in 1991. The next apparent threat came from Asia and the Middle East, followed by refugees trying to reach Australia in their leaky boats. The hysteria and repression this created was out of all proportion.

Almost immediately a new threat was heralded from the Islamist 'caliphate' (ISIS) and its international terrorist networks. But their internecine battles in Syria and Iraq scarcely touched Australia directly. Australians have no interest in defending the brutal Alawite presidency of Assad of Syria, or the 'caliphate'. Their Australian followers were few in numbers, if strongly committed and violent. Whether the elaborate machinery of universal scrutiny through metadata, denial of citizenship, banning of organizations, attacks on belief and ideology, deprivation of citizenship and pressure on one community in a multicultural society are justified should be a major issue for public concern. Whether Australia needs mandatory detention for asylum seekers should be another.

Unfortunately, the two issues have become intertwined in the public mind. The modest request for recognition of some aspects of *shariah* law, have been seized on by opponents of new mosques as evidence of a plot to Islamize Australia (Morgan and Poynting 2012). What is far more serious is the possession of highly destructive weaponry in the hands of dedicated fanatics. They are poisoning community relations in Australia and giving encouragement to reactionary and punitive policies, which rest most heavily on other Muslims. Terrorism is mainly directed against innocent civilians, as are many aerial attacks and advanced weapons. Rejoicing in death and destruction does not win friends, wherever it comes from. Australia has taken part in two unjustified wars, in Vietnam and Iraq, and needs to think carefully before becoming involved in more.

The search for 'cohesion' was weakened by a lack of any concrete definition of what this might mean. To many it simply meant the return to a uniform, Anglo-Australian culture with limited ethnic variety controlled by strict immigration policies; to some the reaffirmation of Christian values; to others simply 'mateship'. Unlike the previous multicultural era no government made any serious, researched and publicized attempt to define what 'cohesion' might look like in real terms. 'Integration', an alternative, was perhaps more concrete as it suggested that newcomers might retain their distinctiveness. As recently as 2017 a revived oath of loyalty was being canvassed, based on discussing 'what being Australian really means'. In a multicultural society this is a silly question.

Relevant research was cut short by John Howard's arbitrary closing of the Bureau of Immigration Research in 1996, the effective monopoly of the

Immigration Department, and the secrecy inherent in security work. The Australian majority was still asking 'Why can't they be like us?', which was often unrealistic for the immigrant generations, but much easier for their children. A more meaningful term for the locally born might be 'adaptation'. Even this did not account for the small minority of young men who became alienated altogether from the society in which they lived and the even smaller number who looked to violent repudiation of majority values and behaviour. These were often locally born converts to Islam without much detailed knowledge of their religion and out of parental control. All terrorist attacks in Australia so far have involved a tiny number of young individuals, some of whom were shot by the police in action. What is consistent through the history of population recruitment and resistance is that Australia cannot be isolated from the world with rigorous, exclusive and unjust decisions that damage its reputation and its aim of creating a planned society in the modern world.

Part II

Chapter 14

THE POST-WAR PROMISE ENDS

Australia has been recruiting and accommodating new settlers for 230 years (Borrie 1994). Policy was more logical and coordinated after Federation in 1901, when immigration became the full responsibility of the Commonwealth government. Before that preference was given to British settlement through free entry and subsidized passages, varying from colony to colony, but advised and organized from London. After that, policy became increasingly uniform and bureaucratized in the hands of colonial and state governments until 1920 and then by the Commonwealth and the Immigration Department, founded in 1945. At all stages, from convicts to the present, there was state involvement to a more active degree than in many other countries. The great exception was the gold rush of the mid-nineteenth century. But even there the state intervened in the form of armed troops at Eureka. After the Commonwealth took over in 1901 the White Australia policy dominated selection for 70 years. After that selection was still based on preferences determined by the Commonwealth, with special favour for British and New Zealand applicants with skills, as it was for the previous century.

Finally, in 2015 a bureaucratic epoch ended. The amalgamation of Immigration and Customs into Border Protection meant that for the first time in 70 years (excepting the brief Whitlam break) there was no Commonwealth department expressly committed to all aspects of immigration, multiculturalism, citizenship and settlement. Controlling and discouraging asylum seekers had become the central priority (Pickering 2005). A backlog of unvisaed asylum seekers were interned in Manus and Nauru with no prospect of settling in Australia, according to ministers from both major parties. The *Migration Act*, amended late in 2014, refined the criteria for granting asylum and left the definition of a refugee in the hands of departmental officials and the Australian Security Intelligence Organisation (ASIO). The UN Convention was reduced to a nullity as far as Australia was concerned. Boats were turned back before they reached the extended Australian sea borders (Corlett 2005). The amalgamation of Immigration and Border Protection and an armed and militarized Australian Border Force was not welcomed by many public servants. Some moved away from the new ministry, whose functions were control rather than settlement (Mackenzie-Murray 2015). One immediate result was a strike wave by public servants, causing serious delays at airports and mainly aimed at pay and conditions. However, bureaucratic leaders went ahead with a proposal to create an amalgam of many border protection agencies in imitation of the US Department of Homeland Security. This increased still further the powers of the Secretary and Minister for Immigration, once fairly minor positions. Selection or rejection would become a primary concern.

Previous policy phases had included White Australia, recruitment of British workers, restrictions during recessions, and eventually the replacement of White Australia by multicultural recruitment (Tavan 2005). Intake totals then were carefully planned in terms of their economic value (FitzGerald 1988) using a points system but allowing for family and humanitarian applicants. However, detailed planning was regularly disturbed by international crises, including wars, which pushed refugees to the centre of controversial emergency recruitments. Eventually these problems were controlled through extensive legislation and the centralized Ministry of Immigration and Border Protection, with its armed and uniformed Border Force, later including the Federal Police.

The *Commonwealth Migration Act of 1958* is one of the most complex and frequently amended pieces of basic legislation. Many of these amendments were designed to close loopholes created by rapidly shifting and often unexpected changes in overseas political and economic situations. Legislation such as the *Citizenship Act*, is also amended to reduce or enhance the chances of immigrants becoming Australians. Since 1986 simply being born in Australia is not enough. By 2014 parents who had not arrived fully visaed might damage the prospects of children then born in Australia. Tests of 'Australian knowledge' were imposed as well as a commitment to Australian 'values'. The great majority passed anyway. It was essentially an exercise to mollify the public and the media, rather than to educate or select the applicants. Knowledge of cricket, a game played seriously in less than a dozen countries, was a prominent item, later modified. Current versions stress Australian 'values' without detailed specification. These were said to be the 'glue' that bound society together but were never given more than a very general definition.

The bureaucratic expectation that a rational overall policy can be constructed and maintained is often frustrated. Apart from several Commonwealth departments, which are also often inconsistent, the major guardian of consistency has been the High Court. The system aims at rationality, but is overcome by a changing and complex world over which Australia has little control. This is particularly so for refugees, who are created by unexpected crises and are defined by international laws (Adelman 1994). Politicians are starting to argue that, as they represent the people, they have the right to interpret the law without the interference of unelected adjudicators, especially from overseas. Yet that is precisely what administrative and international law involves (Vrachnas 2009; Crock 1998; Crock and Saul 2002; Gallagher and David 2014). This argument overlooks the fact that migration is international.

Bureaucracies are founded, amended and sometimes abolished in response to party political objectives and shifting priorities. The Department of Immigration has been the heir of regular name changes since its creation in 1945, reflecting different objectives but retaining its basic staff and collective wisdom (Jupp 2007). Towards the end of the Whitlam government in 1975 it was abolished altogether, only to be restored by Malcolm Fraser on his election. In 2015 it was completely restructured to concentrate on border control. This amalgamation sent off its multicultural and settlement functions to Human Services and its English programme to Education. As in many European states, including the United Kingdom, immigration became part of the controlling and policing machinery.

The newly consolidated Department of Immigration and Border Protection can decide who arrives, who can settle and who can and who cannot become or remain a citizen. It can define methods of arrival across the oceans that surround Australia. Its powers are shared with a range of other Commonwealth departments and agencies such as ASIO, the Australian Secret Intelligence Service (ASIS), Attorney General's Department, the Australian Federal Police, Foreign Affairs and Prime Minister and Cabinet. It shares its knowledge with counterparts in the United States, United Kingdom, Canada and New Zealand. It can refuse entry to Australia and detain or deport those who have entered or remained without its permission. Since 2015 it can prevent travellers from leaving Australia and impound their passports if necessary. It can decide the numbers and origins sought each year and vary them in the light of economic and political considerations. Its recent restructuring has increased its power of control, while sending off areas like settlement, training and language policy elsewhere. Late in 2014 its scope was extended by the Migration and Maritime Powers Legislation Amendment (Resolving the Asylum Legacy Caseload) Bill, as far-reaching as its ponderous name suggests. At last the conservative government seemed to have freed itself from the restrictions explicit in several UN Conventions. The United Nations Refugee Convention remained outside the amended *Migration Act.*

Ever since its creation in 1945 the Commonwealth Immigration Department has been at the centre of the most controversial issue in public policy – who can be allowed to enter and settle as a refugee from less peaceful and attractive societies. It shares this power, often reluctantly, with the legal system centred on the High Court, within the concept of the rule of law

(Gibney 2004; Goodwin-Gill and McAdam 2007). The definition of who qualifies as a refugee still rested with the Immigration Department in the first instance, subject to appeal and specific legal decisions. The appeals system has been expanded or contracted according to the approach of the current government. Nobody who arrives unvisaed by boat can expect permanent residence leading to citizenship, nor do they have access to the Refugee Appeals Tribunal. This was not so in the recent past. Conversely, residence can be obtained by a substantial sum in business or property through the Significant Investment visa for approved applicants.

Since 1945 Australia has faced several challenging issues in its attempt to maintain a socially homogenous and economically productive society. This centres around population policy and planning, as in previous generations. These are not the exclusive concern of the Immigration Department. Multiculturalism was a matter for Immigration, but did not extend to the Indigenous. They were of limited interest to the Commonwealth before 1967. The 2013 transfer of multiculturalism to Human Services may correct that division or simply marginalize multiculturalism as a national policy. Changes to the funding and support for ethnic-based services suggest that the multicultural system developed from the Galbally report of 1978 will be merged into broader social security arrangements and not be managed by ethnic-specific agencies.

An official concern is the growing number of asylum seekers produced by political and social unrest in decolonized societies, many of them in the Asia–Pacific region (Loescher 1993; Kneebone 2003). A recent and worrying problem has been the spread of anti-Western jihadist and salafist ideologies, backed by military and terrorist activity in the Muslim world (Chulov 2006; Neighbour 2004). The founding of an Islamic 'caliphate' in Iraq and Syria in 2014 made the problem acute. This new, if unrecognized, state had a substantial local base in northern Syria and conquests in Iraq, but several rivals. Death rates in military action were killing about one quarter of young Australian jihadist volunteers by 2015. Those wishing to return home were threatened with execution by the 'caliphate'. Should they manage to return, Australia threatened them with criminal penalties and probable loss of citizenship. Citizenship had become disposable.

Many such problems are not historically the direct responsibility of the current generation of Australians. But the escalation of a 'refugee problem' has been. Since 1945 over a million Australian immigrants have successfully sought refuge from persecution, wars, revolutions and disasters. Since 1970 many have come from sources previously closed to aspiring immigrants because of their race. Migrants have been processed through complex and restrictive selection (Mares 2001; Neumann 2015). Australia has tightly controlled entry for those who need it most, while maintaining opportunities for New Zealanders, British and South Africans, some Europeans and North Americans, and extending these for temporary residents, businessmen and those able to invest a substantial amount. With temporary migration by tradesmen, students and working holidaymakers at an historic level of 700,000, it became more difficult than since 1945 for refugees to gain permanent residence, and impossible if they arrive by boat without a visa. Unvisaed arrivals are rigorously inspected by the 'five eyes' security systems of Australia, the United States, Canada, New Zealand and the United Kingdom, a process that may take years to resolve one way or another.

The only alternatives for refugees, other than through the narrowing regulations or favoured categories, is either by unlicensed shipping ('the boats') or by securing a short-term visa and seeking asylum upon landing at an airport. Australian officers overseas have instructions about issuing such a visa, under the concept of 'country at risk'. This distinguishes foreign states on the basis of their visa overstaying rates. Information about political conditions overseas utilizes research by the Immigration Department, the Office of National Assessments, Department of Foreign Affairs, ASIO and the CIA, and the British Foreign Office. These are not always consistent. Regardless of these processes, asylum seekers by boat (Illegal Maritime Arrivals) have been told since 2013 that they will 'never' be allowed to settle in Australia, which is a clear breach of the United Nations Convention, Article 31 (McAdam and Chong 2014).

For 70 years refugees have seldom been out of the headlines, even though they rarely formed a majority of those arriving for settlement. The Attorney General's Department supervised the relevant United Nations Conventions to which Australia was a signatory. Foreign Affairs and Trade provided advice on the international impact of policy changes. Instead of being an all-purpose multicultural agency, Immigration has now become a controller and guardian of the borders. Unlike other situations in Europe, North America or Africa, these borders are at sea and invisible, except to precise locational instruments. Control is usually concentrated at the arrival point by air or by intercepting vessels at sea. Boats stopped at sea do not normally continue to the Australian mainland. Indonesia has officially complained about boats being returned, but Sri Lanka has encouraged this.

By 2015 Immigration had become essentially a bureaucratic control, labour recruitment and detention agency, part of the militarized Operation Sovereign Borders. Migrant and refugee settlement was passed to state government agencies or to the Department of Human Services. Settlement services by ethnic and migrant organizations that had grown up since 1978, were at risk of fragmentation or transfer to the less well-equipped states and local government.

This recent policy was the most important administrative change since Whitlam abolished the Immigration Department altogether in 1974. Calwell's slogan of 'populate or perish' was to be replaced by Howard's 'We will decide who comes and under what circumstances'. Australia has moved closer than ever towards a guest worker system for the benefit of employers, tight security against unwanted refugees and their families, and preference for the highly skilled and wealthy. From recruiting the poor and excluding the Chinese, Australia has moved to excluding the poor and recruiting the Chinese – as investors, students and property owners. Chinese and Indians rapidly became major intakes.

Through many changes, the most politically controversial policies surrounded cultural and racial variety and obligations to refugees. These overlapped as few recent refugees came from British or West European origins. The demands of nation-building, effective defence or increased labour power also required recruitment to industry of a workforce, the race or culture of which were not necessarily important. In Europe and North America, industrialization had sought recruitment from rural and foreign societies, regardless of their social impact on the receiving society. Australia from 1906 tried to avoid this, making it difficult for Pacific Islanders to remain. Recently other Islanders, from Samoa or Tonga, find it hard to get visas, despite being Christians and English-speaking. Many rely on New Zealand instead.

Australia could not depend on an Indigenous, immigrant, convict, indentured or rural population who did not also want to assimilate. Australia had a century of relying on the much-larger population of Britain for recruitment and for social and cultural uniformity. This could not last indefinitely, despite a continuing bureaucratic effort to choose and subsidize appropriate immigrants and even refugees. Britain and Europe were much richer than before and were not liable to suffer warfare or revolution. The 'Bring out a Briton' campaign of 1957 was the last serious attempt to offer passage to healthy British subjects, regardless of their qualifications and preferably with their families. Return rates of British immigrants often frustrated this objective.

The limitations on choosing suitable newcomers were met by varying regulations, of which the White Australia rules had been the most important. These could not be maintained either. Post-colonial independence grew rapidly after 1945. The largest intake of non-British after 1945 was greeted with demands for 'assimilation', which continued for several years before Eastern Europe was closed off by its communist rulers, and Southern Europeans filled the resultant large gap. Departmental officials had assumed that Northern Europeans were close enough to the settled majority to be readily assimilated. This early approach meant becoming identifiably Australian in one generation but was never rigorously defined. The European intakes were racially acceptable but culturally quite varied. They were reluctant to 'assimilate' while it meant giving up all previous languages, religions and cultures. Moreover, they were acquiring the vote and using it. This was the force behind the change to 'multiculturalism' in the 1970s (Lopez 2000; Jupp and Kabala 1993).

Most of the newcomers were Christian (mainly Catholic or Orthodox) and were willing to learn English provided their own languages were preserved for private and social use. Their food was interesting and began the massive gastronomic revolution that eventually swamped even the specifically multicultural Special Broadcasting Service. But many influential Australians never accepted any form of multiculturalism, however limited.

An important factor in the shift towards multiculturalism was the retirement of political leaders who had been brought up under White Australia, most notably Sir Robert Menzies (Liberal) and Arthur Calwell (Labor). A generation change produced the likes of Malcolm Fraser (Liberal) and Gough Whitlam (Labor), both with the election of a younger generation of followers and the support of a changing electorate. Organizational changes in Commonwealth and states consolidated these reforms at least until the inflow of Asian refugees from Vietnam and Timor in 1975. Multiculturalism, like assimilation, was never rigidly defined but assumed not only acceptance but equality for non-English-speaking Europeans. As this group declined and Asians increased, more arrivals were not Christians, distinguishing them from the post-war refugees. Many would not have passed the White Australia barrier. But until the outbreak of violence in the Muslim world, multicultural policies and organizations were able to secure toleration and even a level of influence on public policy.

Australian multiculturalism succeeded in creating a more varied and interesting urban society, which was widely welcomed, except by rigorous conservatives who saw it as a threat to the British inheritance. Among these were the Liberal leader, John Howard, and the founder of the One Nation party, Pauline Hanson. Their counterrevolution began during the Bicentennial year of 1988. It grew with the increasing Asian and then specifically Muslim intakes by the turn of the century. At the core of this intake were a growing number of refugees. The official expectation shifted towards 'cohesion' and 'integration', which under conservative governments began to look like 'assimilation' all over again (Jupp and Clyne 2011). However, the previous search for similar and voluntary immigrants had to give way to refugees from warfare, oppression and serious poverty.

Chapter 15

REFUGEES AND WAR

Much that concerns Australia is determined by the politics of the Asia–Pacific region. Control over migration, the economy and the composition of the society have been increasingly dictated by external influences and threats. Migration policy does not develop in peace. On the contrary, there have been more wars and revolutions than ever before and larger numbers fleeing from them and from persecution. As demand has grown, the Australian response has contracted. Permanent settlement has been modified by temporary visas for employment, education and family reunion. Racism no longer dictates policy, as it did for a century. But virtually all asylum seekers recently interned or returned have been from non-European societies.

Rather than individual persecution, international and civil wars became the major cause of seeking refuge, despite thc official concentration on personal cases (Marrus 1985). This has escalated with the breakup of the French, British, Dutch, Belgian and Portuguese empires in Africa and Asia after 1945. The greatest numbers of those seeking refuge have often been created by persecution on an ethnic minority basis, rather than by international warfare, religious or ideological pressure. Little of this had directly affected Australia before the late 1930s, the rise of Nazi Germany and the persecution of the Jews from 1933. Today persecution is the dominant issue.

There are now more refugees in the world than ever before. They have a special status under the United Nations as deserving care and attention. That status is governed by the 1951 Convention Relating to the Status of Refugees; the Protocol Relating to the Status of Refugees of 1967; and Resolution 2198 (xxi) adopted by the United Nations General Assembly. The Protocol covered the whole of the world and was ratified by Australia in 1967, despite the continuing operation of White Australia in its dying days. It was not ratified by most newly independent countries until recently nor, for different reasons, by the United States or the Soviet Union (Loescher 1993).

Previous mass movements caused by wars, revolutions and persecution had not normally received official refugee status before 1920. Nor were mass emigration movements in the nineteenth century, like the Jews from the Russian

Empire or the Irish from the United Kingdom, been officially regarded as creating refugees. Recent civil wars and revolutions, however, do come within the responsibilities of the United Nations High Commissioner for Refugees (UNHCR). Movements caused by famine, desertification or boundary changes are also of concern to United Nations agencies. These include some four million Palestinians and their descendants, formerly resident in the mandated territory of Palestine before 1947 and the responsibility of the UN Relief and Works Agency. The scope and the reasons for seeking refuge are much greater than they had been for the League of Nations. In effect they are not confined to individual fears of persecution. In crises like the end of the Vietnam War in 1975, whole categories might be admitted (Hawthorne 1992; Hayes and Mason 2012; Neumann 2015). This was especially true for refugees from communism in the post-1945 period (Kunz 1988).

Mass movements in Africa and the Middle East now constitute the bulk of refugees fleeing from civil wars, economic collapse, religious and ethnic conflict, starvation and terrorism. They make up the greatest number of refugees in recent years and are housed in large camps under United Nations protection. Few Africans have come to Australia, apart from white expatriates (P. Browne 2006). Other large numbers of refugees are from Afghanistan into Pakistan or Iran, or from Syria and Iraq into Lebanon and Jordan. The majority of refugees are from underdeveloped regions and are settled also in less-developed neighbours. Should peaceful conditions be restored they frequently return to their homelands, but this is often not possible. Australia has selected a small quota from the camps as part of its humanitarian contribution. These have not normally come from the Pacific region, except for the large Indochinese intakes escaping communism after 1975 (Viviani 1992; 1996).

Compared to the vast numbers in the camps, those achieving residence in developed countries like Australia are a small minority. The largest single recipient of refugees for permanent settlement in recent years has been the United States. Most refugees are living in camps or temporary and insecure accommodation. The priority of the UNHCR is that the vast camp populations should return to their homelands when conditions make it safe, which rarely happens. Australia's role in resettlement from African camps has been marginal, leading mainly to the selection of limited numbers from East Africa. Christian organizations have influenced this process for Sudanese coreligionists. Only in specific crises, like the Vietnam War, the wars in Iraq, Syria or Afghanistan, or the collapse of Yugoslavia, has Australia allowed large numbers from a particular source to be admitted. In 2015 it was announced that 12,000 refugees from Syria in UNHCR camps in Lebanon and Jordan would be admitted for permanent residence in Australia. This was exceptional in the face of the greatest mass refugee movement into Europe since the

1940s. Otherwise, all policy has tried to avoid creating concentrated ethnic minorities, or 'ghettoes'. This is incompatible with the aspirations unleashed by multiculturalism in 1978, which relied on such concentrations for the delivery of services.

Not all refugees arrive in states signatory to the United Nations Convention. Acceptance of newcomers is, therefore, not obligatory. They may be generous, as with Muslim states receiving other Muslims, or India's 1948 settlement of mainly Hindu refugees after partition. As in much international law, there is no effective provision for making this compulsory. One requirement of those claiming refugee status (asylum) is that they should be outside their state of origin. Thus, Afghans seeking asylum must move at least to Iran or Pakistan to register as refugees. Several million have done so.

It is harder to access Australia than a state with neighbouring land borders. States with narrow sea crossings will receive many more refugees in small boats than does Australia. The largest refugee movements are across neighbouring land borders in Africa, central Asia and the Middle East. Australia does not have this experience. Nor was it involved in the mass movements by land from Syria in 2015, whose goal was in Germany. This was used by Australian and British opponents of immigration as a warning, but without validity. Britain is an island, with many states to cross before reaching the Channel. Australia is also an island 'girt by sea' as its national anthem claims.

The UN Convention and Protocol are legal documents subject to legal interpretation. Most states require asylum seekers to submit to a verbal or written examination and provision of documents, if available. Otherwise, the system might be swamped by those simply seeking to emigrate for their own benefit. UN official data show that most asylum applications come from states that have experienced wars, revolutions or social chaos. In some societies there have been mass persecutions or disruptions of whole peoples, rather than of individuals. Examples include the Yazidis in Iraq, Hazaras in Afghanistan, the Tamils in Sri Lanka, the Rohingyas in Myanmar and the Hutus in Rwanda. As racist and religious movements grow in strength this may become even more serious. Most refugees from the caliphate/Islamic State have so far been confined to neighbours like Jordan or Lebanon, while Syrians have been streaming into Europe by land only recently, a million aiming for Germany in 2015 by walking across several national borders.

The Convention defines a refugee as someone who is 'unable or unwilling to return to their country of origin owing to a well-founded fear of being persecuted for reasons of race, religion, nationality, membership of a particular social group or political opinion' (Article 1A(2); Vrachnas et al. 2008). Once this status is established, a number of principled obligations come into operation. These include non-penalization and *non-refoulement*. This latter is a fundamental undertaking not to send back to their own country, against their will, anyone who is likely to be persecuted or even killed. It was inherited from the League of Nations. There should be no discrimination on grounds of sex, age, disability or other prohibited factors. There should be no arbitrary detention as a penalty for entering the receiving state illegally. There should be basic standards of treatment, including access to the courts, education, work and a passport (as previously with the League of Nations). These are optimistic objectives. Australia has departed from most of them over the half century since it ratified the Convention in 1954 and the 40 years since ratifying the Protocol. Because Australia maintains a modest and controlled humanitarian programme and support for the UNHCR it escapes much serious criticism, although not all.

The breakup of empires, states and societies and the intervention of major powers disturbs the former quiet isolation of the Pacific region. This creates refugees where none existed before. Australia feels obliged to involve itself in wider disputes, such as failed wars in Vietnam, Afghanistan, Iraq and Syria. Its changed ethnic character also creates commitments further afield in the former Yugoslavia, Lebanon, Egypt and the Middle East. Most significantly its close relationship with the United States leads it into international conflicts well beyond its capacity to make a major contribution (Goot and Tiffin 1992). This has replaced the former reliance on the British Empire, which no longer has any major strategic interests in the region (Ward 2001; Goldworthy 2002) and no longer exists in its historic form. Australia's transfer of loyalty to the United States does not win it much support in many parts of the region. The Australian treatment of refugees appears suspect as well. It overwhelmingly affects non-Europeans, while its military campaigns affect mainly Muslim civilians subject to bombardment and loss of lives and homes.

Chapter 16

THE UNITED NATIONS AND REFUGEES

When the war in Europe ended in 1945, and the United Nations was founded at San Francisco, it was faced with three major problems: the fate of the Jewish population that had survived mass extermination (Bartrop 1994; Blakeney 1985); the presence in Central Europe of several million displaced persons, forcibly removed or voluntarily escaping from the Nazi concentration and labour camp systems; and the need to de-Nazify or put on trial those responsible for this massive chaos. These issues were complicated by the occupation of the most devastated areas by the Soviet Red Army. By a miracle of organization these problems were roughly solved within four years, with Australia playing a major role through the influence of its foreign minister, Herbert Evatt, and its Minister for Immigration, Arthur Calwell (Calwell 1972). Calwell and his officials took an active part in recruiting 181,000 displaced persons to Australia through the International Refugee Organization (Martin 1989). The unavoidable origins of current refugee policy were established in this major crisis in the hope that peace would prevail. It did not, but current refugees are from a different world.

Jews were not included in this scheme, but had separate arrangements negotiated with Calwell and based initially on family reunion (Benjamin 1998; Neumann 2015). These were met with fierce criticism from Australia's incredibly biased print media. The public identification of refugees with Jews, while inaccurate, forced modifications, like the registration as Jews of intending passengers and a quota of 25 per cent maximum for Jewish passengers.

Germans were barred from Australia altogether, as they had been in 1918. Austrians and *Volksdeutsche* were not. No non-Europeans were allowed. Subsequent research shows that many collaborators with the Nazis, including war criminals, used the International Organization for Migration (IOM) system to slip through to Australia, Canada and the United States (Aarons 2001). Escape routes to Latin America had already been organized before the war ended (Aarons 1989; Cesarani 2001; Neumann 2015).

Refugee labour was essential in the rebuilding process and in Australian industrialization. Citizenship was taken up by the great majority selected. This provided security. Communist states did not recognize changes of nationality and often called for the repatriation of their subjects. The displaced persons were to become citizens, not guest workers or temporary residents. This objective was largely achieved and laid the foundations for official multiculturalism.

Australia was not alone in seeking to attract and settle many thousands of wartime refugees living in large camps in Germany, Austria and Italy. The main competitors for refugees were the United States, Canada and Australia. Many were also accepted in Britain, especially the Poles who had served with the Allied forces. A central problem was that many displaced persons were escaping from communism in the Soviet Union, the Baltic and Balkan states and Yugoslavia.

Two major scandals arose from the repatriation of many Cossacks to Russia and many Croatians to Yugoslavia. Most of these disappeared into prison camps or were summarily executed, like the Croatians returned from Bleiburg, the British base in Austria. In both cases the British officials, who controlled this movement, took the conventional view that prisoners-of-war should be returned to their government forces once a war had ended.

The Bleiburg massacres became an 'historic myth' for refugee Croatians, including the large number who were taken to Australia. The record of the Ustashe government of Croatia was also bloodstained, in terms of civilian massacres and support for the Nazis. Many Russians, Ukrainians and Cossacks had joined pro-Nazi military forces under General Vlasov or Stepan Bandera. They were executed, or imprisoned in the *gulag* labour camps of Soviet Siberia.

Poles and Croatians were among the largest nationalities accepted as post-war refugees by Australia (Sutalo 2004). Their histories and loyalties were quite different. This did not stop them from being collectively known as 'DPs' or 'Balts'. They were also collectively condemned by the Australian communists and welcomed by the Liberal Party, and later by the Democratic Labor Party, after the ALP split of 1955 (Murray 1970). The Cold War had already started, the Australian government changed in December 1949, and the national and international communists had become the new enemy.

The 181,000 post-war displaced persons were recruited to Australia by 1954 and moved by the International Refugee Organization. They represented the largest number of non-British immigrants admitted since Federation. Of the 170,070 arriving between 1947 and 1954, 162,966 were citizens of states already under Soviet or communist control, or became so by the end of the programme (Kunz 1988). The largest intakes were from Poland, Yugoslavia and Latvia, and only 4,451 were registered as 'stateless'.

The displaced persons were lodged in former army camps distant from the major cities, the largest being at Bonegilla (near Albury) (Sluga 1988) and Bathurst. They were obliged to remain there until employment was found, which was often in remote locations. Large numbers of foreigners were admitted in such a short time that they would have been very visible in the major cities, where there were also housing shortages. The fear of 'ghettoes' was frequently expressed. All the DPs were white, of course, and virtually none were Jewish. Settlement policy preventing ghettoization was still being urged for the Syrians in 2015 (*Canberra Times* 18 September 2015).

Most DPs came from societies in Eastern and Central Europe with which Australians had no direct experience. The Protestant churches noted that the majority of refugees were Catholics. The unions were wary about the political and industrial threat from immigrants, as they always had been. It was a major task of the new Commonwealth Immigration Department to persuade the voters that there were no problems and that everything was under control. One advantage in this sometimes-heated debate was bipartisan agreement between Labor and Liberals that Australia must 'populate or perish'. Official news programmes helped to modify extreme criticism and racist reactions appearing in the commercial media. The settlement and acceptance roles of the Immigration Department were assimilative, but more welcoming than in recent years. They laid a foundation for settlement services, which in later years were often neglected.

Control was the operative word in managing this novel situation. Most of the DPs had already lived in camps in Europe, often for years. They did not find Australian accommodation particularly rigorous. There was considerable uncertainty about their futures and especially the chance of finding a paying job, which did not exist around Bonegilla or Bathurst. Military units were alerted at Puckapunyal army base near Bonegilla, but never mobilized. Everyone was obliged to take whatever jobs the Commonwealth thought fit. The 'Snowy Mountains Scheme' was particularly favoured. As a public enterprise it paid union wages. The best-paid workers were Norwegian tunnellers, who were not refugees but contract guest workers, familiar with the many Norwegian hydroelectric schemes. Most managerial positions were held by Australian or British citizens.

All males were classified as 'labourers' and all females as 'domestics'. This tradition went back a century to the assisted migrants following the end of the convict system. Regardless of origins or experience, all displaced persons were obliged to accept work anywhere for two years after their arrival in Australia. This was often resented, although awards and union conditions were normally implemented. There are few expressions of gratitude in the memoirs later written (Borin 1959; Panich 1988). Ethnic dancing was an instrument in the official campaign to gain public acceptance. The pictures of women in their 'native costumes' were lodged by the Immigration Department at the National Archives in Canberra.

The 'New Australians', then, were controlled, isolated, homogenized and patronized. The propaganda was mainly directed at the general public rather than the immigrants. New Australians were given contradictory messages: assimilate and speak English, but maintain your picturesque culture for public display: be grateful for being rescued from communism but do not mention the war, or which side you were on. Quite absurd instructions were given: do not wear a hairnet (for men); do not speak loudly in your language in public places; do not form ethnic groups; do not discuss ethnic politics; do not carry briefcases or wear long raincoats; do not settle in the big cities; in other words, be as invisible as possible. Most refugees were fairly young and survived this with a dry sense of humour. But they did not forget their origins and experiences. Similar advice came 60 years later, in the official *Life in Australia* given to all aliens seeking naturalization in 2007. Official attitudes to migrants change slowly.

The displaced persons were the first visibly non-British arrivals after 1945 and bore the burden of majority prejudice and social isolation. They were the founding fathers and mothers of multiculturalism, a word completely unknown to them and their Australian guardians at the time (Jupp 1966). Their churches, organizations and media survived into the present, eventually getting public funding to do so. This was not what the post-war planners expected.

Part of the control mechanism developed for displaced persons was institutionalized for subsequent non-British immigration (still called New Australians). 'Good Neighbour Councils' were set up locally and in each state from 1950. They were funded by the Immigration Department, which also began to appoint welfare workers and to encourage a controlled degree of ethnic self-organization. This began the long period when Immigration took a leading part in settlement, education, social welfare and research, all now reduced except for the humanitarian intake, which has remained stable but limited.

The Good Neighbour movement lasted until 1978, when it was defunded in response to the major review of settlement programmes by Frank Galbally (1978). The Queensland Bjelke-Petersen government funded one separately for several years to reassert its objection to the multicultural objectives of Galbally and the Fraser government. Good Neighbour's appeal was to the British migrants, the Dutch and some of the displaced persons who were fluent in English. Its annual conferences provided a modest opportunity for migrant complaints, but were essentially propaganda exercises for praising Australia and its government. The experience with the displaced persons opened the way for the United Nations Convention on Refugees of 1951 and its ratification by Australia in 1954.

Assimilation was expected but not forced on aliens. The great majority of former refugees sought citizenship under the *Citizenship Act of 1948*. Incentives included access to some social services, especially public housing, and to many occupations, including public service, which were open only to British subjects. When military conscription for overseas service was introduced in 1965 during the Vietnam War, there was considerable public criticism of aliens who were not eligible and were 'not pulling their weight'. The Returned Services League favoured conscripting aliens. This would have discouraged further immigration and caused resident Americans (among others) to lose their US citizenship. It did not happen.

The post-war refugee and immigration programme created two distinct social groups, based on majority prejudices and perceptions. These were the 'New Australians', who included refugees and free immigrants, and the 'migrants', British and Northern Europeans, which included the Dutch and even the Germans after a time. The former were expected to assimilate and take out citizenship, while the latter were assumed to have passed the appropriate tests of assimilation already. Despite suspicion of this novel intake, there was not the fear and hostility more recently expressed for refugees from states once closed by White Australia or arriving from Southern Europe as assisted migrants.

The 'New Australians' were predominantly working class to start with, while the British and Northern Europeans more often secured white collar or managerial jobs because of their superior English (Lever-Tracy and Quinlan 1988). There was however, considerable recruitment of British assisted migrants into South Australia, Victoria and Western Australia as industrial workers. It was only after the shift in immigration policy towards a skilled intake that non-British trade qualifications were recognized. This had caused a generation of frustrated talent that had limited access to previous occupations.

Over the past 70 years since 1945 Australian immigration has passed through several phases and been controlled by many ministers from both major parties. Some of these have been initiators, while others have only done what their departments advised. Priorities and numbers have changed, and sources of immigrants changed even more radically. Since then Australia has been opened up to the entire world. There is no significant country that has not supplied at least a handful of newcomers. British immigration declined to less than 10 per cent, but has risen again through temporary visas such as working holidaymakers, students and skilled workers (457s) rather than family migration as before. Migration from China, India and Southeast Asia has recently predominated. New Zealanders move freely under the Trans Tasman agreement, subject to restrictions in eligibility and charges for some public services.

Change has often been forced on refugee policy by international events and public opinion. Ideally the aim has been to make rational assessments of national needs. But the major events that have forced change have included the end of the World War in 1945, the rise of communism in Asia, the war in Vietnam, the independence of previously colonial Asian societies, internal strife and warfare in Southeast Asia, the rise of Islamic fundamentalism throughout the Middle East and beyond, the collapse of the Soviet system in Russia and Eastern Europe, the expansion of economies in China, Japan, Korea, Taiwan, India and Singapore, and the withdrawal of Britain from its pre-war strength in the Asia–Pacific region. Few of these were expected in 1945.

In 1945 the whole of East Asia and the Pacific, outside China, Japan and Thailand, had been colonies of Britain, France, the Netherlands, Japan and the United States. By the year 2000 only a few island colonies remained. Australia has had no effective influence on any of these major changes, except in Timor and Papua New Guinea (Brawley 1995; Cesari 2013; Walker 1999). The Liberals in the 1950s elections, and the Democratic Labor Party after them, invented a thrust known as the 'Moscow–Peking–Sydney Axis'. Their map showed an imaginary straight line between the two communist capitals and Sydney. This was used to justify wars in Korea, Vietnam and Malaysia, although it was quite imaginary.

Those who wished to preserve Australia's uniquely white British character, like Calwell and Menzies, saw the answer in increased population to manufacture increased defence. Like most politicians these two were firmly bound to the idea that extra people could and should be drawn from Britain, or at least Europe, and that the ravages of war had made this a possibility that had not existed in the depressed 1930s. With the Labor prime minister, Ben Chifley, they found the answer in refugees. Their successors, Whitlam and Fraser, were more broad-minded and laid the necessary foundations for a multicultural society not based on racial uniformity. That was the path of the future, which neither Chifley nor Calwell would have welcomed any more than Menzies.

The displaced persons recruitment had a finite life (Kunz 1988). The Central European camps were cleared of those acceptable to the receiving states by 1954. The communist rulers of the Soviet bloc banned emigration from their tightly controlled states. Refugee escapes from revolts in Czechoslovakia in 1948 and Hungary in 1956 produced large but short-term departures under the UN Convention. The Czech-born population of Australia jumped to 12,000 by 1954, but was unable to increase much after that. The Hungarian-born doubled to 31,000 by 1961, but then remained unchanged. Only Yugoslavs continued to increase under the less-restrictive regime of Marshal Tito. An official agreement was signed in 1970, the only one with a state still under communist control. Yugoslavs were relatively free to emigrate and had moved up into Germany already as guest workers. Australia disapproved of guest worker systems, but allowed employers to recruit to industry from Yugoslavia, Turkey and Greece, which had also contributed to the German system.

With Eastern Europe largely cut off and Northern Europe recovering its pre-war living standards, Australia turned towards Southern Europe as the largest remaining reserve of white migration with any tradition of coming to Australia. The ending of dictatorships in Greece (1974), Spain (1978) and Portugal (1974) and the independence of Malta (1964) were all followed by increases in emigration to Australia. Italy had been sending immigrants since 1891 and the Italian-born peaked in 1971 at 290,000. Migration from these states was not primarily of refugees, except for some Greeks during the dictatorship of 1967 to 1974. Much of it was subsidized by Australia to recruit a manual, industrial working class. Migration from Spain and Portugal proved transitory, as most preferred the short journey into Western Europe or the Latin countries of South America. Immigration to Australia was high from Yugoslavia, the only European communist state.

Essentially, with the development of the European Union communities, Australia was running out of British and European migrants. Numbers dropped off as democracy was restored. White Australia seemed to be risking declining numbers, but these were later sustained from New Zealand and South Africa and periodic increases in British interest. Public opinion seemed resigned to these trends, although the traditional preference for British and Northern Europeans continued.

Unlike the former Jewish refugees, most did not rise into the professions and business, although their children and grandchildren did. The traditional path of the Southern Europeans was through a factory, to a small business or café, and then as proud parents of university graduates. Most Greeks and Italians remained attached to their language and religion and kept links with their home regions. This developed in the multicultural 'golden age' (1972–1996), when refugee recruitment was starting to move towards new parts of the world. Multiculturalism replaced assimilation as official policy from 1973 (Foster and Stockley 1988).

The 'New Australians' and Southern Europeans gradually merged into local societies, especially in the industrial districts of Melbourne, Sydney, Adelaide and Wollongong. American influence was increased through television, which began transmission in 1956. ASIO had a limited interest in possible security problems, mainly from the very large Italian Communist Party and the guerrilla-hardened Greek Communist KKE. They appear to have left ordinary criminal problems to the federal and state police forces.

Where there were problems, which were not investigated until too late, were in the large Calabrian intake of the 1970s and an active cultivation of marijuana in the Murrumbidgee Irrigation District and close to Canberra. This led to the murder of a local Liberal activist, Donald Mackay, and the flight from Griffith (NSW) of locally born notable, Robert Trimbole. He eventually found refuge in Ireland, later dying in Spain in 1987, aged 56. The majority of Italians moved outwards to the suburbs in the major cities, with a high proportion opening their own small businesses and a select few joining the ranks of the very rich, mainly in building and property. These suburban moves melted the 'ghettoes' that officialdom and the media had worried about, creating space for new ones.

At the same time that multiculturalism was developing as a successful settlement policy for Europeans, Indochina was collapsing into chaos and producing refugees in boats or ending up in southern China, Malaysia, Thailand, the Philippines and Hong Kong. The first boatload landed at Darwin in April 1976. Within 20 years the Vietnam-born population of Australia increased from 2,427 to 151,055 (Grant 1979; Viviani 1996).

Between 1975 and 1982, 509,913 Indochinese emigrated by boat, seeking asylum throughout Southeast Asia, and 515,163 left by land, mainly to China (Viviani 1992). The main points of arrival by water were Thailand and Malaysia, both of which had a policy of sending boats back out to sea. Neither adhered to the UN Convention. The major countries of permanent settlement for Vietnamese between 1975 and 1981 were the United States (269,482), Canada (53,822), Australia (48,054), Germany (15,236) and the UK (15,572). Just over half the total had left Vietnam by boat and the rest by land. The United States and Australia were the only states of these five to participate directly in the war. The French had already left.

Given the controversies then and now about 'boat people' landing on Australian shores, it should be noted that between 1975 and 1982 these totalled only 2,059, compared with 55,711 arriving by air with official approval. Australia also accepted 5,919 from Laos and 6,188 from Kampuchea (Cambodia) in the same period. The central problems of Indochinese refugee policy were resolved at Geneva in 1979 by the Orderly Departure Program. This was based on agreement by Vietnam to discourage refugees from departing, for Southeast Asian states to allow them to land and seek refugee status, and for the major Western recipients to process them quickly. This policy worked.

This cooperative model, to which Australia made a valuable contribution, would not necessarily work in different situations. But it was far more acceptable to the UNHCR and to contributing states than current unilateral Australian policies of stopping the boats altogether and denying anyone on them the right to seek permanent asylum in Australia. Many of these have been from Afghanistan, where Australia had actively involved itself in rather futile warfare, as previously in Vietnam (Maley 2002). Relations with communist Vietnam and China became positively amicable after the Viet Cong and North Vietnamese victory.

The mass exodus from Indochina effectively marked the end of the White Australia policy and the start of a new era of mass evacuation from war-torn or post-war former colonial societies. Apart from Vietnam these included Lebanon, with its established, mainly Catholic, community in Australia, and East Timor, also largely Catholic, with its proximity to Darwin. (Neumann 2015).

Immigration from Britain and Europe was in decline. Problems were not confined to Asian neighbours. Yugoslavia, with 150,000 immigrants in Australia from a variety of backgrounds, burst into chaos and ethnic cleansing in 1990. This flowed over into the contested province of Kosovo. (Silber and Little 1996). The response of Australia to this series of crises was creditable. The Immigration Department counted its response as one of its triumphs. Between 1976 and 2001, numbers born in the former Yugoslavia increased from 143,591 to 192,099. The Kosovars were only eligible for short-term 'safe haven' visas, and most returned to what eventually became an independent country. Their 'safe haven' visas were being quoted as relevant to the mass exodus from Syria in 2015.

The Immigration Department does not normally publish official figures for religion, only for birthplace and nationality. However, the five-yearly Census shows the formation of Christian minorities quite clearly. These included Assyrians from Iraq, Anglican Dinka from Sudan, Maronites and Chaldeans from Lebanon, and Copts from Egypt, all from Muslim states with a revival of religious persecution and nationalism. The Muslim Kosovars were mostly given temporary residence over a short period. One new refugee group from communism were Orthodox Christians from Ethiopia, who mainly set up their institutions in Victoria.

Most of these rescue operations were organized between Australia, the UNHCR and the Anglican, Catholic and Protestant churches. They were not widely publicized. They followed in an earlier tradition of accepting Russian Orthodox from China, organized between Australia and the World Council of Churches. They show the extent to which the visa system is elastic in emergencies and can respond to crises as they arise. During the later restrictions on asylum seekers by boat it was argued that everyone granted residence was taking a place from someone who had gone through the orderly process. This was only true because Australian governments made it so. Twenty years previously they had made it possible.

The refugee system after 1975 became increasingly overcrowded as government after government fell to rebels or by civil war. The relatively small rescue operations for Christians were diminishing in their capacity to solve this problem. Moreover, many civil wars in the Arab world were between different Muslim sects and especially between Sunni, favoured by Saudi Arabia, and Shia favoured by Iran. Muslim populations in Bosnia and Chechnya were severely attacked in response to their rebellion against Serbian and Russian domination respectively. Bosnian Muslims were accepted by Australia as part of its long-term commitment to Yugoslav immigration. Muslims in Syria, Iraq and Libya were at war with each other. In Africa post-colonial governments were falling before internal and external enemies, driving literally millions into UNHCR camps. Australia took a very limited role in most of this, as it was entitled to do. Its large Sudanese refugee intake was cut from 70 per cent of the refugee intake to 20 per cent, by an arbitrary decision of the Liberal Minister for Immigration, Kevin Andrews.

The escalating numbers of refugees put growing pressure on states like Australia, which had taken their responsibilities seriously but carefully. One solution to these problems was suggested by the policy adopted towards Chinese students during the Tiananmen Square demonstrations of June 1989. There were thousands of Chinese students in Australia at the time. Prime Minister Bob Hawke, who was visibly disturbed by television images of students being attacked and crushed, promised that no Chinese students present in Australia at the time need return to China if they preferred to stay. This took the Immigration Department by surprise. They quickly cobbled together a scheme of temporary protection, which came to be used with increasing frequency as crises developed. Many Chinese students returned home, but many remained behind. Between 1986 and 2006 the People's Republic of China–born (excluding Taiwan and Hong Kong) increased by 169,122, a much larger increase than at any time in Australian history. China became the largest source of immigrants by 2015, but many were students on temporary visas.

Temporary visas were criticized as creating uncertainty. They could be terminated or reviewed by the Immigration Department and did not guarantee permanent residence. Nevertheless, Chinese graduates were in great demand in Australia and many eventually achieved permanence and citizenship. This enhanced their chances of family reunion. Visas leading to permanent settlement were recently replaced for guest workers, refugees and working holidaymakers, which did not normally lead to permanent residence. However, temporary visas for refugees were restored in 2014, following major changes in refugee policy.

Temporary visas of a special type were introduced to deal with the ethnic cleansing of Kosovo by Serbia in 1998. The Kosovars are predominantly Albanian Muslims who subsequently achieved independence from Serbia (Silber and Little 1996). Internal warfare produced mass movements, which were handled by the Organisation for Security and Cooperation in Europe. Australia gave its support on condition that Kosovars would not be accepted as permanent residents. Protection Visas satisfied this. Four hundred were shipped out through Macedonia and flown to Australia. They were mainly unskilled rural people, Muslims and possibly members of the Kosova Liberation Army. They were housed in army camps two hundred kilometres from Melbourne. The Melbourne and Shepparton Albanian communities offered their assistance, but were warned off. No possibility of permanent residence or asylum was held out and they were transported back to the Balkans as winter set in. This was a noble gesture and well organized. But it began an era when asylum and permanent residence would become much more difficult or impossible for many. By 1991 the floodgates were widely open. In the view of many officials and politicians it was time to start closing them.

Chapter 17

MANDATORY DETENTION

It was precisely at the peak of Chinese and Yugoslav immigration in 1991 that mandatory and irrevocable detention of asylum seekers arriving by boat without a visa was introduced. These significant numbers represented the only uncontrolled element in the immigration intake. Asylum seekers arriving by air without a valid visa were treated differently. Airline companies were liable to meet their return expenses, a penalty that goes back to the early steamship days. Arrivals by air with a refugee visa issued by Australian authorities overseas were allowed entry. Only refugees approved by the UNHCR were flown in at Australian expense, many of them from Africa. Other arrivals by air seeking asylum were normally given a bridging visa while they were being assessed as refugees.

The new policy, which was to become permanent in 1992, was a response to political events in Cambodia leading to the mass slaughter of civilians by the Pol Pot Khmer Rouge communists. This alerted Immigration Department officers to the possibility of yet another 'flood gate' being opened. They persuaded Labor minister Gerry Hand of the need for this serious restriction. In the light of anxiety among voters, the ALP endorsed the new policy and continued to do so for the next 25 years, with the active support of the Liberal/National coalition and only brief modifications under prime ministers Bob Hawke and Kevin Rudd. This policy of 'irrevocable, mandatory detention' for unvisaed arrivals by boat, opened up the system of prison-like camps in remote areas and eventually outside Australia altogether in Nauru and Manus Island. Apart from deportation, this was the most oppressive policy adopted since 1945 (O'Neill 2008; Pickering 2005).

This new approach was not consistent with the terms of the United Nations Convention Relating to the Status of Refugees. One fundamental principle was 'non-penalization' and 'being arbitrarily detained purely on the basis of seeking asylum'. Asylum seekers rights included 'access to the courts (Article 16), to primary education and the provision for documentation'. There was also an expectation that 'refugees lawfully in its territory' have the right to choose their place of residence, to move freely in its territory, subject to any regulations applicable to aliens generally in the same circumstances' (Article

26). This was clearly incompatible with detention in a remote centre from which there was no lawful escape. The contracting states 'shall not impose penalties on account of their illegal entry or presence, on refugees coming directly from a territory where their life or freedom was threatened, provided they present themselves without delay to the authorities and show good cause for further illegal entry or presence' (Article 31). As Afghanistan is landlocked it could be argued that asylum seekers had not arrived 'directly'. However, this could not be argued for Sri Lankan Tamils with access by sea.

One effect of the mandatory detention policy was to cover Australia and neighbouring islands with detention centres, most of them unfit for prolonged human habitation. Some of these occupied disused army or miners' camps. Some consisted mainly of tents. Some went on being used for many years. Others were abandoned after only a few, having cost millions to construct. It is not stretching historic comparisons too far to say that they replicate some aspects of the convict system in the first half of the nineteenth century, including the use of remote islands and locations. Eventually, enclosed centres became so overburdened that many detainees were released into community detention, with conditions approximating being on bail while awaiting trial. However, they were not on trial for any offence.

Previous reception centres had been open, which encouraged movement and work in the community. They provided food and shelter and were, in many cases, used by approved educational and welfare services as part of the settlement process. They were particularly useful for refugees and most were placed in metropolitan districts. They conformed to the expectation of the UN Convention that contracting states 'shall as far as possible facilitate the assimilation and naturalization of refugees' (Article 34). The new centres did none of this, but left their inmates in a state of anxiety and boredom. The only certainty for most inmates after 2000 was that they would not get permanent residence in Australia. The leaders of both major parties had said so.

Mandatory detention was introduced for boat arrivals from 1991 and validated by law in 1992. Centres assumed punitive functions, were locked and eventually sold off to private prison companies with foreign and inappropriate experience. Large international companies like Serco, Transfield and G4S were already being criticized for conditions in their British detention centres. The distinction between reception centres and detention centres should not be confused. The former were completely consistent with the UN Convention. The latter were not. The Immigration Department claimed to adhere to the basic *refoulement* principle (Article 23), prohibiting return to the persecuting state. By 2010 Australia was offering return as a way of escaping from indefinite detention and agreeing with Iran, Vietnam and China to expedite this. Iran refused to take back anyone forced to return.

By 2014 the Australian navy was assisting in the return to Sri Lanka of asylum seekers who had not yet touched on Australia's already extensive migration zone. They were all transferred to Nauru, where they became 'transferees' awaiting processing, with the warning that none would be settled in Australia. The inclusion of about 50 children did not influence the minister to move them to Christmas Island, where appropriate provision might be made. During the major changes of 2014 it was promised that children would be withdrawn from Nauru. This persuaded some independent senators to support the overall changes, which were not fully implemented. The need to remove children from detention was emphasized in an official report in 2004 (Ozdowski 2004). The practice continued except at all-male Manus.

There was no force other than the public expression of UNHCR criticism, which could ensure the application of the basic Convention principles. Australia steadily and consciously departed from most of them. It removed Christmas Island and Cocos/Keeling from the Australian migration zone by the *Border Protection (Validation and Enforcement) Act of 2001*. This was later extended for the migration zone to include the whole of Australia and its adjacent islands. The UNHCR view was that this was 'unique'. Asylum seekers landing from boats anywhere in Australia, its islands and reefs as far away as Cocos, were now deemed not to have landed in Australia at all and thus had no claim on asylum. By 2014 boats were being turned back to Sri Lanka when they had reached Cocos.

The first detention centre under the new regime was at Port Hedland on the north-western coast, 1,700 kilometres from the nearest city (Perth). It was in a developing mining area and was located in disused miners' premises. The surrounding territory was so thinly inhabited that a group of Chinese refugees, wrecked on the neighbouring coast, walked for two weeks without seeing a human being. Another detention centre, which later gained more notoriety, was in disused hutments at Woomera, the deserted centre of post-war atomic explosions. This was more accessible, and demonstrators were able to reach it in later years, along 200 kilometres of desert road through uninhabited country. During demonstrations a number escaped but voluntarily returned. Because of its relative access from Port Augusta and deteriorating accommodation, Woomera was closed in 2003.

Its replacement, closer to Port Augusta, was the custom-built, prison style, state of the art, Baxter. Despite its modern facilities, close security and considerable cost, it was closed down in 2007, only five years after it was opened. Other remote detention centres included Curtin in the Northern Territory, utilizing former air force buildings, which opened in 1995. Two metropolitan and permanent detention centres remained in Sydney and Melbourne. The official policy of the Abbott Liberal Coalition was to have all refugee processing offshore in Nauru and Manus Island, using Christmas Island as a dispersal point. All mainland detention centres were to be closed from 2015, following the principle that nobody arriving by boat should land on Australian soil. Arrivals by boat were, ideally, never to set foot on Australia, even if their processing showed them to be genuinely escaping from torture or brutality. Women and children were not excluded, although only men were detained on Manus, arguably more unsuitable and unprepared than Nauru or Christmas Island. Women and children were subject to attack and harassment on Nauru, and Manus became known for its regular violent rioting. Australia was said to be the only state in the world to detain children without adequate protection.

Whatever they may have been called, these were undoubtedly prisons in fact and as isolated (comparatively) as Norfolk Island or Macquarie Harbour in the convict days. They were all privatized in 1998, passing under the control of several overseas-owned prison companies, mainly Serco, Transfield and G4S. Their staff expertise, if any, was in handling convicted felons. This did not make inmates easier to control, and rioting became a serious problem. The Immigration Department could pass some of the responsibility back to the companies, but this did not relieve the responsibility of its minister. An official review was held on Manus following rioting leading to a death in February 2014 (Cornall 2014).

Eventually, processing of asylum seekers arriving by boat was concentrated on Christmas Island, Nauru, and Manus Island. These had the advantage that they could not be reached by demonstrators and only by officials and the media by special permission. Media access was made as difficult as possible, with $8,000 being charged for a Nauruan visa. But little stands in the way of an ambitious journalist and a human-interest story. The remote detention centres soon produced a large and telling literature. Having stopped the boats for six months the government was faced with the dilemma of what to do with those it had consequentially detained. Its preferred solution was to send them back to their original countries, even offering to pay their fares. A handful of Sri Lankans and Iranians accepted. Most did not. An agreement with Cambodia saw six 'transferees' sent to Cambodia in 2015 for 'permanent settlement'. With a change of government in Sri Lanka in January 2015 it is probable that more Sri Lankans will return home, depending on policy towards the Tamil north. Cambodia, having taken the considerable sums offered for accepting 'transferees', abandoned the scheme in August 2015.

Australian isolation was beyond the dreams of most other asylum states. The United Kingdom toyed with the idea of remote islands, but could not find any ready or willing to be used. Its major detention centre at Yarl's Wood was managed by Serco and has been a regular source of criticism and complaint. However, it is scarcely 'remote' at Milton Ernest, a village on the main road, four miles north of the county town of Bedford with a fast rail link to London. New Zealand was already remote enough not to receive many refugee boats and did not share Australian anxieties. Australia became unique for its prisons in the Pacific, as it had been two centuries before. Only Russia in the wilds of Siberia had built a complete prison system so remote from major population centres, if on a very much larger scale. The location of comparable Chinese centres is usually unknown.

The punitive aspect of the 'prisons in the Pacific' was expected to discourage a flood of boats as asylum seekers emerged from civil-war situations in Afghanistan or Sri Lanka. Facilities at Christmas Island were becoming stretched, and many of the mainland detention centres were closing down due to the expense of maintenance and control and the policy of offshore processing. The Rudd Labor government, elected in 2007, withdrew from Nauru and its minister, Senator Chris Evans, alleviated some of the more restrictive provisions left by his Liberal predecessors. As might have been expected (and probably was by the Immigration Department) there was an upsurge in arrivals, especially from Afghanistan and Sri Lanka. These created a major backlog, settled under supervision on bridging visas over very long waiting periods. About three thousand, including women and children, were again imprisoned in Nauru and Manus, while a few unfortunates faced lifelong detention, at least in theory. None of those interned had been tried for anything.

The basic problem by then was that organized criminal groups in Pakistan, Indonesia and, to a lesser extent, Sri Lanka, had a highly organized booking system, using incentives to boat owners and bribes to police, catering for a backlog of demand. These also serviced communities within Australia seeking reunification with their relatives, but blocked by the limited and unmoving quota available through family reunion. Obstacles had been placed in the way of Sri Lankan Tamils in particular, leaving women and children behind as the husband pioneered the way, as in most immigration movements. Consequently, many subsequent boats were full of women and children, including some which were unseaworthy. While most boats got through, there were several disastrous losses of life.

This gave Australian officials and politicians an opportunity to denounce the criminal organizers, who were mainly in Indonesia, and to defend policy on the basis of 'saving lives'. It was an example of a complex game being played out which made it impossible to gain asylum except for those granted visas in consultation with UNHCR or by direct ministerial intervention. The object of the game was to prevent any uncontrolled immigration to Australia, while presenting a public face of rectitude and compliance with 'international obligations'. A large and growing official justification, academic literature and legal reasoning arose to back either side in the argument. Most of it deplored mandatory detention and offshore processing but was officially ignored.

This game could have been resolved by closer liaison with the port authorities and security machinery in Indonesia and Sri Lanka and a more generous allowance of places to regional asylum seekers. The massive destruction of the Tamil Tiger forces in their 2009 defeat did not produce any comparable assistance for Sri Lankans. On the contrary, Tamils were regarded with great suspicion by Australian authorities, despite the fact that they have made excellent immigrants in the past. As possible revolutionaries they came into the time-honoured category of security risks (but not as communists or Muslims). No terrorist activities by Tamils in Australia were prosecuted. The only charges ever considered and then abandoned were for making financial donations to the Tamil Tigers, which was not a prohibited organization. The new Sri Lankan government began legal proceedings against the alleged crimes of its predecessors in 2015, but did not refer to asylum seekers.

The Australian bureaucracy does not want to lose control. Refugee situations challenge that. This is not a good reason for holding children in detention or punishing people who want to escape from unbearable conditions, even at the risk of their own lives. It is a good reason for an effective system of distinguishing those entitled to protection from those who are using the asylum system to gain entry to Australia for other reasons. It is also a good reason for more effective intelligence work in the points of departure for the boats, which are mainly in Indonesia, Malaysia and Sri Lanka. In 2011 the main nationalities of those in detention were Afghanistan, Iran, Sri Lanka, Iraq, Indonesia, Vietnam and Myanmar.

These societies have generated refugees in very substantial numbers over the past thirty years for very good reasons, including warfare. They are predominantly in the Pacific region and all have major family and social links with Australia. All except Afghanistan and Pakistan have relatively well-educated populations with English as a *lingua franca*. Three of them are not predominantly Muslim. Iraq and Iran were catered for in the humanitarian stream. Both were Islamic societies. Many refugees from Iraq were actually Christians, which was not made very apparent in official or media arguments. Just as refugees became identified wrongly as Jews in 1948, refugees from these massively destructive wars became identified as Muslim Arabs, which Sri Lankans, Afghans and Orthodox Christians were not. This was not a deliberate lie, but simply a response serving the purpose of turning public opinion away from sympathy. Moving from 'asylum seekers' to 'illegals' was an important shift from the Labor governments of Rudd and Gillard to the Liberal government of Tony Abbott. The involvement of Australian troops in the Muslim world also gave credence to the notion that refugees had been enemies.

Chapter 18

'STOP THE BOATS'

Attempts to discourage the growing refugee flow escalated under Howard, Rudd, Gillard and Abbott. This unleashed a rush of misinformation from the more conservative media. The effective humanitarian argument was used by both major parties that stopping the boats would also stop the deaths at sea, which were the fault of the criminals who provided unseaworthy vessels. Shipwrecks of Suspected Illegal Entry Vessels (SIEVs) were publicized and this moral argument influenced Labor politicians especially. Others raised the counter point that locking up refugees for years in remote islands with no knowledge of their fates and long delays at processing, might not only be cruel, but also fatal, contrary to the UN Convention and liable to create rioting.

One ignoble lie was officially spread in October 2001. A broken-down refugee boat, officially called SIEV 4, with 223 people on board, was stopped by an Australian navy warship and then sent on its way. A man was reported as holding a life-jacketed child overboard. Through an exchange of official messages this became inflated to the untrue statement that refugees were throwing their children overboard. This myth eventually reached the prime minister's Department and prompted John Howard to state publicly that 'I do not want people like this in Australia'. This was not unreasonable, if he accepted the rumour as true. However, a subsequent inquiry showed that it was not (Weller 2002). Media coverage was extensive and produced a strong reaction against asylum seekers, which the government did nothing to modify. The whole incident occurred against the background of an impending general election, which Howard won.

This myth and others like it survived and were widely used in defending the offshore internment policy. Liberal politicians persuaded their Labor counterparts that 'saving lives' was their priority, which was another noble lie. Of the 52,000 boat arrivals during the relaxed Labor rules of 2007, 98 per cent had arrived safely. Tragically, 2 per cent drowned because of unseaworthy boats, but this was not catastrophic enough to form the centrepiece of years of propaganda attacks on liberalization. If the Border Protection fleet could turn boats around (as it does) it could also return them to safety. In fact, under military-style secrecy, the 'noble lie' that mandatory detention had stopped the boats and saved lives became quite untrue. Boats continued to come, but were turned around to their place of origin, which was usually Indonesia. Lives were saved by breaching the Convention veto on *refoulement*. The notion that refugee protection was an obligation remained alive but scarcely very central. Governments of both persuasions agreed on the need to control intakes as strictly as possible. Unfortunately, the demand for asylum did not diminish as it had done after the world wars.

Chapter 19

FINDING A DECENT DUMPING GROUND

Successive Australian governments have adopted various devices for 'solving' their rather modest problems of unvisaed arrivals by boat. One problem was the limited number of Convention signatories in the immediate region. Australia and New Zealand were almost alone, until Australia started offering financial and aid inducements to sign, which appealed to small and impoverished states. The United States did not sign international conventions, which required Congressional approval. Their traditional view was that the 50 states were independent parties who should not be committed to international agreements. This did not prevent the United States from being very active in the acceptance of refugees. Indonesia, Malaysia, Thailand, Singapore, Sri Lanka, India, Pakistan, Nepal, Brunei, Myanmar, Malaysia, Vietnam, Laos, Micronesia, Maldives, Bangladesh, Vanuatu and several minor Pacific states, were not signatories. The larger of these had considerable refugee populations already.

Most who are signatories, have only recently signed: Cambodia (1992), Fiji (1968), China (1982), Nauru (2011), Papua New Guinea (1986), Philippines (1981), Samoa (1988), Solomons (1995), Timor Leste (2003), Tuvalu (1986). The majority of these are very small and undeveloped. It is not surprising that Australia saw itself as limited to Timor, Nauru, Papua New Guinea and Cambodia, all poor and unsuitable. Australia is the richest state in this corner of the world, and neighbours may feel that its 'burden' is rather slight compared with theirs. The High Court has blocked relocation of non-signatories like Malaysia on the grounds of their inability to meet the Convention requirements.

Moreover, some of these unsigned states produced refugees who sought asylum in Australia, creating a mutual obligation of sorts once peace was restored. These included Timor Leste, Fiji, China, Sri Lanka, Nepal, Myanmar, Bangladesh and, of course, Vietnam, Cambodia and Laos. Few of these had any intention of being used by Australia for its unwanted arrivals. Some, like China or Vietnam might have considered the proposal insulting. Many regional states that are not Convention signatories have taken in very large numbers of refugees, especially India. Their refugee situation is not always secure or pleasant, but it is judged by them as safer than staying at home. The boats, trucks, buses and trains will still be moving refugees in Southeast Asia, whatever Australia does.

The Liberal/National government committed itself to a 'Pacific Solution' for the arriving boatloads by using distant Nauru, an independent state of about 10,000 people, which had always relied on Australia for economic support. Boats were initially unloaded at the Australian Christmas Island territory, and the passengers sent on to Nauru as the 'Pacific Solution'. Those accepted as genuine refugees were given temporary protection visas rather than permanent residence in Australia. After a strike by detainees the great majority were allowed to settle in Australia. They included nearly all the 4,000 rescued from the *Tampa* in 2001, the largest single number of asylum seekers ever rescued, causing a standoff between the Norwegian tanker ship and the Australian government. The 'Pacific Solution' had temporarily failed (Brennan 2003; Marr and Wilkinson 2003).

The use of two small islands to isolate the unwanted was strangely reminiscent of the convict days, when recalcitrants were sent to Norfolk Island or Macquarie Harbour. Nauru was rejected as a detention centre in 2008 by the newly elected Labor government of Kevin Rudd. Faced with increased arrivals of Sri Lanka Tamils after the defeat of the Tamil Tigers in 2009, the government tried to get the cooperation of Indonesia in settling asylum seekers. This failed and began a series of increasingly bizarre programmes of trying to unload Australia's modest problems on poorer countries. The brief Labor attempt to liberalize the system and bring it closer to the original Convention changed to became more hostile to boat arrivals than ever before, with governments from both parties competing over various 'solutions'. All of these depended on the acquiescence of states smaller and poorer than Australia, including two (Timor and Nauru), which had been totally dependent. Timor graciously declined, but Nauru accepted, was then cancelled by Labor and then recommissioned by the Liberals.

An agreement with Malaysia to exchange asylum seekers from Australia with others from Malaysia was rejected by the High Court in 2010. The offer made by Julia Gillard's Labor government was to exchange four hundred refugees for one thousand asylum seekers from several different states. What the advantage of this to Australia might have been was never revealed. The 'solution' was rejected by the High Court on the basis that a non-signatory could not be legally obliged to implement the full requirements of the Convention and Protocol. A brief attempt to send asylum seekers to Cuba on an exchange basis quietly died.

The 'Malaysian Solution' followed the 'Pacific Solution' into the dustbin of history, only to be taken out again in a different form by the Liberal/National government elected in 2013. Malaysia was not a Convention signatory, but it took in a substantial number of asylum seekers, mostly from Muslim countries. An Australian media campaign showed that these lived in squalid and insecure conditions, were subject to arbitrary deportation at the whim of the Malaysian government, and were regularly harassed by the Malaysian police. The Malaysian government, no doubt insulted by this criticism, ceased negotiating. Indonesia and Sri Lanka assisted Australia in preventing the departure of boats, but neither was interested in retaining the passengers, apart from their own citizens.

This was followed by a hurried attempt to sign up several very small countries that were heavily dependent on Australian aid, most notably Nauru and Timor Leste. Christmas Island remained a holding station. The latest addition to 'prisons in the Pacific' was Manus Island, two hundred miles off the north coast of Papua New Guinea. Like Nauru, PNG had been signed up to the Convention to meet the earlier objections of the High Court. As with the convict islands of nearly two centuries ago, Nauru was too remote for escape. It was 300 miles from the nearest other small island. Despite the approval of the PNG government, the political and social situation on Manus was relatively explosive, and the scandalous conditions in the tent-based detention centre were soon exposed to the Australian public. These included violence, rape and murder, as well as suicide attempts.

The final punishment in the policy of dumping asylum seekers on poorer countries was imposed after a foolish claim by Labor prime minister, Kevin Rudd, during the election of 2013, which he lost. Without any debate or legal challenge he announced that nobody who had arrived by boat without a visa would 'ever' secure permanent residence in Australia. This was seized upon by the Liberals after their victory and became their official policy. A similar claim had been made by John Howard while prime minister, but it disappeared. It caused considerable unhappiness among those in various detention centres and was claimed by many to have sparked riots that took place in Nauru, Christmas Island and eventually Manus. This was the first occasion on which boat arrivals could not expect Australian residence, even if they were judged to be genuine refugees. The suggestion that they should settle in PNG or Cambodia indicates the desperation and contempt of the Australian government. The ancient British principle that no government should seek to bind its successor was ignored.

The boats were stopped or turned around for six months between 2013 and 2014, when two set out from Pondicherry in South Indian Tamil Nadu. Passengers were surrounded in mystery under the naval operations practice of secrecy, but were believed to be Sri Lankan and Indian Tamils. The smaller of the two boatloads was returned to Sri Lanka, where the passengers were tried at Galle for leaving the country without permission. The much larger of the two boats was not in Australian or Sri Lankan migration zones, and its crew claimed to be heading for New Zealand. The passengers were locked away in a lower deck without windows on an Australian Customs boat, awaiting a High Court decision. Failing any agreement to talk with Indian government representatives, they were transferred to Christmas Island and flown directly to Nauru to await processing, with the warning that they would 'never' be settled in Australia, whatever their status might prove.

Australia and Sri Lanka had been working together since the end of the civil war in 2009. Australian leaders, including the prime minister, Tony Abbott, had gone out of their way to praise post-war restructuring and to deny the criticism of other governments, including Canada and the United Kingdom. Australia and Sri Lanka created a joint naval exercise, which made departure from Sri Lanka increasingly difficult. The election of a different Sri Lankan government in 2015 made it possible that asylum pressures from there will decline. Sri Lanka has been an important source of immigrants to Australia for many years. Its new government would expect that to continue without undue pressures and obstacles, if only to reduce the unhappy population.

Sri Lanka is not a signatory to the Convention nor a recipient of many refugees. Its interest is to restrain its large and critical Tamil diaspora by preventing its citizens from leaving without permission. With Sri Lanka unable to take anyone back because of *refoulement*, Australia began negotiations with India. These resolved that India would take back Indian citizens and possibly others who could establish their refugee claims against Sri Lanka. This would only be done if the 157 passengers on the larger boat were landed in Australia and then interviewed by Indian officials. Australia accepted this highly unusual arrangement. The asylum seekers were flown from Cocos to Derby in Western Australia, to be held for questioning at the Curtin detention centre in a remote location, 235 kilometres from Broome and 2,416 kms from Perth. They were transferred through Christmas Island to Nauru after they had refused to talk with Indian officials.

Thus, the new century ushered in a de facto Australian departure from the UN Convention and the imposition of a system under which only those chosen by Australian official processes could expect to settle in Australia, however dire were their homeland experiences. All other asylum applicants arriving by boat were given a choice: they could return home, however dangerous that might be; they could settle in one of the poor countries that agreed with Australia to take them; they could remain in detention until policy changed; they could employ a lawyer to plead any special case; or they could try to get support from refugee advocates, especially if their family was broken up. These opportunities are in declining order of likely success. The most unfortunate are those with an unfavourable security clearance from ASIO. The otherwise sympathetic High Court had ruled that they could be lawfully kept in detention forever. One hundred and eighty years ago a convict with a ticket of leave would have been in a much more favourable position.

Unless policy changes for the better (which would require bipartisan support) this means that 'refugees' are now those chosen by the Department of Immigration in consultation with the UNHCR and ASIO and are normally well qualified for future employment. They will not necessarily come from anywhere near Australia or a particularly oppressive state. The 'transferees' will be in detention, awaiting transfer back home or to an agreed country, other than Australia. They will be moved as quickly as possible from Christmas Island to Nauru to be processed by Nauruans, or interned on Manus Island until their case is resolved and the responsibility has passed to the Papua New Guinea government. Australia will pay for this, supervise it through private companies and pass any blame over to the Nauruans or PNG if anything goes wrong. It did in the rioting of February 2014, which led to a violent death. Blame for this serious disorder was shifted between the Iranian 'transferees', the private company guards, the local police and the villagers. The Australian Minister for Immigration, Scott Morrison, was visibly disturbed, but ignored Australian criticism that he should resign. He was later promoted.

This very neat system for depriving 'transferees' of any power or rights is obviously not without problems. It sparked violent reactions, notably at Manus. It will not be well received by the United Nations and its agencies, including the UNHCR. Department of Foreign Affairs and Trade officials still place some importance on good international relations, which has often led to different policy positions from Immigration. Australia spent much labour and money on being elected to the UN Security Council. A well-organized, well-educated and very vocal minority opinion has grown up and influenced policy marginally. The major obstacle for this large group has been the recalcitrance and electoral sensitivity of the ALP. That party is in a state of flux and cannot be written off completely, especially as it might need Green support to govern.

As argued throughout, immigration and refugee policy comprise an area in which international events are often more important and unpredictable than Australian opinion and politics. The 'problem' is not insoluble and the UN Convention remains a good guide, if too optimistic. The orderly departure programme following the Vietnam War worked well with international cooperation. With previously stable societies like Sri Lanka and Thailand following the path of Afghanistan, Nepal and Ukraine, Australia will find it difficult to avoid its obligations under the Conventions it has signed. Neighbouring states like Indonesia or Malaysia, which are not Convention signatories, will feel unwilling to take over Australia's responsibilities. Australia continues to turn around boats from Indonesia. In June 2015 it was alleged to be paying boat crews to return to Indonesia. It has extended temporary visas to Ukrainians, who are not from the region, but were in Australia at a time of severe dispute with Russia and are white Europeans.

No policy that stands up before Asia and says, 'Go away and take these unwanted people with you' can last forever. Australia has the legal right to limit the numbers seeking refuge and to determine the validity of their applications. But it lacks the moral right to exclude genuine asylum seekers from 'ever' settling in Australia; or the use of remote prison camps for men, women and children in dangerous environments; or to assist in the vilification of refugees and asylum seekers in general; or to evade the Convention that it has signed and operated under for decades; or to twist and turn in the courts and the media with evasions, secrecy and misstatements.

Australia can afford to take a larger humanitarian quota than it does and to settle refugees in a civilized and humane way – as it did for many years from the 1950s. At last in 2015 the mass exodus from Syria began to modify Australian policy. It came too late to save the Abbott government, which was removed by his own party. They remained committed to the legacy of John Howard and Tony Abbott. The farce continued under the next (Turnbull) government, with the 'liberalization' of the Nauru centre. This was to be unlocked, its inmates given the choice of staying in Nauru, going to Cambodia, or returning home. Australia would pay the bills, but Nauru would make the decisions and maintain order. A serious limitation was that nobody who had sought unvisaed asylum through the boats would ever be allowed to settle in Australia. This arrangement is also likely to fail in due course, as Nauru lacks the capacity to manage it. Cambodia has already benefitted from a grant of $22 million for taking precisely two 'transferees'.

Chapter 20

HISTORY AS TRAGEDY AND FARCE

From 1945 until 1990 Australia gradually humanized its immigration and refugee programs. It was accepted that refugees had genuine problems in an unsafe world, that Asians could settle in as well as Europeans, and that organizations and policies should be developed to cater for the needs of new citizens, regardless of their origins. There were still older traditions: submerged historical prejudices against unfamiliar and unfortunate immigrants who might not fit into the dominant British-created society. Some of these prejudices originated in Britain even before 1788. A continuing strand of racism was inherited originally from the British Empire. Fear that Asian numbers might 'open the floodgates' and swamp the small Australian population was time-honoured. These attitudes sustained One Nation between 1997 and 2017 and some relatively minor racist and extremist groups recently. They were also latent in many Australian minds.

These traditions appealed to those within the Immigration Department who had operated the White Australia policy and regretted its ending, as well as hard-line staff within the Compliance Branch of the department who were responsible for ensuring that the 'floodgates' remained firmly locked against unauthorized entrants. These fulltime officials were able to influence their short-term ministers. In practice the 'floodgates' were open to temporary workers, working holidaymakers, students and investors, in larger numbers than for refugees. Those depositing investments of two million dollars or more could look forward to permanent residence and citizenship in due course. The great majority of these were prosperous Chinese.

Other favoured groups were seen as economically productive, but not as permanent residents. Hundreds of thousands of them were living and working in Australia without citizenship by 2010. Some were being exploited by their employers. Most were not and came from countries to which they could return as they thought fit. Others were originally asylum seekers, offered Safe Haven Enterprise Visas if they moved to provincial areas with labour shortages. This was an echo of the directed labour of displaced persons in the 1940s. It was introduced in 2014, but did not guarantee permanent residence to those who had arrived by boat.

Many in the Liberal Party still subscribed to the idea of Australia as a homogenous society dedicated to British traditions. These found their leadership in John Howard, prime minister between 1996 and 2007. However, mandatory detention, the administrative revision that changed the refugee situation and reflected public opinion, was made by the Labor government and Minister for Immigration Gerry Hand. This began an escalation of repression and exclusion with strong echoes of White Australia. All repressive and exclusive policies were, in effect, directed against non-Europeans and especially Muslims. The mandatory detention records show that almost no Europeans were admitted, detained, or processed as asylum seekers. Even the Kosovars, who are predominantly Muslim Europeans, were merely allowed a temporary respite from the self-evident collapse of their society. Bosnian Muslims were accepted under an existing international agreement covering former Yugoslavia.

The most blatant departure from liberal and humane policies in the recent past centres around the adoption and implementation of 'mandatory and irrevocable' detention of those seeking to enter Australia by boat as asylum seekers under the United Nations Convention and the Protocol. This denial of obligations effectively reversed Australian commitment to rescuing and settling individuals and families threatened by other governments, by warfare, revolution and repressive religions and ideologies. The efforts of the Immigration and Border Protection Department were being dedicated to avoiding, ignoring or redefining these obligations, enrolling the support of the Australian Navy and the governments of Papua New Guinea, Sri Lanka and Nauru.

The greatest step in this direction was legislation passed between 2014 and 2015, which effectively freed Australia from its obligations under the UN Convention. This ended the role of appeals tribunals for asylum seekers, denied the legitimacy of the Convention ban on *refoulement*, permitted the turnaround of asylum seeker boats and reserved the right to send unvisaed asylum seekers anywhere in the world. Journalists claimed that 'Scott Morrison [the Minister] is now the most powerful person in government' (*Guardian* 5 December 2014). His movement up the Liberal party hierarchy led to the major portfolio of Social Services and then to Treasurer with the change of government. Promises to restore temporary protection visas, to release children from Nauru detention and to allow bridging visa holders to work, were sufficient to secure support from senators representing minor parties. Labor and the Greens voted against the entire package. The Senate majority was by two votes. The children are still there.

Mandatory and irrevocable detention for boat arrivals has been the key to everything that has developed since 1990. The policy implemented by the

Keating Labor government in 1991 in the face of the Cambodian holocaust, reversed the generous and successful policies pursued since 1950 and the national and international reputation developed over forty years. It was further developed by the Howard and Abbott/Liberal national governments and never denied by the Gillard or Rudd Labor governments. Like White Australia it publicly endorsed no specific racial prohibitions. But like White Australia its impact fell overwhelmingly upon non-Europeans and non-Christians. It breached international conventions on human rights, refugees and children and obstructed the liberation of many thousands from intolerable situations. It was defended by 'noble lies', clever evasions, dishonest appeals and, in the last analysis, by cruelty and inhumanity. It denied the very humane values that popular myth claims to be part of the national inheritance.

The central hypocrisy of the 'Stop the Boats' slogan is that what Australian governments were really trying to do is 'stop the people' in the boats. The quite recent concern with preventing deaths at sea provides a convenient moral cover for keeping out refugees of predominantly Muslim faith and Asian origins. Most are escaping from blood-stained, collapsing societies that can no longer provide them with any security or future. Many are hoping to be reunited with relatives already in Australia. In excluding them, Australia is breaching at least three United Nations conventions to which it is a signatory (Refugees, Human Rights and Rights of the Child). Rescuing unseaworthy boats at sea is hazardous, but central to the law of the sea. It is a task worthy of the Australian navy. In 2001, when the Norwegian captain of the *Tampa* rescued asylum seekers from a sinking boat, the Australian government refused permission for him to enter Australian territorial waters. When he did, seeking medical help for his passengers, armed Australian troops boarded the ship. International comment was unfavourable. Captain Arne Rinnan was awarded a medal by the King of Norway for upholding the best traditions of one of the world's leading shipping nations. Most *Tampa* passengers were eventually admitted to Australia, although after long delays (Brennan 2003; Marr and Wilkinson 2003).

All this undermines the basis of civilization in international law, which Australian statesmen and women have urged since H. V. Evatt. Even more important is the internment of refugees off the boats, with no Australian government having the slightest idea how to get rid of them. Every 'solution' – Pacific, Malaysian, Manus and Nauru, Cambodian and Timorese – has failed or been abandoned. This is both farce and tragedy. Farce because no sensible advice from the political and bureaucratic system has mastered this escalating issue, despite an expenditure of about $2 billion per annum; tragedy because there is no visible hope for the thousands locked away in remote corners, with no idea of what their future might be. Many rioted when told that they would 'never' be settled in Australia. They were then disqualified from any future consideration as troublemakers and threatened with criminal prosecution. The 'no advantage' principle, which harks back to the early workhouse days in England, places the great majority not drowned at sea in an impossible situation. Some may even face indefinite detention. The inclusion of children has promoted the widest concern, nationally and internationally (Ozdowski 2004). Attacks on Manus and Nauru detainees by local people are a further problem.

The British colonizers of convict Australia gave their prisoners the right, as British subjects, to expect release when their incarceration had expired, and even reduced the penalty for good behaviour. These options are not open at present to the two or three thousand living in Manus, Nauru or even Christmas Island, or the 15,000 waiting in Australia on temporary bridging visas for resolution of their asylum claims. Even if these are favourable, they no longer guarantee residence. Governments of both parties are paralysed by the worst fear of all – that they may lose the next election if they let go. In the convict colonies of New South Wales and Van Diemen's Land, that was not a problem. But public opinion was, as in the case of the Tolpuddle martyrs and eventually of the entire convict system. Public opinion prevented the imprisonment of the Eureka rebels. Public opinion did not save Ned Kelly, but there were many thousands who regarded his execution as undeserved and petitioned the Victorian government accordingly, making him a dubious national hero.

Public opinion defeated the illegalization of the Communist Party and associated organizations, leaving time for them to wither away. Public opinion later ended the settled policy of White Australia, after 70 years of exclusion and expulsion. Public opinion did not stop participation in the failed wars in Vietnam, Iraq or Afghanistan. But it prevented them from being glorified. Public opinion rallied round behind Dr Mohamed Haneef, both in Australia and India. In due course he was paid an unrevealed sum for wrongful treatment. Public opinion was sufficiently shocked by the mass movements from Syria in 2016 to secure a promise of 12,000 extra humanitarian visas.

Opponents of vindictive policies include many lawyers, academics, Christians, Catholic bishops, social media networks, NGOs, doctors, the Greens, the Socialist Alliance, the Refugee Council of Australia, many thousands working in migrant and refugee organizations and so on. These do not add up to a majority of Australians. Nor do they include the Australian Labor party (officially). The normally very moderate Federation of Ethnic Communities Councils strongly criticized the proposed changes to the citizenship law as having the potential 'to create two classes of citizens' (FECCA 2015). They include a substantial proportion of those who take a professional interest in immigration and refugees. They include the same sort of reformers who spoke out against slavery and transportation and for parliamentary democracy and social justice in the Australian past.

Eventually there has to be an end to leaving thousands of people in limbo, or giving ASIO the final power to decide who is a refugee or a loyal citizen and who is not. Australia is a rich and stable society with ample resources and a long history of settling people from around the world. Refusing to accept any refugees who arrived by boat became its official policy by 2014. Timor Leste, Cambodia, PNG or Nauru were offered as alternatives, simply because Australia had persuaded them to sign the Convention. They were among the poorest societies on earth and desperately needed Australian aid. Of the four, only Timor had the courage to say 'No'.

Eventually an agreement was signed with Cambodia in September 2014, which left a narrow opening for those registered as refugees, but denied permanent settlement in Australia because they had arrived by boat. They were free to settle in Cambodia. Australia would deny all further responsibility for them once they did that. Cambodia took the money and then ended the agreement at the end of March 2016, by which time only two refugees had accepted the offer of settlement. Those who refused were offered three-year temporary protection visas in Australia, which denied them permanence and family reunion. Sections of the *Migration Act* referring to the UN Convention were to be removed and replaced by statements about Australia's right as a sovereign state to do whatever it liked with refugees. In effect Australia would end its role as a major recipient of asylum seekers, settling only those chosen by the government through annual quotas and plans and arrangements with the UNHCR.

Sri Lanka, also aid-dependent to a lesser extent, had actively encouraged Australian policy by taking back returnees under the former president, Mahinda Rajapaksa. These were promptly tried under the local law prohibiting free departure from their birthplace and imprisoned. This Sri Lankan law was previously condemned by the UN Human Rights Commission. It also ignored the Convention on Refugees (which Sri Lanka did not sign) and which forbade *refoulement.*

At the same time, Australia was actively increasing the transitory elements of its population through favouring short-term working and student visas and making those who could invest a modest $5 million, or a more attractive $50 million, most of them Chinese, eligible for permanent residence. This was not what the post-war settlement was about.

Stopping the boats by naval force against small and unseaworthy launches is relatively easy, if ignoble, once they are located. But Australia is permanently in the Asia–Pacific region and has major populations from there already and from the Middle East. It is always likely to be under pressure to give some relief to those seeking asylum, unless it cancels its international commitments altogether. This inescapably means that humanitarian and family reunion categories must be maintained and expanded, along with emergency capacity for unpredictable political crises. It is necessary to maintain a reserve, as intakes vary annually. Major crises have been dealt with efficiently before, by cooperation with neighbouring states, rather than with welfare-dependent small societies. Jordan and Lebanon have been bearing burdens that should be shared by richer societies.

Australian foreign policy requires respect and tolerance from major countries, both within the region and internationally. It has risked much of that in recent years. The cost of all this is running at over a billion dollars annually, which could be spent more fruitfully on humanitarian and respected policies, as in the past. Apart from useful aid to small and poorer neighbours, much more needs to be done effectively for the Indigenous peoples, a vital policy area in which much effort has been exerted with limited results. Australia's international reputation has suffered through refugee and Indigenous policy, despite the 'noble lies' of its statesmen to the contrary. Australia has been more enthusiastic about joining in futile military adventures than in sustaining its previous record as a safe haven.

Australia is certainly entitled to limit the acceptance of those claiming asylum if numbers exceed the capacity to settle and find employment without creating mass welfare dependence. Such a challenge has not been experienced at any time since 1945, when the population was much smaller and poorer than it is today. Australia is entitled and obliged to submit asylum seekers to rigorous inspection of their credentials and experience, against reliable knowledge of the political and social situation in their country of origin. This has been the case for all applicants for permanent settlement for at least forty years, since favourable treatment was removed from British subjects. Australia has a duty to investigate rigorously the claims of widespread corruption with visa issues.

Policy need not be based on detention in remote locations on islands, except for the small minority of indubitable security risks, as determined by law and their activities. Nor should it be unduly restrictive to prevent intakes from societies in crisis like Syria and Iraq. Rules for admission for permanent or temporary residence exist and should be publicly available and subject to appeal, as they were until recently. There are about 175 visa subclasses, so there is enough flexibility to meet all problems if needed. The introduction of privileged admission and settlement for favoured investors contrasts with the growing discrimination against asylum seekers. This is a moral rather than an economic judgement, which has attracted almost no public comment. The visa system is wide and flexible and can be adjusted by departmental decision, as it has often been in the past.

Most of those detected as a threat to national security have so far been Australian-born. They are a target for ASIO and the Australian Federal Police, not Immigration and Border Protection. In the past Australia has been able to implement special visa arrangements for refugees from crises within the region, and these can be reactivated when needed. Australia has been taking rising numbers of temporary settlers, while reducing the chances of those in genuine need. These increased numbers refute earlier clams that Australia was 'full up'. Even accepting that much of the country is uninhabitable, Australia ranks with Mongolia as the most thinly peopled state on earth and one of the richest.

It is in the interest of all Australia's neighbours to combat terrorism, piracy and people smuggling, which are a threat to stable government and human life. With unstable regimes disintegrating between Syria and Iraq over to Thailand and Fiji, there will always be a need for regional cooperation in managing refugee movement. Australia was willing to send military support against the 'Islamic Caliphate' set up in Syria and Iraq in 2014. This assumes an obligation on Australia, as a rich and stable society, to be actively engaged in any humane solution of regional problems. The suspicion that Australia is only interested in protecting its own rich and essentially 'European' society, damages fruitful cooperation. Its alliance does not oblige it to follow the United States in all its military activities.

In his inaugural address to the UN Human Rights Council on 8 September 2014 the new High Commissioner for Human Rights, Zeid Ra'ad Al Hussein, claimed,

> Australia's policy of off-shore processing for asylum seekers arriving by sea, and its interception and turning back of vessels, is leading to a chain of human rights violations, including arbitrary detention and possible torture following return to home countries. It could also lead to the resettlement of migrants in countries that are not adequately equipped.

The response by Australia's government marked the end of an era when policies were justified in terms of 'fulfilling international obligations'. Replying to criticism from the UN Committee Against Torture, prime minister Tony Abbott replied: 'Australians were sick of being lectured by the United Nations, particularly as we have stopped the boats' (*Australian*, 10 March 2015: 8). However, there was a rapid reversal of policy late in 2015 in response to media coverage of the massive refugee exodus from Syria into Europe. As in the past, public opinion shifted once refugees were seen as human beings.

A total of 12,000 extra humanitarian places were added for women, children and members of persecuted minorities from Syria and Iraq. Not surprisingly among the latter were Christians, likely to be Syrian Orthodox and Catholics. The earlier success of various rescue missions for the Chinese students, the Russian Christians in China, and the Kosovars were officially quoted. Other states, notably Germany, had already made a major commitment. A special place was reserved for the persecuted Yazidis, a remnant of Zoroastrianism, brutally decimated by the Islamic State of Iraq and the Lebanon (ISIL) and relocated at Wagga in New South Wales in 2017.

Chapter 21

FACING THE 'REAL WORLD'

Australia has changed its character and its traditions of nation-building and asylum away from permanent refugee settlement. Its region was facing the possibility of escalating warfare and consequent increases in refugee numbers. Much of the Muslim world was disintegrating in internecine wars, with the exception of Indonesia and Malaysia, Australia's largest and closest neighbours. The creation of the long-awaited Islamic 'caliphate' (ISIL) in Syria and Iraq was built on nations in which Australia had intervened as an ally of the United States. Australia was also a participant in the inter-communal warfare of Afghanistan. These were futile attempts to create democracies by force in societies that had never accepted democracy, a system some Islamic teachers have described as *haram* or forbidden. 'Crusading' intervention was almost certain to fail and leave much bitterness behind. Military intervention to change an unpopular culture is too high a price to pay unless it directly challenges Australia.

In the view of Australian governments, which their Oppositions endorsed, the propaganda and recruiting power of the 'caliphate' was such that young Muslim Australians were being attracted and trained in terrorist tactics ultimately directed against Australia. This was undoubtedly true, although the numbers going to Syria were little more than a hundred and included converts and non-Arabs. This fear, which was publicly endorsed by ASIO and the Federal Police, created the dilemma of endorsing multicultural principles and practices, while greatly expanding supervision and control over half a million Australian Muslims. This approach has failed in France and Britain. It unleashed the dormant hostility that underlay much Australian and Muslim public opinion. To focus public antagonism on one small section of society is not conducive to social cohesion (Chulov 2006). 'Deradicalization' programs were developed and revised to appeal to the Muslim communities, but were failing to reach the locally born youth with their social media networks, which the 'caliphate' used with great skill. One problem was that rebellious youth had assimilated to Australian street life, with its long and violent traditions, which were scarcely 'Islamic' at all and mainly inspired from the United

States. Terrorist attacks that focused on Australian and British targets in the Lindt Café, Sydney (2014) and Westminster, London (2017) were the work of single, mentally disturbed individuals, known to the police but not regarded as Islamic terrorists until after they had been shot dead during their damaging attacks. The process by which individuals may become terrorists are more complex than simply being recruited by Islamist organizations. As with the much earlier Black Muslims in the United States, many are being recruited while in prison.

The difference between this threat and previous ones was that genuine jihadist terrorists were far more determined, vicious, irresponsible and positively dangerous than Asian immigrants, local communists or the Irish rebels in the past (Coolsaet 2011). The massive expansion of social media created a network of information and propaganda aimed at the potential for terrorist recruitment among 20- and 30-year-old youths and even a few younger boys (Yusuf 2009). Huge reserves of weapons in the Middle East had been acquired from incompetent and corrupt armies in Iraq and Afghanistan and spread through militarized groups and training camps to which a few young Australians were attracted. The tactics of random murders and kidnapping sustained fear and resentment, without leaving any prospect of a negotiated peace. It damaged the long-term interests of all Muslims living in Australia, Canada, Britain, Europe and the United States. Many of the perpetrators were young converts, shaming their own parents and relatives and being killed in substantial numbers. Most were not immigrants, but locally born into Western societies (Aly 2007). One 15-year-old shot and killed a police employee in Parramatta (NSW) in October 2015, being shot and killed in return. Evidence of connections with others showed that he had previously been 'unknown to the police'. His contacts had been questioned in the major 'Appleby' campaign of the previous year and ranged from mosques to criminal networks.

It was in Australia's national interest to reduce the appeal of the 'caliphate', which was militant and murderous against all Western influences. It was also in Australia's interest to disown the vocal minority who wanted to stop all Muslim immigration or refugees from Muslim origins, to close down Islamic institutions and to emulate the French by banning the burqa, mosques, beards and all the symbols of difference. This just annoys people without achieving anything, but is inevitable in a democratic society. France has suffered far more serious Islamic rioting and terrorism than either Britain or Australia.

Governments have a duty to calm things down, but many politicians are frightened by the polls and the popular media. By 2017 national and overseas politics had become so confused that many of the old beliefs were in ruins. Voters in Britain and the United States had turned against conventional leadership to vote against the European Union and the US Democrats. Loyalties became fluid in what some believed to be a revolt of the masses against the élites, for which the evidence is weak. By abandoning UN Conventions in practice and adopting an exclusive and discriminatory refugee policy against those escaping from some Asian states, political leaders were sustaining the very antagonisms on which the jihadists and salafists seized. Local intensive policing exacerbated tension. Picking out 'visible' Muslims at airports and delaying their departure or even confiscating their passports, soon builds up resistance. The rule of law should apply equally to all. In effect laws were being created and implemented that only focused on those Australians who are Muslims or even look like them.

The half-century of abandoning White Australia and building a multicultural alternative was replaced by laws and punishment that only really applied to a religious and ethnic minority of less than 3 per cent. The jihadist fanatics and their indignant critics were part of the same problem, a refusal to accept human variety. The jihadists were bloodthirsty and threatening, but were more dangerous to other Muslim movements, rulers and civilians than to Australia. Their warfare and mass murders have far more impact on fellow Muslims. This condemns their cause to the factionalism and brutality that marred previous failed attempts to unify the Muslim world. Growing hatred between Shia Iran and Sunni Saudi Arabia threatens an international battle even more prolonged and bloody than the earlier seven-year war between Iran and Iraq. The intervention of major powers such as Russia and the United States only increases the destruction and the flow of refugees.

Whether Australia should play any role in this, or be active in rescuing some of the refugees from it, must remain a central issue in local and regional politics for the foreseeable future (Goot and Tiffin 1992). Some of the leaders of the major regional powers, such as Iran, Saudi Arabia and Turkey, might sort out the chaos without the military intervention of Australia, the United States, Russia or the United Nations. Meanwhile hundreds of men, women and children have been detained without trial by Australia, denied any possibility of settling and at risk of losing their health and sanity. Accepting new refugees does not solve the problem of detaining thousands of others. As officially stated, nobody from Syria or Iraq who had reached Australia by boat and been detained would qualify for settlement in Australia from the huge intake of refugees reaching Europe in early September 2015. Their punishment without crime will continue.

The statesmanship that resolved the post-war and Vietnam crises was lacking. As elsewhere, refugees and Muslims have become objects of prejudice and even fear (Esposito 1995; Cesari 2013). Party politics have not provided the best solutions for humane, diplomatic and moral issues. Perhaps the rescue operation for Syrians in 2015 marks a shift back to previous generosity. But it was not extended by Australia to those detained in Manus and Nauru, and was limited to those already in UNHCR and other camps in Lebanon and Jordan. It was the 'humane face' of a concerted US/Australian aerial bombardment of Syrian strongholds of the 'caliphate', but not of president Assad. Judgement on these developments must wait on policies pursued by the Liberal/National government, which replaced Tony Abbott in September 2015. Governments have been changing rapidly in Australia and alternatives are always possible. The detention systems on Nauru and Manus have become unviable and their abolition is long overdue. But refugees are not the problem so much as the result of regional instability in Australia's international environment. Limited policies that only seek to solve Australian problems are unlikely to be effective. Yet another attempt to unload the Nauru and Manus detainees on Costa Rica, in an exchange with the United States, collided with President Trump's determination to exclude Latin Americans in 2017.

Chapter 22

COHESION AND HUMANITY

Official attempts to find satisfactory titles and descriptions for the post-war settlement of a multicultural immigrant population have gone through many stages from 'New Australians' to 'Culturally and Linguistically Diverse'. Descriptions of desirable outcomes have gone from 'assimilation' to 'cohesion'. All these formulations have been developed within a bureaucracy corresponding to political imperatives, rather than emerging from the ethnic or religious communities, expert opinion or the general public. None have much of a basis in community demands or in serious academic inquiry. As in the United States a century ago, many of the majority population have resented 'hyphenated' terms (even 'Anglo-Australians') but many of the newcomers have been happy to use them. Indigenous Australians (also a bureaucratic term) have preferred North American terminologies like First Nations, stressing prior occupation during many centuries. What has been lacking is in-depth analysis of public opinion about a multicultural society and the attitudes of the several million Australians whose ancestors were not derived from the British Isles. This lack has partly been due to the limited interest in such issues by the Commonwealth bureaucracy and its monopoly of official definitions and funding. The growth of a controversial Muslim population has revealed the importance of knowing whether this threatens 'cohesion', even when cohesion has not been effectively defined. Undue reliance on opinion polling has tended to blur the complexity of Australian society and its responses.

The Monash University and Scanlon Foundation research programme, 'Mapping Social Cohesion', tackles cohesion through opinion polls and focus groups (Markus 2013). The ongoing surveys suggest a high degree of satisfaction with immigration and multiculturalism. There is very little alternative study in Australia that might modify or endorse these regular findings. A Scanlon-Monash Index (SMI) of Social Cohesion explains and develops this. It brings into question the excited media treatment of relevant issues. It distinguishes the opinions of respondents by their ethnicity, which is normal in North America but very rare in Australia. It has been produced in a period when ethnic relations and immigration were apparently tense in response to the Islamic revival and the corresponding organization of racist and militant opposition.

Over the past 15 years there has been little to justify the high excitement of organizations like Pauline Hanson's One Nation or the recent and more militant Australian Liberty Alliance. The Alliance, which is made up partly of fundamental Christians, aims 'to stop the Islamization of Australia'. Clearly, there is a wide gap between the Scanlon research and the street demonstrations against mosques by the organizations making up the Alliance. This raises the question of what is cohesion? How can it be measured, and is it important?

In 2007 I argued in a joint academic collection that, although Australia was a rather 'anxious society', most of the perceived threats to social cohesion have been based on worst-case scenarios, which never materialized in reality (Jupp and Nieuwenhuysen 2007:17). This was after 9/11, the wars in Afghanistan and Iraq and the false optimism of the 'Arab Spring', none of which were directly threatening Australia. This was rather optimistic and was responding to movements such as Pauline Hanson's and the opposition of leading conservative politicians to multiculturalism. However, much that has been examined in this book comes to similar conclusions. Neither the communists, nor the Far Right, or the Irish nationalists, or the Chinese miners seriously threatened Australian social cohesion once the convict era and the chaos of the gold rushes were concluded. The greatest threat came not from immigrants or even European colonial rivals, but from Japanese imperialism, leading to its destruction in the 1940s of the colonial systems on which Australia depended for security. Nor have Chinese or Vietnamese communism lived up to the fears of those who developed the mythical Moscow–Peking–Sydney axis in the 1950s. The only dangerous relic of that era is the isolated dictatorship of North Korea, which exerts itself in preserving its own cohesion while threatening others.

We now know what lack of cohesion really looks like in the Middle East, and how this affects life as far away as the United States, France and Britain. The Australian Coalition government was sufficiently alarmed to devise a programme to enhance cohesion, which soon disappeared, like many other optimistic but unfocussed schemes. An illustrated outline of the programme was published in 2017 as *Multicultural Australia: United, Strong, Successful*. This propaganda piece put the emphasis on 'shared values' as the 'glue' that bound Australians together. One unmentioned attitude was already emerging from opinion polling – the relative suspicion about Muslims as opposed to other non-British immigrants. However, there was not the opposition to multiculturalism of Pauline Hanson, who wanted it 'abolished'. Indeed, the official report praised multiculturalism as unifying society, without detailing the extent to which current practice varies from the original model.

Recently, the reasons to be anxious about cohesion in Australia have become stronger, but still not overwhelming. There is probably more reason to be worried about the impact of the drug trade. Serious crime and violence pose a greater threat to individuals than does ethnic variety. Despite one mass riot in Cronulla in 2005 and justified Asian and Aboriginal complaints of racism, Australia is certainly not falling apart. But it does maintain a cruel, vicious and essentially racist detention policy towards asylum seekers, who come from societies that are certainly not cohesive. That is repression without adequate reason and for political advantage. Locking the floodgates, turning around the boats and even the predicted losses at sea, are not sufficient reasons for this persecution of asylum seekers, who had not been advised of their likely fate of 'never' settling in Australia. Cohesive societies are preferable to chaos, but need not secure their objectives by punishing the victims of shattered and war-torn neighbours arriving as refugees.

Chapter 23

FROM NATION-BUILDING TO BORDER PROTECTION

Years of crisis followed the attack in 2001 on the Twin Towers in New York and major terrorist activity in London, Bali, Paris, Moscow, Iraq and Syria. The powers of ASIO and Border Protection were steadily increased to detect and prevent any terrorist activity in Australia. Political instability in the Philippines, Indonesia, Thailand and Sri Lanka all affected areas with which many Australians were familiar, either as immigrants or tourists. The Bali tourist deaths of 2002 were the largest loss of Australian life through terrorism in 15 years. Nothing comparable has struck Australia itself. The Australian dilemma is living securely and comfortably among dangerous regional neighbours about whom they know little. Australian terror attacks have been very rare and committed by individuals, usually young, locally born and mentally deranged. Three were shot.

Australian troops were engaged in Afghanistan, a country that has never been conquered. Yugoslav immigrants watched the breakup of their Titoist state and the resulting chaos and ethnic cleansing. Arab and Egyptian Christians were conscious of the likely impact of the 'Arab Spring', unlike Western observers. However, the majority of Australians only slowly came to grips with the long-term prospects these disparate events might have on their secure, comfortable and prosperous lives. There was more concern, but limited progress, in Indigenous advance and wellbeing, which few knew much about.

A limited media, based mainly in the ABC, SBS and even the *Australian*, kept those informed who wanted to be. However, there was plenty of information, public and secret, for the élite who studied population and immigration policy as well as defence, security and foreign trade. Public servants, military officers, public intellectuals, business executives and even a few politicians were very interested in the rise of China, the nuclear aims of North Korea and Iran, the movement of manufacturing industry to Asia (causing local unemployment), and the need to protect the Australian economy from international crises. One of the benefits of multiculturalism was the growing number of educated and expert immigrants from Asia who understood these issues and had relevant overseas connections. These skilled international settlers were not usually consulted by locally born Australians, of whom few are familiar with Asian languages or cultures. Schools and universities moved rather slowly towards the changing world. Arabic, the fourth language of Australia, was hardly taught at all and most of those studying Chinese were Chinese. Even academic debates about politics were largely confined to upmarket journalism reporting puerile local squabbles between politicians.

The greatest observable threats to Australian social cohesion include an urban subculture of violence, political instability and corruption, youth unemployment, the organized drug trade, racist organizations, the isolation of the Muslim communities, and simple ignorance and indifference about what is actually going on. This is not new. What is new is the ready availability of weapons for alienated youth, the use of social media for communications, and the indifference of many terrorists to their own death and that of others. This is a social failure, which immigration control has not helped and for which no political or religious creed so far has the answer, including attempts at assimilation. Australia has proved quite capable of cohesion, provided it does not try to impose national stereotypes, restrict variety or deny the needs of the less advantaged. But local cohesion is not the only factor in a world that has become unstable.

In the first part of this century the world seemed to lose its mind. Elections in the United States and a referendum in the United Kingdom stood everything on its head, with unpredictable consequences. Britain voted, by a very narrow margin, to leave the European Union, threatening EU viability. The United States elected a president whose views on foreign policy veered so far away from previous wisdom that many experts were rendered speechless. His first act was to withdraw the United States from the Trans-Pacific Partnership, of which Australia was an applicant. The old wisdoms of Right and Left had little to offer. The elected leader of the USA was a billionaire with radical ideas. The prime minister of Britain, Theresa May, was a Conservative lady from the Home Counties, who was critical of immigration. Australian political leaders were barely on speaking terms, while still agreeing that Australia was 'multicultural' and harmonious.

Two things seemed certain. Immigrants and racial minorities could lose many of the gains they had made; and the old party systems of liberals and reformists, were in ruins. Neither of these trends seemed to offer cohesion to a society like Australia's. Immigration was under threat in Britain and the United States and not only for refugees. President Trump planned to build a wall against Mexico, while prime minister Theresa May started to restrict movement to the United Kingdom and to aim at an annual immigrant intake of 100,000. This was very small by normal British levels and likely to damage major industries, such as tourism, for no particular purpose.

Chapter 24

AN UNSTABLE WORLD

The start of the New Year in 2017 saw an unstable political system in Australia and more serious divisions in Europe and the United States, with the election of US President Donald Trump and the British departure from the European Union. Journalistic wisdom claimed a hypothetical revolution against the élites. Disruptions were caused by populist trends in voting and polling, which shattered the Democrats in the United States, drove the British Conservatives into disunion and Labour into oblivion. The underlying ideology was simple nationalism and the aim of making America or Britain 'great again'. But below this was a thick layer of old-fashioned racism directed mainly against foreigners – Mexicans in the United States and Poles (unusually) in Britain. If this was a populist revolt through the ballot box, its inspiration came from the Right rather than the Left. The world order, which so much effort had gone into creating since 1945, was starting to crumble under nationalism and ethnic prejudice. This was reflected in the rise of reactionary and racist parties in Europe, Britain and Australia. Most of these kept links with each other and with Australians and Americans. European radicals had more electoral appeal than the English-speaking parties. Exceptions have been Pauline Hanson's One Nation and the UK Independence Party (UKIP) in the 'Anglosphere', well organized for electoral gains, but yet to make many. Even so the Australian party system was more volatile than for many years, as is the case in Britain..

The main impact of these changes on Australia is likely to be in trade with Europe and the United States. Tariffs may be raised or lowered, depending on how they benefit American companies. China is one of the world's major traders and is well established in Australia, with investments in agricultural estates, the port of Darwin, mining and banking, retail trade and property development. China's main dispute with the democracies is on access to the South China Sea, where disagreement is with the United States and Taiwan. The immediate political impact of this dispute on Australia was not as disturbing as in Europe or North America. China will remain a one-party state, despite internal struggles. It is unlikely to suffer the popular instabilities of the democracies or, at least, to reveal them. Australia has, in general, been a close friend of China for longer than has the United States. Domestic politics are unlikely to change this.

Most commitments by the democracies were directed towards a military shield against Russia or China or North Korea. These were of most value to the United States in making America 'great' again and retaining its overpowering military domination. Other arrangements shared with Australia were directed to improving the lot of modest island states and former colonies, by aid and sharing some defence knowledge. Australia's reputation as a haven for refugees was already tarnished. The protection once offered by the British Empire was a tattered relic. Its revival was being urged by some British Conservatives as a potential element in the Anglosphere along with the United States, Canada, Britain and New Zealand. Australia turned again towards the United States as its protector, but with a US president who was critical of China and, according to rumour, more favourable to Russia. The first few weeks of 2017 concerned Australia directly because of the US/Australian refugee exchange agreement left by President Obama for his successor. It favoured predominantly Muslim detainees when President Trump was actively banning entry from the same sources. Trump's complaint that Germany was not paying enough for defending Europe is unlikely to sway Australia very much as it seeks to sustain its own economy.

The most visibly dangerous threat came from the inscrutable leaders of North Korea, with their long-range missiles aimed at the Pacific and its countries. Neither the United States, China nor Australia had an answer for that. This extraordinary combination of major issues in 2017 underlines that however well Australia has managed its affairs over the past two centuries the outcome has not always been what was intended. Major changes had to be made to adjust to circumstances.

The convict system was ended because slavery was ended, and British official opinion was critical of any similar system. The preference for British immigrants continued much longer but could not be maintained past the 1970s as the economic benefits of moving across the world faded away. European immigrants and then Chinese and Indians filled the gaps. White Australia could not be sustained because of regional and local criticism and the continuing need for recruiting labour regardless of race. Uncontrolled immigration continues to produce increasingly controversial human rights problems and the stubborn insistence of politicians and public servants on mandatory detention. The dilemma of Indigenous disadvantage and alienation continues, despite many bureaucratic schemes for resolving the issues. The disappearance of a protective British Empire from the Australian Pacific has been accepted, despite the appeal of the Anglosphere to conservative and British optimists. Former British colonies and dominions in Asia are not guaranteed allies, and the United States has potential problems elsewhere. Australia is likely to remain a managed society with rigorous control over immigration, a less generous approach to welfare, and concerns about relations with its neighbours. It will still be socially engineered by a bureaucracy and nominally ruled by national and local politicians. Whether they will learn much from the past two centuries may depend on their ability to forget optimistic myths and entrenched prejudices from remoter times and ancestors. They may also encourage the creation of enlarged security organizations, a trend already under way and likely to affect civil liberties. With this tightening of control came the new threat of aerial bombardment from North Korea, a potential danger not seen in a lifetime – since the war with Japan. Australia has no prepared answer to this except to rely on the United States.

CHRONOLOGY

1718	UK Transportation Act.
1770	Lieutenant James Cook claims New South Wales for the British Crown.
1788	Arrival in Sydney Cove of male and female convicts with British military units, under governor-designate Arthur Phillip.
1792	System of assigning convicts to employers begun.
1801	Ticket of leave system introduced.
1803	British colony at Van Diemens Land (later Tasmania).
1804	Suppression of Irish rising at Castle Hill.
1823	New South Wales Act (UK) establishes courts and Legislative Council.
1819–21	Bigge Commission reports, critical of Governor Macquarie.
1833	Abolition of slavery in the British Empire.
1834	Poor Law reform in England allows funding assistance by local authorities for emigration to British colonies.
	Massacre of Aborigines at Pinjarra (WA).
1835	Tasmanian Aborigines removed to Flinders Island.
1836	South Australia proclaimed as a convict-free 'province'.
1837	New township at Port Phillip named Melbourne.
1840	Ending of transportation to New South Wales after 52 years.
1848	First Chinese arrivals.
1850	Colony of Victoria created from New South Wales.
1851	Start of the first gold rush and population explosion.
1853	Ending of transportation to Tasmania (VDL) after 50 years.
1854	Eureka Stockade.
1855	Chinese Immigration Act (Victoria) (repealed in 1865).
1856	Responsible government in three colonies.
1858	Irish Revolutionary Brotherhood (Fenians) founded.
1861	Chinese population of Australia reaches 38,398.
1863	Pacific Islanders brought to Australia as indentured labourers.
1868	Ending of transportation to Western Australia after 18 years.
	Fenian convicts transported to Fremantle on the *Hougoumont.*

1869	Victorian Board for the Protection of Aborigines.
1870	British troops withdrawn.
1876	Fenians escape on the *Catalpa*.
1877	Chinese Immigrants Regulation Act (Queensland).
1881	Uniform census across Australia records a population of 2,271,102.
1881	Influx of Chinese Restriction Act (NSW).
1886	Chinese Immigration Act (WA).
1891	Foundation of Australian Labor Party in Queensland and New South Wales.
	Queensland shearers strike.
1892	Long-term economic depression begins in Victoria.
1897	Aborigines Protection and Restriction of the Sale of Opium Act (Queensland).
1899	Queensland Labour government formed briefly.
1901	Federation and Constitution of the Commonwealth of Australia.
	Immigration Restriction Act and Pacific Island Labourers Act consolidate the White Australia policy.
1905	Western Australia Aborigines Act.
1906	Deportation of the Pacific Islanders.
1910	Election of the majority Labor government of Andrew Fisher.
1911	South Australia Aborigines Act.
1914–18	World War I.
1915	ANZAC engagement at Gallipoli.
1916	Australian Labor Party splits over conscription.
	Arrest of IWW members in Sydney.
1917	Referendum on military conscription fails.
1919	'Red flag' rioting in Brisbane.
1920	Communist Party of Australia founded.
1922	UK Empire Settlement Act subsidizes British immigration.
1930	Worldwide economic depression.
1931	Australian Labor Party splits over the Premier's Plan.
1932	Jack Lang dismissed as NSW premier by the state governor.
1934	Egon Kisch lands in Australia.
1939–45	World War II.
1940	Communist Party banned for opposing the war.
1941	Japan attacks Pearl Harbour in Hawaii; US enters World War II.
1944	Cowra breakout of Japanese prisoners-of-war.
1945	End of World War II .
	Department of Immigration founded.

1947	First displaced persons arrive.
1948	Nationality and Citizenship Act passed.
1949	Foundation of ASIO by Chifley Labor government.
	Menzies Liberal/Country coalition elected.
1951	United Nations adopts the Status of Refugees Convention.
	Referendum to allow the banning of the Communist Party narrowly defeated.
1954	Australia ratifies the UN Convention on Refugees.
	Royal Commission on Espionage.
	Soviet embassy withdraws from Canberra.
1955–56	Australian Labor Party splits over industrial groups.
1958	Migration Act replaces the Immigration Restriction Act.
1959	Soviet embassy returns to Canberra.
1962	Aborigines granted the vote in Federal elections.
1965–71	Troops committed to the war in Vietnam.
1967	Protocol to the Refugee Convention extended to the whole world.
	Constitution amended giving power over Aborigines to the Commonwealth.
1972	Whitlam Labor government elected.
	Final ending of White Australia policy.
1973	Ratification of the Protocol to the Refugee Convention.
1974	Immigration Department temporarily abolished.
1975	Whitlam government dismissed and then defeated by Fraser Liberal and National Country parties.
1976	First amnesty for overstayers.
	Department of Immigration and Ethnic Affairs re-established.
	Vietnamese refugees land by boat at Darwin.
1978	Galbally report lays the basis for multiculturalism.
1979	Numerical Multifactor Assessment System (NUMAS) introduced.
	Federation of Ethnic Communities' Councils founded.
	Australian Institute of Multicultural Affairs established.
1982	Assisted passages for all but refugees ended.
1983	Hawke Labor government elected.
1984	Geoffrey Blainey criticizes Asian immigration.
1986	Review of Migrant and Multicultural Services.
	Australia Act establishes final legal autonomy.
1987	Office of Multicultural Affairs in Prime Minister's Department.
1988	FitzGerald report advocates greater emphasis on migrant skills.
1989	Chinese students resident in Australia allowed to remain due to Tiananmen repression in Beijing.

	Comprehensive Plan of Action for Indochinese refugees (until 1996).
1991	Mandatory detention for asylum seekers by boat and opening of Port Hedland detention centre.
1992	Migration Reform Act validates mandatory detention.
	Mabo case establishes native title.
1995	Curtin detention centre opened near Derby (WA).
1996	Howard Liberal/National Coalition elected.
1997	One Nation party founded by Pauline Hanson.
1998	Immigration detention centres privatized.
1999	Referendum on a republic defeated.
	Temporary protection for Kosovars and Timorese.
	Woomera detention centre opened.
2001	Destruction of the Twin Towers in New York by terrorists.
	Tampa incident and 'Pacific solution' introduced, based on detention in Nauru and excision of Australia from its own migration zone.
2002	88 Australian tourists die in terrorist attack in Bali.
	Custom-built Baxter detention centre opened.
2003	Woomera detention centre closed.
2005	Race riot at Cronulla (NSW) against young Lebanese.
2007	Dr Haneef arrested on suspicion of terrorism and then freed.
	Baxter centre closed.
	Kevin Rudd (Labor) wins Federal election.
2008	Trial of Islamists following Operation Pendennis.
2009	Sri Lankan civil war ends with a massacre and increased refugee flow.
	Citizenship tests introduced.
2013	Liberal National Coalition wins election on slogan 'stop the boats'.
2014	Rioting on Manus Island involving local people and asylum seekers leads to one death.
	Immigration and Customs merged under the title Department of Immigration and Border Protection (DIBP).
	New security laws directed against local recruitment to Islamic 'caliphate' (Syria/Iraq).
	Migration and Maritime Powers Legislation Amendment (Resolving the Asylum Legacy Caseload) Act 2014 passed.
2015	Passports seized and travel prohibited for selected passengers at Australian international airports.

Government proposals to withdraw citizenship for participation in terrorist activities or overseas warfare.

Border Force Act prohibits statements by detention centre staff and professionals.

Labor Party conference endorses Liberal policy on unauthorized arrivals by boat, but supports an enhanced refugee programme.

Australia increases refugee intake from Syria by 12,000 after mass exodus of one million between Syria and Germany.

2017 US presidential election of Donald Trump makes refugee transfers to United States from Australia doubtful but later accepted.

Temporary bans by the United States on immigration from seven mainly Muslim countries.

Amalgamation of Australian immigration, security and intelligence agencies on the US model as Immigration and Border protection Department.

Terror attack on London Parliamentary district by a single jihadist.

North Korea launches missiles capable of reaching Australia, Japan and the United States.

2018 President Xi Jinping tells 19th Chinese Communist Party Congress that China would become the strongest state in the world by 2050.

Amalgamation of Home Affairs and Immigration and Border Protection under a single minister and privatization of visa and immigration facilities.

REFERENCES

Aarons, Mark. 1989. *Sanctuary*. Melbourne: Heinemann.

———. 2001. *War Criminals Welcome*: Melbourne: Black Inc.

———. 2010. *The Family File*. Melbourne: Black Inc.

Adelman, Howard et al. (eds). 1994. *Immigration and Refugee Policy: Australia and Canada Compared*. Melbourne: Melbourne University Press.

Alexander, A. 2010. *Tasmania's Convicts: How Convicts Built a Free Society*. Sydney: Allen & Unwin.

Altman, Jon and Nieuwenhuysen, John. 1979. *The Economic Status of Australian Aborigines*. Cambridge: Cambridge University Press.

Aly, Waleed. 2007. *People Like Us*. Sydney: Picador.

Amos, Keith. 1976. *The New Guard Movement: 1931–1935*: Melbourne: Melbourne University Press.

———. 1988. *The Fenians in Australia 1865–1880*. Sydney: UNSW Press.

Anderson, Warwick. 2002. *The Cultivation of Whiteness: Science, Health and Racial Destiny in Australia*. Melbourne: Melbourne University Press.

Appleyard, Reginald. 1988. *The Ten Pound Immigrants*. London: Boxtree.

Atkinson, Alan. 1997. *The Europeans in Australia: The Beginning*. Melbourne: Oxford University Press.

Attwood, Bain. 2005. *Telling the Truth about Aboriginal History*. Sydney: Allen & Unwin.

Aulich, Chris and Evans, Mark (eds). 2010. *The Rudd Government*. Canberra: ANU E Press.

Aulich, Chris and Wettenhall, Roger (eds). 2008. *Howard's Fourth Government*. Sydney: UNSW Press.

Australian Dictionary of Biography. 1966–. Melbourne: Melbourne University Press.

Australian Human Rights Commission (AHRC). 2010. *Immigration Detention on Christmas Island*. Sydney: AHRC.

———. 2014. *The Forgotten Children*. Sydney: AHRC.

Australian Security Intelligence Organisation (ASIO). 2013. *Report to Parliament 2012–2013*. Canberra: ASIO.

Ayres, Philip. 2007. *Prince of the Church*. Melbourne: Miegunyah Press.

Ball, Desmond and Horner, David. 1998. *Breaking the Codes: Australia's KGB Network*. Sydney: Allen & Unwin.

Bartrop, Paul (ed.). 1990. *The Dunera Affair*. Melbourne: Jewish Museum of Australia.

———. 1994. *Australia and the Holocaust 1933–45*. Melbourne: Scholarly Publishing.

Bashford, Alison and Macintyre, Stuart (eds). 2015. *The Cambridge History of Australia*. Vols. 1 and 2. Melbourne: Cambridge University Press.

Bate, Weston. 1979. *Lucky City: The First Generation at Ballarat 1851–1901*. Melbourne: Melbourne University Press.

Bean, Clive et al. (eds). 1997. *The Politics of Retribution*. Sydney: Allen & Unwin.

Beaumont, Joan et al. 2008. *Under Suspicion: Citizenship and Internment in Australia during the Second World War*. Canberra: National Museum of Australia.

Beckett, Jeremy. 1987. *Torres Strait Islanders: Customs and Colonialism*. Melbourne: Cambridge University Press.

Benjamin, Rodney. 1998. *'A Serious Influx of Jews'*. Sydney: Allen & Unwin.

Beresford, Quentin. 2008. *The Godfather*. Sydney: Allen & Unwin.

Berndt, Ronald and Berndt, Catherine. 1988. *The World of the First Australians*. Canberra: Aboriginal Studies Press.

Bevege, Margaret. 1993. *Behind Barbed Wire: Internment in Australia during World War Two*. St Lucia: University of Queensland Press.

Bialoguski, Michael. 1955. *The Petrov Story*. Melbourne: Heinemann.

Birrell, Bob. 1995. *A Nation of Our Own*. Melbourne: Longman Cheshire.

———. 2001. *Federation: The Secret Story*. Sydney: Duffy & Snellgrove.

Blainey, Geoffrey. 1969. *The Rush That Never Ended*. Melbourne: Melbourne University Press.

———. 2003. *Black Kettle and Full Moon: Daily Life in a Vanishing Australia*. Melbourne: Viking.

———. 2008. *A History of Victoria*. Melbourne: Cambridge University Press.

Blakeney, Michael. 1985. *Australia and the Jewish Refugees 1933–1948*. Sydney: Croom Helm Australia.

Blaxland, John. 2015. *The Protest Years: The Official History of ASIO 1963–1975*. Sydney: Allen & Unwin.

Blaxland, John and Crawley, Rhys. 2016. *The Secret Cold War: The Official History of ASIO 1975–1989*. Sydney: Allen & Unwin.

Bollen, John. 1972. *Protestantism and Social Reform in New South Wales 1890–1910*. Melbourne: Melbourne University Press.

Bolton, Geoffrey. 1970. *A Thousand Miles Away: A History of North Queensland until 1920*. Canberra: ANU Press.

———. 1994. *A Fine Country to Starve In*. Perth: University of Western Australia Press.

Border, Ross. 1962. *Church and State in Australia 1788–1872*. London: SPCK.

Borin, V. L. 1959. *The Uprooted Survive*. London: Heinemann.

Borrie, Wilfred David. 1954. *Italians and Germans in Australia*. Melbourne: Cheshire.

———. 1994. *The European Peopling of Australasia*. Canberra: ANU Press.

Bouchard, Gérard. 2008. *The Making of the Nations and Cultures of the New World*. Montreal: McGill-Queens University Press.

Bouma, Gary. 1994. *Mosques and Muslim Settlement in Australia*. Canberra: Bureau of Immigration Research.

Brawley, Sean. 1995. *The White Peril: Foreign Relations and Asian Immigration to Australasia and North America*. Sydney: UNSW Press.

Brennan, Frank. 2003. *Tampering with Asylum*. St Lucia: University of Queensland Press.

Breward, Ian. 2001. *A History of the Churches in Australasia*. Melbourne: Oxford University Press.

Bridge, Carl and Federowich, Kent (eds). 2003. *The British World: Diaspora, Culture and Identity*. London: Frank Cass.

Briskman, Linda et al. 2008. *Human Rights Overboard*. Melbourne: Scribe.

Broadie, Alexander (ed.). 2003. *The Cambridge Companion to the Scottish Enlightenment*. Cambridge: Cambridge University Press.

Broome, Richard. 1984. *Arriving*. Sydney: Fairfax Syme & Weldon.

———. 1994. *Aboriginal Australians: Black Responses to White Dominance 1788–1994*. Sydney: Allen & Unwin.

———. 2005. *Aboriginal Victorians: A History since 1800*. Sydney: Allen & Unwin.
Browne, Peter. 2006. *The Longest Journey: Resettling Refugees from Africa*. Sydney: UNSW Press.
Burchett, Wilfred. 2005. *Rebel – Journalist: The Autobiography of Wilfred Burchett*. Sydney: UNSW Press.
Burgmann, Meredith. 2014. *Dirty Secrets: Our ASIO Files*. Sydney: New South.
Burgmann, Verity. 1985. *'In Our Time': Socialism and the Rise of Labor 1885–1905*. Sydney: Allen & Unwin.
———. 1995. *Revolutionary Union: The Industrial Workers of the World*. Melbourne: Cambridge University Press.
Burke, Anthony. 2001. *In Fear of Security: Australia's Invasion Anxiety*. Sydney: Pluto Press.
Cain, Frank. 1983. *The Origins of Political Surveillance in Australia*: Sydney: Angus & Robertson.
———. 2008. *Terrorism and Intelligence in Australia: A History of ASIO and National Surveillance*. Melbourne: Australian Scholarly Publishing.
Calwell, Arthur. 1972. *Be Just and Fear Not*. Melbourne: Lloyd O'Neil.
Campbell, Andrew. 1978. *The Australian League of Rights*. Melbourne: Outback Press.
Campbell, Christy. 2002. *Fenian Fire*. London: Harper Collins.
Campbell, Eric. 1965. *The Rallying Point*. Melbourne: Melbourne University Press.
Campbell, Judy. 2002. *Invisible Invaders: Smallpox and Other Diseases in Aboriginal Australia 1780–1880*. Melbourne: Melbourne University Press.
Capp, Fiona. 1993. *Writers Defiled: Security Surveillance of Australian Authors and Intellectuals*. Melbourne: McPhee Gribble.
Carey, Hilary. 1996. *Believing in Australia: A Cultural History of Religions*. Sydney: Allen & Unwin.
Castles, Stephen et al. 1988. *Mistaken Identity*. Sydney: Pluto Press.
Cathcart, Michael. 1988. *Defending the National Tuckshop: Australia's Secret Army Intrigue of 1931*. Melbourne: McPhee Gribble.
Cesarani, David. 2001. *Justice Delayed*. London: Phoenix Press.
Cesari, Jocelyne. 2013. *Why the West Fears Islam*. Basingstoke: Palgrave Macmillan.
Chesterman, John and Galligan, Brian. 1997. *Citizens without Rights: Aborigines and Australian Citizenship*. Melbourne: Cambridge University Press.
Childe, V. Gordon. 1923. *How Labour Governs*. Melbourne: Melbourne University Press.
Choi, C. Y. 1975. *Chinese Migration and Settlement in Australia*. Sydney: Sydney University Press.
Christopher, Emma. 2010. *A Merciless Place*. Sydney: Allen & Unwin.
Chulov, Martin. 2006. *Australian Jihad*. Sydney: Pan Macmillan.
Cigler, Michael. 1986. *The Afghans in Australia*. Melbourne: AE Press.
Codrington, Robert Henry. 1972 [1891]. *The Melanesians*. Oxford: Clarendon Press.
Cole, Phillip. 2000. *Philosophies of Exclusion: Liberal Political Theory and Immigration*. Edinburgh: Edinburgh University Press.
Coleman, Peter. 1974. *Obscenity, Blasphemy and Sedition: 100 Years of Censorship in Australia*. Melbourne: Angus & Robertson.
Commonwealth of Australia. 1993. *Report of the Investigations of War Criminals in Australia*: Sydney: Attorney General's Department.
Commonwealth Parliament. 2000. *A Sanctuary under Review*: Canberra: Senate Legal and Constitutional References Committee.
Connell, Raewyn and Gould, Florence. 1967. *Politics of the Extreme Right*. Sydney: Sydney University Press.
Coolsaet, Rik. 2011. *Jihadi Terrorism and the Radicalisation Challenge*: Farnham: Ashgate.

Corlett, David. 2005. *Following Them Home: The Fate of the Returned Asylum Seekers*. Melbourne: Black Inc.

Cornall, Robert. 2014. *Review into the Events of 16–18 February 2014 at the Manus Regional Processing Centre*. Canberra: Department of Immigration and Border Protection.

Corris, Peter. 1973. *Passage, Port and Plantation: A History of Solomon Islands Labour Migration 1870–1914*. Melbourne: Melbourne University Press.

Crean, Frank and Gillard, Julia. 2002. *Protecting Australia and Protecting the Australian Way*. Canberra: Australian Labor Party.

Cresciani, Gianfranco. 1980. *Fascism, Anti-Fascism and Italians in Australia 1922–1945*. Canberra: ANU Press.

Crock, Mary. 1998. *Immigration and Refugee Law in Australia*. Sydney: Federation Press.

Crock, Mary and Saul, Ben. 2002. *Future Seekers: Refugees and the Law in Australia*. Sydney: Federation Press.

Crock, Mary et al. 2006. *Future Seekers II: Refugees and Irregular Migration in Australia*. Sydney: Federation Press.

Curthoys, Ann and Markus, Andrew (eds). 1978. *Who Are Our Enemies? Racism and the Working Class in Australia*. Sydney: Hale & Iremonger.

Daniels, Kay. 1998. *Convict Women*. Sydney: Allen & Unwin.

Davidson, Alastair. 1969. *The Communist Party of Australia: A Short History*. Stanford: Hoover Institution.

———. 1997. *From Subject to Citizen*. Melbourne: Cambridge University Press.

Davies, Norman. 2000. *The Isles: A History*. London: Macmillan.

Deen, Hanifa. 1995. *Caravanserai: Journey among Australian Muslims*. Sydney: Allen & Unwin.

Deery, Phillip (ed.). 1978. *Labour in Conflict: The 1949 Coal Strike*. Sydney, Hale & Iremonger.

De Lepervanche, Marie. 1984. *Indians in a White Australia*. Sydney: Allen & Unwin.

Department of Immigration and Border Protection (DIBP). 2015. *Opening Statement to the Senate Select Committee on Conditions and Circumstances at the Regional Processing Centre in Nauru*. Canberra: DIBP.

Douglass, William A. 1995. *From Italy to Ingham*. St Lucia: University of Queensland Press.

Dutton, David. 2002. *One of Us? A Century of Australian Citizenship*. Sydney: UNSW Press.

Dutton, Peter. 2015. Commonwealth Parliamentary Debates, House of Representatives. 24 June: p. 7369.

Edwards, Coral and Read, Peter. 1989. *The Lost Children*. Sydney: Doubleday.

Elkin, A. P. 1956. *The Australian Aborigines*. Sydney: Angus & Robertson.

Elkner, Cate et al. 2005. *Enemy Aliens*. Ballarat: Connor Court.

Erickson, Charlotte. 1994. *Leaving England: Essays on British Emigration in the Nineteenth Century*. Ithaca, NY: Cornell University Press.

Esposito, John L. 1995. *The Islamic Threat: Myth or Reality*. New York: Oxford University Press.

Evans, Raymond. 1989. *The Red Flag Riots: A Study of Intolerance*. St Lucia: University of Queensland Press.

Evans, Raymond et al. 1993. *Race Relations in Colonial Queensland*. St Lucia: University of Queensland Press.

Ewart, Jacqueline. 2009. *Haneef: A Question of Character*. Canberra: Halstead Press.

Farrell, Frank. 1982. *International Socialism and Australian Labor*. Sydney: Hale & Iremonger.

FECCA (Federation of Ethnic Communities Councils of Australia). 2015. S*ubmission to the Joint Parliamentary Committee on Intelligence and Security*, 3 August.

Fischer, Gerard. 1989. *Enemy Aliens: Internment and the Homefront Experience in Australia 1914–1920*. St Lucia: University of Queensland Press.

Fitzgerald, Alan. 1981. *The Italian Farming Soldiers 1941–1947*. Melbourne: Melbourne University Press.
Fitzgerald, John. 2006. *Big White Lie: Chinese Australians in White Australia*. Sydney: UNSW Press.
FitzGerald, Stephen (chair). 1988. *Immigration – A Commitment to Australia*. Canberra: AGPS.
Fitzpatrick, David. 1994. *Oceans of Consolation*. Cork: Cork University Press.
Fitzsimons, Peter. 2012. *Eureka: The Unfinished Revolution*. Sydney: Heinemann.
Ford, Patrick P. 1966. *Cardinal Moran and the ALP*. Melbourne: Melbourne University Press.
Foster, Lois and Stockley, David. 1988. *Australian Multiculturalism: A Documentary History and Critique*. Clevedon: Multilingual Matters.
Frame, Tom. 2007. *Anglicans in Australia*. Sydney: UNSW Press.
Francis, Ronald David. 1981. *Migrant Crime in Australia*. St Lucia: University of Queensland Press.
Fraser, Charles Frederick 1940. *Control of Aliens in the British Commonwealth of Nations*. London: Hogarth Press.
Frost, Alan. 1980. *Convicts and Empire: A Naval Question*. Melbourne: Oxford University Press.
———. 2012. *Botany Bay: The Real Story*. Melbourne: Black Inc.
Galbally, Frank (chair). 1978. *Migrant Services and Programs*. Canberra: AGPS.
Gallagher, Anne T. and David, Fiona. 2014. *The International Law of Migrant Smuggling*. Melbourne: Cambridge University Press.
Galligan, Brian and Roberts, Winsome. 2004. *Australian Citizenship*. Melbourne: Melbourne University Press.
Galligan, Brian and Roberts, Winsome (eds). 2007. *The Oxford Companion to Australian Politics*: Melbourne: Oxford University Press.
Gascoigne, John. 2002. *The Enlightenment and the Origins of European Australia*. Melbourne: Cambridge University Press.
Getzler, Israel. 1970. *Neither Toleration nor Favour*. Melbourne: Melbourne University Press.
Gibney, Matthew. 2004. *The Ethics and Politics of Asylum*. Cambridge: Cambridge University Press.
Goldsworthy, David. 2002. *Losing the Blanket: Australia and the End of Empire*. Melbourne: Melbourne University Press.
Gollan, Robin. 1960. *Radical and Working Class Politics: A Study of Eastern Australia 1850–1910*. Melbourne: Cambridge University Press.
———. 1975. *Revolutionaries and Reformists*. Canberra: ANU Press.
Goodwin-Gill, Guy and McAdam, Jane. 2007. *The Refugee in International Law*. Oxford: Oxford University Press.
Goot, Murray and Tiffin, Rodney (eds). 1992. *Australia's Gulf War*. Melbourne: Melbourne University Press.
Gott, Ken. 1965. *Voices of Hate*. Melbourne: Dissent.
Grant, Bruce. 1979. *The Boat People: An 'Age' Investigation*. Harmondsworth: Penguin Books.
Gray, Peter. 2009. *The Making of the Irish Poor Law 1815–43*. Manchester: Manchester University Press.
Greenland, Hall. 1998. *'Red Hot': The Life and Times of Nick Origlass*. Sydney: Lane Press.
Griffin, Carl J. 2014. *Protest, Politics and Work in Rural England, 1700–1850*. Basingstoke: Palgrave Macmillan.
Gumpl, Gary and Kleinig, Richard H. 2007. *The Hitler Club*. Melbourne: Brolga Publishing.
Habib, Mamdouh and Collingwood, Julia. 2008. *My Story*. Melbourne: Scribe.
Haebich, Anna. 1988. *For Their Own Good*. Perth: University of Western Australia Press.
Haines, Robin F. 1997. *Emigration and the Labouring Poor*. London: Macmillan.

Hall, Richard. 1978. *The Secret State*. Sydney: Cassell.
Hamilton, Clive and Maddison, Sarah (eds). 2007. *Silencing Dissent*. Sydney: Allen & Unwin.
Hammerton, A. James and Thomson, Alistair. 2005. *Ten Pound Poms*. Manchester: Manchester University Press.
Harcourt, David. 1972. *Everyone Wants to Be Fuehrer*. Sydney: Angus & Robertson.
Harper, Marjory. 2003. *Adventurers and Exiles: The Great Scottish Exodus*. London: Profile Books.
Hartz, Louis. 1964. *The Founding of New Societies*. New York: Harcourt Brace & World.
Hasluck, Alexandra. 1978. *Unwilling Emigrants*. Melbourne: Oxford University Press.
Hassan, Riaz. 2008. *Inside Muslim Minds*. Melbourne: Melbourne University Press.
Hawthorne, Lesleyanne (ed.). 1992. *Refugee: The Vietnamese Experience*. Melbourne: Oxford University Press.
Hayes, Anna and Mason, Robert. 2012. *Cultures in Refuge: Seeking Sanctuary in Modern Australia*. Farnham: Ashgate.
Haynes, John Earl and Klehr, Harvey. 1999. *Venona: Decoding Soviet Espionage in America*. New Haven: Yale University Press.
Hazlehurst, Kayleen M. 1987. *Migration, Ethnicity and Crime in Australian Society*. Canberra: Australian Institute of Criminology.
Head, Brian and Walter, James (eds). 1988. *Intellectual Movements and Australian Society*. Melbourne: Oxford University Press.
Herman, Arthur. 2003. *The Scottish Enlightenment: The Scots' Invention of the Modern World*. London: Harper Collins.
Hicks, David. 2010. *Guantanamo: My Journey*. Sydney: Random House.
Higgins, Claire. 2017. *Asylum by Boat*. Sydney: UNSW Press.
Hill, David. 2010. *The Gold Rush*. Sydney: Random House.
Hirst, John. 1983. *Convict Society and Its Enemies*. Sydney. Allen & Unwin.
———. 1988. *The Strange Birth of Colonial Democracy: New South Wales 1848–1854*. Sydney: Allen & Unwin.
———. 2008. *Freedom on the Fatal Shore*. Melbourne: Black Inc.
Hobsbawm, Eric and Rudé, George. 1969. *Captain Swing*. Harmondsworth: Penguin.
Hocking, Jenny. 1993. *Beyond Terrorism: The Development of the Australian Security State*. Sydney: Allen & Unwin.
———. 2004. *Terror Laws*. Sydney: UNSW Press.
Hogan, Michael. 1987. *The Sectarian Strand*. Melbourne: Penguin.
Hope, Justice Robert Marden. 1986. *Royal Commission on Australia's Security and Intelligence Agencies*. Canberra: AGPS.
Horton, David (ed.). 1994. *The Encyclopaedia of Aboriginal Australia*. Vols. 1 and 2. Canberra: Aboriginal Studies Press.
Horner, David. 2014. *The Spy Catchers: The Official History of ASIO 1949–1963*. Sydney: Allen & Unwin.
Hughes, Robert. 1987. *The Fatal Shore*. London: Collins Harvill.
Human Rights and Equal Opportunity Commission (HREOC). 1998. *Those Who've Come across the Seas: Detention of Unauthorised Arrivals*. Sydney: HREOC.
———. 2004. *Kisma-Listen: National Consultations on Eliminating Prejudice against Arab and Muslim Australians*. Sydney: HREOC.
Huntington, Samuel P. 1996. *The Clash of Civilizations and the Remaking of World Order*. New York: Simon & Schuster.
Immigration Reform Group (IRG). 1960. *Control or Colour Bar? A Proposal for Change in Australia's Immigration Policy*. Melbourne: IRG.

Inglis, Amirah. 1987. *Australians in the Spanish Civil War*. Sydney: Allen & Unwin.
Jakubowicz, Andrew and Ho, Christina (eds). 2013. *'For Those Who've Come across the Seas [...]': Australian Multiculturalism Theory, Policy and Practice*. Melbourne: Australian Scholarly Publishing.
Jamrozik, Adam. 1995. *Social Change and Cultural Transformation in Australia*. Melbourne: Cambridge University Press.
———. 2004. *The Chains of Colonial Inheritance*. Sydney: UNSW Press.
Jayasuriya, Laksiri et al. 2003. *Legacies of White Australia: Race, Culture and Nation*. Perth: University of Western Australia Press.
Jeffery, Keith. 2010. *MI6: The History of the Secret Intelligence Service 1909–1949*. London: Bloomsbury.
Joint Standing Committee on Migration. 2008. *Immigration Detention in Australia: A New Beginning*. Canberra: Parliament of the Commonwealth of Australia.
Jupp, James. 1966. *Arrivals and Departures*. Melbourne: Cheshire Lansdowne.
———. 1998. *Immigration*. Melbourne: Oxford University Press.
——— (ed.). 2001. *The Australian People*. Melbourne: Cambridge University Press.
———. 2004. *The English in Australia*. Melbourne: Cambridge University Press.
———. 2007. *From White Australia to Woomera*. Melbourne: Cambridge University Press.
——— (ed.). 2009. *The Encyclopedia of Religion in Australia*. Melbourne: Cambridge University Press.
Jupp, James and Kabala, Maria (eds). 1993. *The Politics of Australian Immigration*. Canberra: AGPS.
Jupp, James and Nieuwenhuysen, John (eds). 2007. *Social Cohesion in Australia*. Cambridge: Cambridge University Press.
Jurgensen, Manfred and Corkhill, Alan (eds). 1988. *The German Presence in Queensland*. St Lucia: University of Queensland, Department of German.
Kabir, Nahid. 2005. *Muslims in Australia*. London: Kegan Paul.
Keneally, Thomas. 1998. *The Great Shame*. Sydney: Random House.
Kent, David and Townsend, Norma. 2002. *The Convicts of the Eleanor*. London: Merlin.
Kisch, Egon. 1969. *Australian Landfall*. Sydney: Australian Book Society.
Kneebone, Susan York (ed.). 2003. *The Refugee Convention 50 Years On: Globalisation and International Law*. Aldershot: Ashgate.
Kobal, Ivan. 1999. *The Snowy: Cradle of New Australia*. Rydalmere: Self-published.
Koivukangas, Olavi and Westin, Charles (eds). 1999. *Scandinavian and European Migration to Australia* and *New Zealand*. Turku: Institute of Migration.
Kristianson, Gerald Lawrence. 1966. *The Politics of Patriotism*. Canberra: ANU Press.
Kumar, Krishan. 2003. *The Making of English National Identity*. Cambridge: Cambridge University Press.
Kunz, Egon. 1988. *Displaced Persons: Calwell's New Australians*: Canberra: Australian National University Press.
Lake, Marilyn and Reynolds, Henry. 2008. *Drawing the Global Colour Line*. Melbourne: Melbourne University Press.
Lamidey, Noel W. 1974 *Aliens Control in Australia 1939–1946*. Sydney: Noel Lamidey.
Leach, Michael et al. 2000. *The Rise and Fall of One Nation*. St Lucia: University of Queensland Press.
Lever-Tracy, Constance and Quinlan, Michael. 1988. *A Divided Working Class*. London: Routledge & Kegan Paul.
Loescher, Gil. 1993. *Beyond Charity: International Cooperation and the Global Refugee Crisis*. New York: Oxford University Press.

London, Herbert Ira. 1970. *Non-White Immigration and the 'White Australia' Policy*: New York: New York University Press.

Lopez, Mark. 2000. *The Origins of Multiculturalism in Australian Politics 1945–1975*. Melbourne: Melbourne University Press.

Lovell, David and Windle, Kevin (eds). 2008. *Our Unswerving Loyalty*. Canberra: ANU E Press.

Lynch, Andrew, McGarrity, Nicola and Williams, George. 2015. *Inside Australia's Anti-Terrorism Laws and Trials*. Sydney: New South.

Macdonagh, Oliver. 1996. *The Sharing of the Green*. Sydney: Allen & Unwin.

MacFarlane, Ian. 2012. *The Kelly Gang Unmasked*. Melbourne: Oxford University Press.

Macintyre, Ben. 2014. *A Spy among Friends: Kim Philby and the Great Betrayal*. London: Bloomsbury.

Macintyre, Stuart. 1985. *Winners and Losers: The Pursuit of Social Justice in Australian History*. Sydney: Allen & Unwin.

———. 1998. *The Reds: The Communist Party of Australia from Origins to Illegality*. Sydney: Allen & Unwin.

———. 2015. *Australia's Boldest Experiment: War and Reconstruction in the 1940s*. Sydney: New South.

Macintyre, Stuart and Clark, Anna. 2003. *The History Wars*. Melbourne: Melbourne University Press.

Maddock, Kenneth. 1983. *Your Land is Our Land*. Ringwood: Penguin.

Maley, William. 2002. *The Afghanistan Wars*. Basingstoke: Palgrave Macmillan.

Mann, Tom. 2003. *Desert Sorrow: Asylum Seekers at Woomera*. Adelaide, Wakefield Press.

Manne, Robert. 1987. *The Petrov Affair*. Sydney: Pergamon Press.

———. 1994. *The Shadow of 1917*. Melbourne: Text.

———. (ed.). 2004. *The Howard Years: A Political Interpretation*. Melbourne: Black Inc.

Mansouri, Fethi and Lobo, Michele (eds). 2011. *Migration, Citizenship and Intercultural Relations*. Farnham: Ashgate.

Mares, Peter. 2001. *Borderline*. Sydney: Allen & Unwin.

Markus, Andrew. 1979. *Fear and Hatred: Purifying Australia and California 1850–1901*. Sydney: Hale & Iremonger.

———. 1994. *Australian Race Relations 1788–1993*. Sydney: Allen &Unwin.

———. 2001. *Race: John Howard and the Remaking of Australia*. Sydney: Allen & Unwin.

———. 2013. *Mapping Social Cohesion: The Scanlon Foundation Surveys*. Melbourne: Monash University.

Markus, Andrew, Jupp, James and McDonald, Peter. 2009. *Australia's Immigration Revolution*. Sydney: Allen & Unwin.

Marlow, Joyce. 1971. *The Tolpuddle Martyrs*. London: History Book Club.

Marr, David. 1984. *The Ivanov Trail*. Melbourne: Nelson.

Marr, David and Wilkinson, Marian. 2003. *Dark Victory*. Sydney: Allen & Unwin.

Marrus, Michael R. 1985. *The Unwanted: European Refugees in the Twentieth Century*. New York: Oxford University Press.

Martin, Ged (ed.). 1978. *The Founding of Australia: The Argument about Australia's Origins*. Sydney: Hale & Iremonger.

Martin, Harry. 1989. *Angels and Arrogant Gods*. Canberra: AGPS.

McAdam, Jane and Chong, Fiona. 2014. *Refugees: Why Seeking Asylum is Legal and Australia's Policies Are Not*. Sydney: UNSW Press.

McAllister, Ian and Pietsch, Juliet. 2011. *Trends in Australian Political Opinion*. Canberra: Australian National University.

McClymont, Kate and Besser, Linton. 2014. *He Who Must be Obeid*. Sydney: Random House.
McConville, Chris. 1987. *Croppies, Celts and Catholics*. Melbourne: Edward Arnold.
McGregor, Russell. 1997. *Imagined Destinies: Australian Aborigines and the Doomed Race Theory*. Melbourne: Melbourne University Press.
McKenna, Mark. 1996. *The Captive Republic*. Melbourne: Cambridge University Press.
McKenzie-Murray, Martin. 2015. 'Inside Border Force's Power'. *The Saturday Paper*, No. 76: 8–9.
McKnight, David. 1994. *Australia's Spies and Their Secrets*. Sydney: Allen & Unwin. McMaster, Don. 2001. *Asylum Seekers*. Melbourne: Melbourne University Press.
McNair, John and Poole, Thomas. 1992. *Russia and the Fifth Continent*. St Lucia: University of Queensland Press.
McQueen, Humphrey. 1986. *A New Britannia*. Ringwood: Penguin.
Medding, Peter Y. 1968. *From Assimilation to Group Survival*. Melbourne: Cheshire.
Menghetti, Diane. 1981. *The Red North: The Popular Front in North Queensland*. Townsville: James Cook University History Department.
Merritt, John. 1986. *The Making of the AWU*. Melbourne: Oxford University Press.
Metcalfe, Susan. 2010. *The Pacific Solution*. Melbourne: Australian Scholarly Publishing.
Mills, Richard C. 1974. *The Colonization of Australia 1829–42*. Sydney: Sydney University Press.
Mol, Hans. 1971. *Religion in Australia*. Melbourne: Nelson.
Molony, John. 1969. *The Roman Mould of the Australian Catholic Church*. Melbourne: Melbourne University Press.
———. 1984. *Eureka*. Melbourne: Viking Press.
Moore, Andrew. 1989. *The Secret Army and the Premier*. Sydney: UNSW Press.
———. 1995. *The Right Road: A History of Right-Wing Politics in Australia*. Melbourne: Oxford University Press.
Moore, Clive. 1978. *The Forgotten People: A History of the Australian South Sea Island Community*. Sydney: Australian Broadcasting Commission.
Moore, Tony. 2010. *Death or Liberty: Rebels and Radicals Transported to Australia*. Sydney: Allen & Unwin.
Morgan, George and Poynting, Scott (eds). 2012. *Global Islamophobia*. Farnham: Ashgate.
Muirden, Bruce. 1968. *The Puzzled Patriots: The Story of the Australia First Movement*. Melbourne: Melbourne University Press.
Murphy, Denis (ed.). 1975. *Labor in Politics: The State Labor Parties in Australia 1880–1920*. St Lucia: University of Queensland Press.
Murray, Robert. 1970. *The Split*. Melbourne: Cheshire.
Nagata, Yuriko. 2000. *Unwanted Aliens: Japanese Internment in Australia*. St Lucia: University of Queensland Press.
Nairn, Bede. 1975. *Civilising Capitalism*. Canberra: ANU Press.
Nasiri, Omar. 2006. *Inside the Global Jihad*. Melbourne: Scribe.
Neighbour, Sally. 2004. *In the Shadow of Swords*. Sydney: Harper Collins.
Neumann, Klaus. 2006. *In the Interest of National Security: Civilian Internment in Australia during World War II*. Canberra: National Archives of Australia.
———. 2015. *Across the Seas: Australia's Response to Refugees*. Melbourne: Black Inc.
Nicholas, Stephen (ed.). 1988. *Convict Workers: Reinterpreting Australia's Past*. Melbourne: Cambridge University Press.
Nicholls, Glenn. 2007. *Deported: A History of Forced Departures from Australia*. Sydney: UNSW Press.

O'Farrell, Patrick. 1977. *The Catholic Church and Community in Australia: A History*. Melbourne: Nelson.

———. 1987. *The Irish in Australia*. Sydney: UNSW Press.

Oliver, Pam. 2004. *Allies, Enemies and Trading Partners: Records on Australia and the Japanese*. Canberra: National Archives of Australia.

O'Neill, Margot. 2008. *Blind Conscience*. Sydney: New South.

Oxley, Deborah. 1996. *Convict Maids: The Forced Migration of Women to Australia*. Melbourne: Cambridge University Press.

Ozdowski, Sev. 2004. *A Last Resort? National Inquiry into Children in Immigration Detention*: Sydney: Human Rights and Equal Opportunity Commission.

Palfreeman, Anthony C. 1967. *The Administration of the White Australia Policy*: Melbourne: Melbourne University Press.

Panich, Catherine. 1988. *Sanctuary?* Sydney: Allen & Unwin.

Papers on Parliament 65. 2016. Canberra: Department of the Senate.

Parliament of the Commonwealth of Australia. 2001. *A Report on Visits to Immigration Detention Centres*. Canberra: Joint Standing Committee on Foreign Affairs, Defence and Trade.

———. 2004. *Report of the Inquiry into Australian Intelligence Agencies*. Canberra: Joint Standing Committee on ASIO, ASIS and DSD.

———. 2009. *Immigration Detention in Australia*: Canberra: Joint Standing Committee on Migration.

———. 2015. *Advisory Report on the Australian Citizenship Amendment (Allegiance to Australia) Bill*. Canberra: Parliamentary Joint Committee on Intelligence and Security.

Parliament of the Commonwealth of Australia. Joint Standing Committee on Migration. 1994. *Asylum, Border Control and Detention*. Canberra: AGPS.

Partington, Geoffrey. 1994. *The Australian Nation: Its British and Irish Roots*. Melbourne: Australian Scholarly Publishing.

Patkin, Benzion. 1979. *The Dunera Internees*. Sydney: Cassell.

Pearl, Cyril. 1983. *The Dunera Scandal: Deported by Mistake*. Sydney: Angus & Robertson.

Phillips, Walter. 1981. *Defending a Christian Country*. St Lucia: University of Queensland Press.

Pickering, Sharon. 2005. *Refugees and State Crime*. Sydney: Federation Press.

Pietsch, Juliet and Clark Marshall (eds). 2015. *Migration and Integration in Europe, Southeast Asia and Australia*. Amsterdam: University of Amsterdam Press.

Pike, Douglas. 1967. *Paradise of Dissent*. Melbourne: Melbourne University Press.

Poynting, Scott et al. 2004. *Bin Laden in the Suburbs: Criminalising the Arab Other*. Sydney: Institute of Criminology.

Prasser, Scott et al. 1990. *Corruption and Reform*. St Lucia: University of Queensland Press.

Prentis, Malcolm. 2008. *The Scots in Australia*. Sydney: UNSW Press.

Price, Charles. 1946. *German Settlers in South Australia*. Melbourne: Melbourne University Press.

———. 1963. *Southern Europeans in Australia*. Oxford: Oxford University Press.

———. 1974. *The Great White Walls Are Built*. Canberra: ANU Press.

Reece, Bob. 1989. *Irish Convicts: The Origins of Convicts Transported to Australia*. Dublin: University College: Department of Modern History.

———. 2001. *The Origins of Irish Convict Transportation to New South Wales*. Basingstoke: Palgrave Macmillan.

Reid, Janice and Strong, Timothy. 1987. *Torture and Trauma: The Health Care Needs of Refugee Victims in NSW*. Sydney: Cumberland College of Health Sciences.

Reynolds, Henry. 1995. *Fate of a Free People*. Ringwood: Penguin.

———. 1999. *Why Weren't We Told?* Ringwood: Penguin.

———. 2003. *North of Capricorn: The Untold Story of Australia's North*. Sydney: Allen & Unwin.
———. 2012. *A History of Tasmania*. Melbourne: Cambridge University Press.
Richards, Eric. 1985. *A History of the Highland Clearances*. Vol. 2. London: Croom Helm.
———. (ed.). 1995. *Female Immigrants in Colonial Australia*. Canberra: Australian National University.
———. 2004. *Britannia's Children*. London: Hambledon & London.
———. 2008. *Destination Australia*. Sydney: UNSW Press.
Richelson, Jeffrey and Ball, Desmond. 1985. *The Ties That Bind: Intelligence Cooperation between the UKUSA Countries*. Sydney: Allen & Unwin.
Robinson, Portia. 1985. *The Hatch and Brood of Time*. Melbourne: Oxford University Press.
———. 1993. *The Women of Botany Bay*. Melbourne: Penguin.
Robson, Leslie Lloyd. 1965. *The Convict Settlers of Australia*. Melbourne: Melbourne University Press.
Roe, Michael. 1965. *The Quest for Authority in Eastern Australia 1831–1851*. Melbourne: Melbourne University Press.
———. 1995. *Australia, Britain and Migration 1916–1940*. Melbourne: Cambridge University Press.
Rolls, Eric. 1992. *The Sojourners*. St Lucia: University of Queensland Press.
———. 1996. *Citizens*. St Lucia: University of Queensland Press.
Rose, Michael E. 1971. *The English Poor Law 1780–1930*. Newton Abbot: David & Charles.
Ross, Lloyd. 1980. *William Lane and the Australian Labor Movement*. Sydney: Hale & Iremonger.
Rowley, Charles Dunford. 1970. *The Destruction of Aboriginal Society*. Canberra: ANU Press.
Rowse, Tim. 1978. *Australian Liberalism and National Character*. Melbourne: Kibble Books.
———. 2071. *Indigenous and Other Australians*. Sydney: UNSW Press.
Rubinstein, William D. 1991. *The Jews in Australia*. Melbourne: Heinemann.
Rudé, George. 1978. *Protest and Punishment: The Story of the Social and Political Prisoners Transported to Australia 1788–1868*. Melbourne: Oxford University Press.
Rutland, Suzanne D. 1997 *Edge of the Diaspora*. Sydney: Brandl & Schlesinger.
Ryan, Lyndall. 2012. *The Tasmanian Aborigines*. Sydney: Allen & Unwin.
Saeed, Abdullah. 2003. *Islam in Australia*. Sydney: Allen & Unwin.
Saeed, Abdullah and Akbarzadeh, Shahram. 2001. *Muslim Communities in Australia*. Sydney: UNSW Press.
Santamaria, Bob. 1981. *Against the Tide*. Melbourne: Oxford University Press.
Sasson, Molly. 2015. *More Cloak than Dagger*. Ballarat: Connor Court.
Saunders, Kay. 1982. *Workers in Bondage: The Origins and Bases of Unfree Labour in Queensland 1824–1916*. St Lucia: University of Queensland Press.
Saunders, Kay and Daniels, Roger (eds). 2000. *Alien Justice*. St Lucia: University of Queensland Press.
Saville, Margot. 2007. *The Battle for Bennelong*. Melbourne: Melbourne University Press.
Sayer, Mandy. 2017. *Australian Gypsies*. Sydney: New South.
Scott, Andrew. 1991. *Fading Loyalties: The ALP and the Working Class*. Sydney: Pluto Press.
Senate Legal and Constitutional References Committee. 2000. *A Sanctuary under Review*. Canberra: Commonwealth of Australia.
Senate Select Committee on a Certain Maritime Incident. 2002. *Report*. Canberra: The Senate.
Serle, Geoffrey. 1963. *The Golden Age: A History of the Colony of Victoria: 1851–1861*. Melbourne: Melbourne University Press.
———. 1980. *The Rush to Be Rich: Victoria 1883–1889*. Melbourne: Melbourne University Press.

Shaw, Alan George Lewers. 1977. *Convicts and the Colonies*. Melbourne: Melbourne University Press.

Short, Susanna. 1992. *Laurie Short: A Political Life*. Sydney: Allen & Unwin.

Silber, Laura and Little, Allan. 1996. *The Death of Yugoslavia*. London: Penguin/BBC.

Simms, Marian (ed.). 2001. *1901: The Forgotten Election*. St Lucia: University of Queensland Press.

Simms, Marian and Warhurst, John. 2000. *Howard's Agenda*. St Lucia: University of Queensland Press.

Sluga, Glenda. 1988. *Bonegilla: 'A Place of No Hope'*. Melbourne: University of Melbourne History Department.

Small, Clive and Gilling, Tom. 2016. *Evil Life: The True Story of the Calabrian Mafia in Australia*. Sydney: Allen & Unwin.

Souter, Gavin. 1976. *Lion and Kangaroo*. Sydney: Collins Fontana.

Splivalo, Anthony. 1982. *The Home Fires*. Perth: Fremantle Arts Centre Press.

St John, Edward. 1972. *The Australian League of Rights*. Sydney: UNSW Press.

Staffordshire Record Society. 1992. *Staffordshire Assize Calendars 1842–1843*. Stafford: Staffordshire Record Society.

Strahan, Lachlan. 1996. *Australia's China: Changing Perceptions from the 1930s to 1990s*. Melbourne: Cambridge University Press.

Sullivan, Martin. 1985. *Men and Women of Port Phillip*. Sydney: Hale & Iremonger.

Sutalo, Ilija. 2004. *Croatians in Australia*. Adelaide: Wakefield Press.

Suttor, Timothy Lachlan. 1965. *Hierarchy and Democracy in Australia 1788–1870*. Melbourne: Melbourne University Press.

Svensen, Stuart. 1989. *The Shearers' War*. St Lucia: University of Queensland Press.

Symons, Beverley et al. 1994. *Communism in Australia: A Resource Bibliography*. Canberra: National Library of Australia.

Tampke, Jürgen and Doxford, Colin. 1990. *Australia Willkommen*. Sydney: UNSW Press.

Tatz, Colin, Arnold, Peter and Heller, Gillian. 2007. *Worlds Apart*. Sydney: Rosenberg.

Tavan, Gwenda. 2005. *The Long, Slow Death of White Australia*. Melbourne: Scribe.

Thom, Vivienne. 2011. *Inquiry into the Actions of Australian Government Agencies in Relation to the Arrest and Detention Overseas of Mr Mamdouh Habib from 2001 to 2005*. Canberra: Inspector-General of Intelligence and Security.

Thomas, Mandy. 1999. *Dreams in the Shadows*. Sydney: Allen & Unwin.

Thompson, Roger Clark. 1980. *Australian Imperialism in the Pacific: The Expansionist Era 1820–1920*. Melbourne: Melbourne University Press.

Toohey, Brian and Pinwill, William. 1989. *Oyster: The Story of ASIS*. Melbourne: Heinemann.

Turner, Ian. 1979. *Industrial Labor and Politics: The Dynamics of the Labour Movement in Eastern Australia 1900–1921*. Sydney: Hale & Iremonger.

———. 1979. *Sydney's Burning: An Australian Political Conspiracy*. Sydney: Alpha Books.

Tyler, Heather. 2003. *Asylum: Voices behind the Razor Wire*. Melbourne: Lothian Books.

Vickers, Jill and Isaac, Annette. 2012. *The Politics of Race*. Toronto: University of Toronto Press.

Victoria. 1855. *Chinese Immigration Act*. Melbourne: Government Printer.

Viviani, Nancy (ed.). 1992. *The Abolition of the White Australia Policy: The Immigration Reform Movement Revisited*. Brisbane: Griffith University Press.

———. 1996. *The Indochinese in Australia 1975–1995*. Melbourne: Oxford University Press.

Vrachnas, John et al. 2008. *Immigration and Refugee Law*. Melbourne: Cambridge University Press.

US Committee for Refugees. 2002. *Sea Change: Australia's New Approach to Asylum Seekers.* Washington: US Committee for Refugees.
Walker, David. 1999. *Anxious Nation: Australia and the Rise of Asia 1850–1939.* St Lucia: University of Queensland Press.
Ward, Russell. 1965. *The Australian Legend.* Melbourne: Oxford University Press.
Ward, Stuart. 2001. *Australia and the British Embrace: The Demise of the Imperialist Ideal.* Melbourne: Melbourne University Press.
Wawn, William T. 1973. *The South Sea Islanders and the Queensland Labour Trade*, ed. Peter Corris. Canberra: ANU Press.
Webb, Leicester. 1954. *Communism and Democracy in Australia: A Survey of the 1951 Referendum.* Melbourne: Cheshire.
Weiner, Tim. 2012. *Enemies: A History of the FBI.* London: Allen Lane.
Weller, Pat. 2002. *Don't Tell the PM.* Melbourne: Scribe.
Welsh, Jennifer M. (ed.) 2006. *Humanitarian Intervention and International Relations.* Toronto: Oxford University Press.
West, Nigel. 1999. *Venona: The Greatest Secret of the Cold War.* London: Harper Collins.
White, Charles. 1975. *History of Australian Bushranging.* Melbourne: Lansdowne Press.
Willard, Myra. 1923 (1967) *History of the White Australia Policy.* Melbourne: Melbourne University Press.
Windschuttle, Keith. 2004. *The White Australia Policy.* Sydney: Macleay Press.
Winter, Barbara. 1986. *Stalag Australia: German Prisoners of War in Australia.* Sydney: Angus & Robertson.
Yarwood, A. T. 1964. *Asian Migration to Australia: The Background to Exclusion.* Melbourne: Melbourne University Press.
Year Book of Australia. 1908–. Canberra: Australian Bureau of Statistics.
Yong, Ching Fatt. 1977. *The New Gold Mountain.* Adelaide: Raphael Arts.
Yusuf, Irfan. 2009. *Once Were Radicals.* Sydney: Allen & Unwin.
Zamoyska, Betka. 1988. *The Ten Pound Fare.* London: Viking.
Zogbaum, Heidi. 2004. *Kisch in Australia.* Melbourne: Scribe.

INDEX